Y OU
ALREADY
KN OW

YOU ALREADY KNOW

How to access your intuition & find your divine life path

HELEN JACOBS

murdoch books

Sydney | London

Murdoch Books Australia
83 Alexander Street, Crows Nest NSW 2065
Phone: +61 (0)2 8425 0100
murdochbooks.com.au
info@murdochbooks.com.au

Murdoch Books UK
Ormond House, 26–27 Boswell Street, London WC1N 3JZ
Phone: +44 (0) 20 8785 5995
murdochbooks.co.uk
info@murdochbooks.co.uk

 A catalogue record for this
book is available from the
National Library of Australia

A catalogue record for this book is available from the British Library

ISBN 978 1 76052 437 1 Australia
ISBN 978 1 91163 252 8 UK

Cover design by Arielle Gamble

Internal design by Madeleine Kane

Printed and bound in Australia by Griffin Press

10 9 8 7 6 5 4 3 2 1

CONTENTS

INTRODUCTION 9

CHAPTER 1

BREADCRUMBS 17

How a surprise visit from spirit made
me sit up and pay attention.

CHAPTER 2

REMEMBERING 23

Connect to your heart and soul,
over your mind.

CHAPTER 3

A NEW PATH EMERGES 33

Let go of your mind's limited life
plan to allow your soul's divine
life path to unfold.

CHAPTER 4

ALL OF LIFE
SUPPORTS YOU 43

Life is not inhospitable, but
geared in your favour.

CHAPTER 5

YOUR DIVINE
INVITATION 53

Listen to the whispers calling you
back to your divine life path.

CHAPTER 6

STILLNESS. SPACE.
SILENCE. 63

Create the perfect conditions
to hear your guidance.

CHAPTER 7

LIFE'S MESSENGERS 75

Meet the myriad messengers
delivering you guidance.

CHAPTER 8

SIGNS & SYMBOLS 89

Discover the symbolic language of
your intuition and your guides.

CHAPTER 9

INTUITION 99

Journey into the layers of your
inner world, and all the
wisdom stored there.

CHAPTER 10

SPIRITUAL SUPPORT
TEAM 113

Meet your own personal team
of advisors working with you
from the spirit realm.

CHAPTER 11

WORKING WITH
MESSENGERS:
A PROCESS 125

Follow this step-by-step
process for working with your
intuition and your guides.

CHAPTER 12

FOLLOW THAT
THREAD 139

Discover the threads of guidance
and how they weave together
to form a complete picture.

CHAPTER 13

INNER TRANSFORMATION
149

Activate the change to take
you from where you were to
where you're going.

CHAPTER 14

HEALING TOOLKIT 163

Work with the specific tools and
techniques best for each phase
of the inner transformation.

CHAPTER 15

IN THE FLOW 183

Unblock your energy flows to
experience a life of flow.

CHAPTER 16

THE MANUAL 195

Receive the energetic imprint
of your soul blueprint, with help
from your blueprint guides.

CHAPTER 17

LESSONS 207

Life's lessons are the path, not
a sign you're off your path. Learn
to handle them with grace.

CHAPTER 18

PURPOSE 219

Now, your purpose begins to
emerge. Discover what treasure
is buried inside of you.

CHAPTER 19

ALCHEMY 231

All this knowledge now
needs to come into form.

CHAPTER 20

FROM THE INSIDE, OUT 243

All you've unearthed needs to make its way out, into the world around you.

CHAPTER 21

MANIFESTING 255

Work with the Law of Attraction to draw to you what you desire, and also create it in physical form.

CHAPTER 22

EXPRESS YOURSELF 267

Your gifts, talents, ideas and unique perspective must move through you. Unleash your expression!

CHAPTER 23

PITFALLS & TROUBLESHOOTING 279

Some pitfalls are all too common along this adventure. Learn from these common mistakes and frequently asked questions.

CHAPTER 24

SEASONS & CYCLES 291

Your pathway is far more cyclical than linear. Knowing your season and cycle can remove many frustrations.

CHAPTER 25

GUIDED PATHWAY 307

Once you walk this new pathway, you'll never really go back. Welcome to your new normal.

CHAPTER 26

SOUL JOURNEY 319

With time, we move beyond these foundations and spiritual awakening into a deeper soul awakening.

CHAPTER 27

ONWARD JOURNEY 331

Final thoughts and insights to prepare you for your own adventure, in situ.

RESOURCES 340

ACKNOWLEDGEMENTS 341

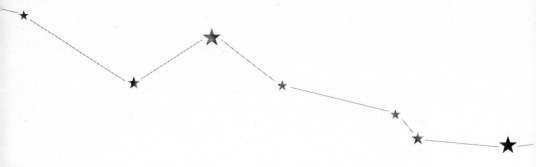

To Isla and Rose: may you always know
and live out your own wondrous life path.

And to my seven-year-old self:
you were right; we did it!

INTRODUCTION

Why do you think you're here, in this very moment, reading this book? What if it's not by chance you're reading these words but because some greater forces conspired to place this message in front of you, right now? What if you're here reading this because you already know deep down you're supposed to.

What if these forces have *always* been at play in your life, not just to bring you this book but also to bring you into each and every moment of your life? Imagine life has delivered you a series of breadcrumbs, or clues, leading you in and out of each moment — what a shame it would be if you've missed these clues (and the opportunities they represented). Can you entertain, just for a moment, what might be possible for you if you came to see that life is working quite differently from how your mind perceives it to be. What if you're not actually lost, off-path or mistaken, but instead you already know you've outgrown where you are and something new is now calling you forward? Would you listen?

> Our life's experiences aren't designed for our heads
> to understand, but for our hearts and soul to feel.
> Through *feeling*, we can recall what we already know
> at this deeper level, and align with it.

Recalling everything we already know, buried deep down within, requires a new approach.

Trusting your own, innate inner wisdom and entertaining the idea your life is unfolding in ways your mind might not yet understand can open the doorway to an adventure full of possibility, serendipity and synchronicity. It's a treasure hunt to discover yourself and your potential.

You don't have to figure it out alone. You'll encounter a team of advisors — who act both as cheerleaders and as guides — who will support you on this journey. This team is quite unlike any other, largely because they aren't a *physical* team of advisors, but a spiritual collective. Comprised of a range of higher vibrational guiding beings, they are privy to your path and purpose and are specifically assigned to you to help you remember it. There is one main guiding being, with each team member playing a specific role. I call them a Spiritual Support Team (SST).

SPIRIT SPEAK

Your **Spiritual Support Team** is a group of non-physical, higher vibrational guiding beings, individually and collectively assigned to your growth and development. Each guide plays a specific role as they counsel you along your life path.

Without physical form, they can't quite communicate with you in the same way as others in your life, so instead they'll begin to communicate with you via your intuition. Listening to their guidance, you'll come to recognise these greater forces at play in your life (and how to work with them). Your SST will ask you to trust that they give you the most relevant information and guidance, even when it doesn't immediately form a clear picture or appease your logical mind (actually, *especially* then).

Your SST will remind you of your path and purpose. It will tug at your intuition, reminding you of all you already know deep within, before asking you to apply what you discover to radically transform yourself and your life path. Your SST already knows the lessons and purpose your soul chose to explore in this lifetime, as encoded in your soul's blueprint, and it wants you to remember that you already know these details, too.

SPIRIT SPEAK

Think of your **soul blueprint** not as a physical document, but as an energetic imprint containing the agreements and areas for exploration your soul committed to in this lifetime.

The journey of this book

You haven't picked up this book by chance. I don't believe in mere coincidences; all things are connected and happen for a reason, even if we never become consciously aware of those reasons in this lifetime. Your own SST has most likely led you to this book because you're called to this new way; you're on the frontier of soul-led living.

This book will help you
* confidently make choices that appear risky and illogical with soul-aligned clarity;
* determine if you're on the 'right' path;
* transform feelings of being lost, confused, jaded or disconnected into authentic and inspired living;
* connect to your truth, life and others in brilliant and meaningful new ways;

- freely express who you really are; and
- identify what you really want — and how to get it.

You'll do this by
- tapping into your own internal navigation system — your intuition, wisdom and guidance — to understand what it's asking of you and where it's leading you;
- opening to the higher guidance of your own team of advisors, or SST;
- unlocking the secrets of your life path and purpose, by accessing your soul's blueprint; and
- living the life you were born to live, by walking what I call your divine life path.

A new way of living awaits

Choosing this new way, you begin to see yourself and your life through new eyes. Connections are made, realisations come into focus and you suddenly find meaning where before there was none. Purpose wafts in where before confusion hung thickly. You begin to feel alive and pulsing with the current of your own dazzling life. Like the hidden image in a 3D magic eye illustration, your life will come into sharper focus and clarity; a beautiful experience emerges from the background to supersede the life once at the fore. You cannot un-see or un-know what you're about to uncover. I doubt you'll ever want to.

For more than a decade, I've been on such an adventure. This was not where I started, though. Back in my early twenties, intuition and spirit communication were the furthest things from my mind. Instead, I worked in fast-paced communications of another kind: public relations. After eight years in PR, I was disconnected from my life and on antidepressants. From the outside looking in, it might have appeared picture perfect. From the inside looking out, I felt numb. Little by little, I followed the threads of guidance, working with my own team of advisors and connecting with my intuition daily. Like an archaeologist, I intuitively began to dig for treasure. I accessed my own innate wisdom revealing myriad hidden gems within.

SPIRIT SPEAK

Spirit communication refers to the ability to communicate via non-verbal or non-physical means with non-physical beings in the spirit realm.

This excavation put into context one of my life's most pivotal moments and had me suddenly recognising the breadcrumbs life was giving me. At age nineteen, while studying at university (and with very different priorities), my recently deceased aunt visited me in spirit. She jarringly reminded me of my ability to connect with guidance from a source beyond my own mind, but it still took me a while to listen. Once I did, I quickly course-corrected, pivoting from PR to giving psychic readings, booking a six-month wait list, almost overnight. Totally surprising myself (and those who knew me), I've worked as a psychic, channel and mentor for thousands of people globally since. My divine life path showed up and one hell of an adventure unfolded.

Almost immediately, this new approach delivered me my now-husband, Gary. I clairvoyantly saw the life Gary and I could build together, including our children (which, you might imagine was a tad overwhelming at the outset of a new relationship!). Gary, and now our two daughters, Isla and Rose, are all along for this wild adventure with me.

Another key relationship at the heart of this adventure is with my own SST. Early in my relationship with Gary, we would often be in the middle of a public crowded area, with me talking at length about guiding beings and psychic predictions. Gary affectionately named my SST 'Chris', as the pseudonym helped us feel a little less awkward, and it stuck. I still regularly refer to my SST as Chris in conversation.

SPIRIT SPEAK

Chris is an affectionate pseudonym referring to the entire group of non-physical guiding beings in my SST. Although I refer to Chris in the masculine, he's not really male, physical or even one being. Chris is my entire team of guides, each their own mix of masculine and feminine energies.

Chris' guidance helps me immensely — in creating and running a business, buying and selling houses, understanding my children, navigating friendships and relationship dynamics, and even leading me to writing this very book. Your SST can do the same for you, too. You'll hear from Chris — and even your own SST — throughout this book.

Rest assured, you needn't become a professional psychic to access the secrets of your divine life path (although you will tap into your own latent ability). I've worked with thousands of private clients, from all walks of life, over the years via psychic readings, mentoring, workshops, retreats, online programs and now, with you, via this book. Despite each client's unique circumstances, lessons and purpose, they've each created a significant life change by applying these same principles. This change isn't just in their outer world — their careers, relationships and homes — although that is a nice by-product.

Instead, this is deep, inner-world change, led by your own inner knowing. Step by step, your intuition and SST will lead you through an exciting pilgrimage of self-discovery, radically transforming how you see yourself and your place in the world, delivering you squarely onto your unique life path.

While fun, this is not for the faint-hearted! Your guidance will often ask you to take blind leaps of faith, to act on irrational information — but when you understand the process, you'll do so confidently. Don't see this as a sign to rush into some major life change just yet. Instead, see this as a long-term, sustainable lifestyle change.

How to use this book

Here, the practical everyday meets the mystical and otherworldly. Not only is working with your intuition rather like learning a new language, so, too, is much of the terminology. You'll notice throughout the book I've included 'Spirit Speak' sections, with explanations of terms and ideas that may be new to you.

A series of self-reflection prompts are also included throughout, and these are perfect for self-enquiry in your journal. You'll notice them by the little journal icons beside them. You'll also find practical exercises at the end of each chapter, as 'Choose your adventure' sections. On your first read, work through the exercises, in order. However, life is less likely to unfold in such a linear, chronological fashion; our soul adventure is far more cyclical. For this reason, after your first read through, I envisage this book becoming a reference guide for your divine life path, in situ. Life will rapidly rise to meet you, bringing you opportunities to 'test' your new knowledge. Refer back here as you begin to interact with your life and guidance from this new perspective.

To keep you moving through this transformation, I also share the potential pitfalls and perceived setbacks this adventure may serve up. You'll learn from my personal experiences, as well as a few of my clients throughout this book (or at least, an amalgamation of their stories to protect their privacy).

Above all else, I ask you to trust your own guidance for what's ahead. The life you were born to live awaits you; it's time to remember what you already know.

CHAPTER 1

★

BREADCRUMBS

My world changed dramatically during the early hours of 8 September 2001. I awoke abruptly after dreaming of my aunt Cathy, who had died a few weeks earlier. In that dream, she led me through the timeline of her life, showing me people, relationships and events that, as her niece, I'd never known. I remember waking with a start that morning, before my radio alarm clock went off. I don't recall seeing Cathy at the end of my bed, but I certainly felt her. I'm not sure why I spoke out loud to her, but I did. I asked why she came back to visit me instead of my mum (her sister), her mother (Granny) or her own children.

Then my alarm went off — but not at the time I had set it for. A song blared out, seemingly in response to the very question I had just asked. Usher's voice sang out the lyrics of his song, 'U Remind Me', explaining that I reminded her of a girl she once knew and that she sees her face whenever she looks at me. Was Cathy saying I reminded her of herself? Usher goes on to sing he can't get with this girl who reminds him of someone else, but I didn't hear it that morning. I'd already burst out crying and thought I was going crazy. But, seeing as my alarm had gone off and I had a university assignment to write before working my casual job that day, I tried to shrug it off as a weird dream.

I couldn't shake the feeling Cathy was still with me. Boiling the kettle to make a cup of tea, I remember whipping around, feeling her behind me. I still couldn't see her; I could just feel her presence. Later, I walked down to the other end of the house, passing an internal window. I jumped as I passed it, throwing myself into the wall. Not realising anyone else was awake, my mum had startled me, sitting on the couch on the other side of the house.

She joked, 'Geez, it's like you saw a ghost.'

She was the first, but not the last, person to unknowingly say that to me that day. Walking over to Mum, I asked her about the people and events Cathy had shown me in the dream. Mum confirmed much of what I'd just experienced. These were indeed details of Cathy's life I had just witnessed.

What unfolded next has never happened to me again in quite the same way. As I sat there talking with my mum on the couch, Cathy began to inhabit my body. I later learned this is called transmediumship — a form of communicating with the spirit world — but I had no understanding of that at the time. It was as if I stood aside while Cathy popped in and proceeded to interact with my mum — Irish accent and all. I was aware of what was happening, but not in control of it. This continued to unfold over the next few hours. Yes, *hours*. By the time I, or more correctly, Cathy, was through, one of my sisters and my dad had also awoken to what was unfolding in my family's living room.

Towards the end of the episode, in a conversation I can only describe as happening inside my head, I met with Cathy in a darkened space where she pleaded with me words I will never forget.

'My children. My children. Tell my children I love them.'

I didn't complete my assignment that morning and I called in sick to work. Instead, my mum and I went to see my cousins. I relayed the details of the dream to two of Cathy's three children. Coming to the end of the story, sharing Cathy's last words to me, I saw my cousins' faces change. They exchanged a knowing look, before explaining to me they'd stayed up late the night before, talking about their mum and wondering why she hadn't told them more often that she loved them.

It wasn't until many years later that that particular moment of confirmation would send me on a new trajectory. But, at the time, I wasn't ready.

For many days, weeks, months and even years after Cathy's visit, I pondered what happened that morning. So many questions swirled. The most pressing, and the one I'm now asked most often, is how did I know I could communicate with the world of spirit? Until Cathy's visitation, I had forgotten that I could. Suddenly, I could see all the breadcrumbs that had led me there.

Looking back, I realised life had hinted all along to this ability I seemed to have. I just wasn't listening; I wasn't looking for the clues. So much of my early childhood in particular came rushing back. Like the two spirit men who'd visit me in my family's living room. One stood tall and thin in his tails and top hat, arms folded across his chest. He never spoke to me, but I always felt safe in his presence. There was also an older man, dressed in a checked flannelette shirt, sleeves rolled up, braces holding up his pants and a grey flat cap atop his balding head. He always seemed so inviting, this man, but I had no idea who he was. As no one else could see him, I thought I'd never know.

Hindsight suddenly brought clarity to much of my childhood. I often felt I was being watched. A cousin used to poke fun at me for always singing in the bathroom — but I suddenly recognised I'd picked up the habit as a kid to distract me from feeling like I was being watched.

Then there was the time my parents bought a new pet bird.

'You'll never guess what we called it,' Mum said as I walked into the kitchen that day.

'Ringo!' I casually shot back, to her amazement (and mine!).

The breadcrumbs had always been there, like little nuggets of wisdom arriving with clues of my own potential, inviting me on an exciting treasure hunt. I've always communicated with the spirit world, I just didn't know that's what I was doing.

SPIRIT SPEAK

Life delivers us clues, or signposts, highlighting our way forward, which I like to think of as a trail of **breadcrumbs**. When we notice, then follow them, an entirely new pathway emerges — one aligned with our divine life path.

Steve Jobs shared a similar sentiment to this breadcrumb idea in his commencement address to Stanford University students in 2005, a few years after Cathy died. As he advised those students, we cannot always see how the dots, or our life's events, will connect up until we can look back on them.

Trusting our intuition propels us to follow the dots leading forward, even when they lead us onto a less-worn path. Nothing really happens by chance, and we must believe it will all make sense eventually.

Since the time of Cathy's visitation, all I could do was trust that this ability to connect with spirit would make clearer sense in the future. I didn't know what to do with it, let alone what to make of it. But I wasn't ready to veer off the well-worn path, yet. Waiting for the dots to connect up, I completed a Bachelor of Journalism degree, then a Bachelor of Business, majoring in public relations and marketing.

After eight years in PR, I felt miserable, disconnected and dissatisfied. I was finally ready to explore the world of spirit again.

I'll share the turn of events that led me from PR to psychic readings later, but as this happened, the dots weren't just connecting looking back; they started leading me forward. Following that trail has been the greatest adventure of my life. For the past decade, I've dedicated my life to it. A crazy little experiment in following my intuition has become my livelihood and life's work. In the following pages, I'll share everything I learned from following my intuition and working with inner guidance — my SST — as my life dots began to connect into a pathway forward.

My hope for you, dear reader, as you continue through these pages, is that you not only see your own trail looking back, but that you start to see the dots guiding your way. Embarking on this new approach, following your intuition and connecting with your SST holds vast realms of possibility and potential. Savour each moment of magic, taking it one breadcrumb at a time. And even if you don't yet recognise this moment as one of magic, trust that this, too, is part of your divine life plan. Everything connects up eventually.

CHAPTER 2

★

REMEMBERING

I never set out to work as a psychic, but life had other plans. After Cathy's visitation, I carried on the well-worn path until it came to a grinding stop. After a few years, I was on medication for depression, completely disconnected from myself and my life. My outer world, though, appeared to tell a different story.

I managed PR projects and campaigns for household consumer brands, top-rating radio stations and an island resort in the Whitsundays. I hosted corporate boxes for media and attended launch parties. All-expenses-paid trips to New York and London featured. My career was burgeoning; I'd bought my first property and I was surrounded by plenty of friends and family.

Despite ticking all the boxes of my supposed 'right' path, I wasn't any happier for it. I couldn't shake the feeling something was wrong. Although I loved living alone in my own apartment, singledom was wearing thin. No matter what I did to try and change my situation — my job, my love life, my happiness — nothing brought me the feelings I sought. My own thinking got me into this mess, but it couldn't get me out. I decided to see a psychic.

Growing up in a religious family, there was an underlying mistrust of psychics and mediums. As a kid, I remember Mum and Aunty Cathy having their tea leaves or cards read, only to giggle retelling their stories afterwards. Ironically, this was the same aunt who visited me; this was not lost on my family. Suddenly, we all found a renewed curiosity in the paranormal in Cathy's physical absence, even if we couldn't immediately logically reconcile it. Some extended family members had seen a local psychic medium after Cathy's death. I thought maybe this psychic might have answers for me, too, especially about my career and love life. It felt to me that Cathy's spirit visitation somehow confirmed she was no longer shy or mistrusting of these methods, so I tried not to be either.

I don't remember too much of the psychic's advice, other than her response to a question I almost didn't ask. As I left, I asked her opinion on Cathy's visitation all those years ago. She explained the event as transmediumship and invited me to her upcoming workshop to explore things further. I had no idea how it happened, but the psychic information just poured out of me at that workshop. The same psychic then suggested I didn't really need to learn *how*. I just had to practise.

My sisters sent me their friends to practise with; people I knew and trusted, but whose intimate life details were far enough removed from my knowledge. They then sent me more people to practise on. Word quickly spread. Before long, people quite removed from my own social circle contacted me. When they asked me what my fees were, I knew the answer to my original question regarding my career direction was right under my nose.

Soon, I worked PR by day, psychic by night. Long after a psychic reading client had gone, I continued working with spirit. The tap was on, so I carried on asking my own questions. What were these ideas and concepts I saw in sessions? How the heck I was doing this? And what was ahead for me?

Around this time, I discovered the practice of automatic writing, a form of channelling messages from spirit, verbatim, into written form. To facilitate the connection, I would first meditate to move into a transcendental state. Then, I'd write my question for Chris on the page, and transcribe his response when it arrived. I filled pages and pages of journals with my observations and questions. (I have 200+ journals at last count.) These pages contained all the proof I needed. Breadcrumbs were being given — and these predictions were coming true!

I had tapped in to an intuitive mind and began tasking my logical mind as its servant, allowing a new way of living to emerge.

How do you already know?

Yes, this book is called *You Already Know,* but you're probably feeling that you really *don't* already know. So, before I lose you entirely, allow me to remedy this. I promise you *do* already know. It's just not coming to you in the same way you know other things.

I've just shared a story of how I suddenly remembered my psychic medium abilities, even though I didn't immediately cognitively know how I did it. This wasn't some ordinary recalling of facts and figures my mind had intellectually absorbed. I didn't study to become a psychic or medium. Instead, this was a deep awakening of stored inner knowledge arising from deep within me, like remembering a dream as you rouse from sleep. Like our SST, we, too, are spiritual beings, but our human form seems to scramble our inner wisdom. As we embark on this intuitive treasure hunt to discover ourselves, we are moving through a *Process of Remembering* — and feeling like you don't yet know your path and purpose is an important part of the process. At least now you're on your way to remembering.

SPIRIT SPEAK

A **Process of Remembering**, or 'remembering', is about awakening to your soul, your true essence and nature, and the details of your soul's agreements and blueprint. Latent knowledge arises in your awareness, bubbling to the surface like information remembered upon awakening from a dream.

In my early practise psychic readings, I didn't know *how* I knew what I knew; I just knew. Without intellectually learning or researching the information, I just knew details as plainly as I knew my name is Helen. What I told those strangers sitting opposite me was beyond my own cognition. Somehow, I'd tapped into the inner wisdom of my heart and soul, and a higher guidance beyond me, too. Chris led those sessions, communicating with me via my intuition and latent psychic ability, not my own mind. I simply became a vessel through which spirit could relay its messages.

> You know more than your logical, rational mind thinks you do. What you already know is more feeling-based, intuitive and wise. What you already know isn't mental, cognitive knowledge, but heart and soul knowledge. Too much thinking dulls the soul's wisdom.

To tune in to this wisdom, you cannot rely on the rational mind at the expense of your intuitive mind. We can't think ourselves out of the problems our rational minds have created. We must turn to our intuitive mind and feel our way out.

SPIRIT SPEAK

The **soul** is the aspect of us beyond our physical form that has incarnated through a number of prior lifetimes, each to explore, learn and grow in accordance with its blueprint. As the soul accumulates experiences, lessons and relationships across each lifetime, it influences what is explored in this particular lifetime — and creates a memory of deep soul wisdom.

CHANNELLED GUIDANCE: Process of Remembering
Below is an excerpt from an automatic writing journal entry I channelled from spirit on 11 February 2016, explaining this Process of Remembering after our Process of Forgetting.

'At this time, just about every soul moves through a Process of Remembering, which is to say you also go through a Process of Forgetting.

'At the time of birth into the physical realm, your soul begins the Process of Forgetting. That is to say all prior soul knowledge is superseded and becomes foggy. It is most uncommon — until now — for souls to remember details of their agreement and blueprint from birth. You move through a Process of Forgetting. Too much soul knowledge from birth would be overwhelming on Earth at this time.

'And, so, for much of your early life you live in a fog ... more and more people are moving through the Process of Remembering at once. And, in time, you will no longer need to forget to remember, but you'll always know. Some of these souls are now arriving.

'The Process of Remembering is about awakening to your soul ... your true essence and nature, and the truth and essence of humankind. It's about ... removing the barriers put in place during the Process of Forgetting. Indeed, much of your early life is forgetting; then you must remember who you are.

'Before now, only a few had awakened while most continued to sleep. For the awakened ones, it was quiet and peaceful, perhaps even lonely. It was like rising before others in your household, the

---

calm before the storm. Now, as many awaken at once, there's a lot of "noise" disrupting those moving from forgetting to remembering. It's important to take time to find your centre, calm and balance for your own remembering amidst the bustle of the mass awakening. Don't lose your dreams before you're bombarded with the noise.

'Once you remember, you will set forth with greater clarity and focus to offer your soul's gifts, talents and skills.

'A mass Process of Remembering brings the mass rising of soul-led relationships, businesses, healthcare, financial structures. As each individual remembers who they are and the soul-role they play in the greater collective blueprint, then your earthly structures are remodelled. As an individual remembers, so does the collective.'

We're more than our minds

Our inner wisdom doesn't arrive in the logical, linear, clearly defined manner our rational mind desires. Instead, it's rather piecemeal, like breadcrumbs being dropped in between all our other plans. If we aren't paying attention, we can easily miss the guidance. In my case, clues to my channelling ability were present from early in my life. My mind, however, attached to other stories about who I was meant to be in the world. While my mind was busy making other plans, I was missing the divine life path offered up before me.

Our breadcrumbs, then, are like signposts leading us deeper into our unique life path. Our SST and intuition remind us of the vault buried deep within us, holding the secrets of our life path. We are programmed with a unique soul mission, as recorded in our soul blueprint, before we arrive in this lifetime, and assigned our SST and intuition to lead us back to it. Accessing our soul's knowledge requires trusting our guidance and opening our hearts. There's more to us than we *think*.

Our rational mind is incredible but, when compared to the vast knowledge beyond it, it's really rather limited. Our soul's knowledge is connected to something far greater than our rational mind. Loosening a reliance on logic and opening to something we may not immediately intellectually understand will feel, at least to our heart and soul, like a deep remembering.

I'm not asking you to never think again. That would be impossible while in a human body. We need our mind. But a sole reliance on our mind disrupts our soul reliance. To remember what we already know, we need less thinking, more feeling.

Think less, feel more

Thinking overshadows feelings. We're taught to squash them, ignore them, hide them or disguise them. From the time our mothers are 'shooshing' us as crying infants — and I have been that mother — we absorb how unwelcome our feelings are. As adults, many of us struggle to label our feelings, let alone sit with them for too long. We're too busy self-medicating and fuelling unhealthy addictions. We're also ignoring one of the first clues we have to our soul's wisdom and inner imprint of our divine life path.

This is often my starting point with many of my clients, who arrive feeling disconnected from themselves and their lives. This feeling, that so many of us try to fill, override or ignore, is a huge clue. Paying attention to our feelings provides us with a litmus test for whether we're living in alignment with our divine life path or not. As a general rule, feelings of openness, expansiveness, happiness and positivity are pretty good signs we are 'on path'. Feeling disconnected, angry, sad and dissatisfied signals the opposite; something is off kilter.

Soul's knowledge, then, is communicated through our feelings, but our mind has convinced us not to trust them.

Self-reflection: How do you feel about your life right now? What does this feeling tell you? Do your head and heart interpret this differently? How do you know this information?

Head versus heart

A battle will rage between your head and your heart, or your rational and intuitive mind. Really, this is the same tussle between love and fear, and intuition and logic. I see them all as variants of the same thing. Working with your heart means you're working with love, intuition and feminine energy. Your head, then, is more fearing, logical and masculine in its approach. An intuitive mind (the heart) requires a faithful servant in the rational mind (the head).

The heart

I don't just mean your physical heart, or even your emotional heart, but also the core of who you are. Whether or not you connect to this as 'being in your heart', this is the pure part of you that is open, loving, non-judgmental, spacious, free and flexible. This part of you already knows your divine life path.

The head

This is the rational, thinking, logic-loving mind. Your inner critic may also reside here. The critic's constant mind chatter is usually judgment-focused, relying on facts and figures, pros and cons. It wonders, 'What if?' Tasked to keep you safe from perceived threats, your head's viewpoint tends to be rather limited; it doesn't know *all* the answers. Our heads rely on history, ideas, experiences and stories — and these all have an element of perception, rather than truth.

Which wins?

That's up to you. There may be phases where one takes the lead. Our ultimate goal is to have them working in unison.

CHOOSE YOUR ADVENTURE

At the end of each chapter, in a 'Choose your adventure' section, I'll ask you to complete a task. I suggest having a dedicated journal for the work you'll do here, as you'll expand your use of it throughout the book and may want to keep your findings in one place. Work with the journaling prompts below to remember and notice your breadcrumbs.

Journaling prompts

Date your journal entry and write your initial responses to the questions below. Please don't censor yourself — you'll want the truth on these pages for later. Now consider your life path to date. Looking back, can you recognise the signposts (or breadcrumbs) that led you to where you are right now? In your journal, answer the following questions:

- What have been the big turning points in your life? How have they impacted the path's direction? What have you learned? Is there more you can learn, now with the advantage of hindsight?
- Where are you on your path, today? Is this where you thought you'd be? Why/why not?
- Do you think this is where your soul intended you to be? Why/why not? How do you know this?
- What were the subtle signs or breadcrumbs pointing you along the way? Did you trust them? Why or why not?
- Are there new breadcrumbs in your life right now? What are they, and where might they be leading you?

★

CHAPTER 3

A NEW PATH EMERGES

Life has a funny way of taking us where we need to be, if we only pay attention. Chris nudged me to leave PR behind as a new path needed to emerge. But, before I tell this story, I need to catch you up on an important storyline.

As my evenings filled up with psychic readings, my day job had changed. During my last year at the PR agency, an ex-colleague tried several times to entice me over to the online travel company where she now worked. I continued to decline. Another of her emails landed in my inbox, but this time I paid attention. This one arrived while I was in a meeting with the agency's director and general manager, resigning with no other plans in place. Not surprisingly, I successfully interviewed and was offered the job of PR manager at the online travel company.

I also want to remind you of my interest back then in my love life, a hot topic of enquiry in my automatic writing sessions. Chris assured me I'd meet someone in January 2009. Guess when I started at the online travel company? January 2009.

Alas, I certainly did *not* start a new romance that month.

Feeling led astray on the romance front, I gave up hope. My psychic reading work was growing, so Chris prompted me to resign from the travel company after just six months. I coached myself through the belief that I'd forever remain single if I forged a new career as a psychic. 'What guy in his twenties would want to date a psychic?' I wondered. I was about to find out. Word of my plans quickly spread around the office. People were intrigued. I remember one particular email from a colleague, a user experience designer, offering to help me with my blog. He still helps me with all things technical from time to time — he's now my husband.

I met Gary within the first few minutes of walking into that building in January 2009. It just took another six months, and a decision on my career and personal truth, for us to make the move from friendship to romance. For that whole six months, he sat just one desk away.

Life had other plans my rational mind could not fathom. I learned an important lesson in allowing a new path to emerge. I kept following my intuitive mind.

Path to date

Hundreds of psychic readings later, I realised I'm not the only one with a 'life plan'. Maybe you, too, have mapped out a linear, chronological order of events, scheduling the time frame of your life? Mine focused on establishing my career, a committed relationship and property ownership by an age I'd plucked from thin air. In my rational mind, if these things didn't happen when I wanted them to, I would have failed.

This is not the same thing as our divine life path. Instead, my divine life path was dropping breadcrumbs — spirit communication as a child; practising psychic readings; working at the online travel company; now quitting. Many of my life's more recent milestones never even featured in my original life plan, but they're so much better than I could have planned for myself. My rational mind was no match for the treasure I've unearthed from within.

It wasn't just the milestones or markers of the life plan, either. It was also *how* I thought I had to make everything happen and *who* I thought I had to be to do so. Of course, we won't all have concocted the same 'life plan', but I'm sure you have your own version of it lurking somewhere. As you're about to find out, your expected life plan may never have really been *your* plan to begin with.

You don't have to ditch your life plan — by which I mean the overarching list of destination points — but *how* and *when* you get there is not up to you. Your desires are important and so are your dreams. But these desires and dreams are breadcrumbs for your divine life path and not a structure of the life plan for your rational mind to map and implement.

Just beneath the surface, a new divine life path wants to emerge.

You're not off-path

Let me be clear: you haven't been on the 'wrong path' to date. Nor is there any one 'right path' for you, either. To our soul, it's all data. All your experiences thus far are part of the process. There is certainly a point where the divine life path becomes clearer, but we've always been on it. We can never truly be 'off-path'. Our mind may judge the path and attach meaning to where we find ourselves. But, to our soul, it's exactly where we need to be (even if our rational mind can't comprehend that at the time, or ever!). Soul does not judge where we are. All roads lead to Rome — or soul, as the case may be.

I wasn't off-path studying journalism or business. I wasn't off-path when I worked in PR. I wasn't even off-path when I ignored the world of spirit. Nor was I off-path as I ignored every email inviting me to join the online travel company. In fact, these things *created* the path I would soon walk. My divine life path cleared *because* of those earlier experiences. I was preparing my lessons, as you will be, too. Please trust that where you are is purposeful. Soul hasn't led you here to only lead you here.

If you catch yourself thinking you're not 'there' yet, please know where you are is important, valid and contributing to some bigger life plan your mind may not yet be able to see.

The divine life path

Imagine your life as a Choose Your Own Adventure book. Many pathways open up based on the choices and decisions you make. You have free will; you can always decide. But what you decide will play out within the boundaries of that particular book's adventure pathways. Similarly, our choices play out in accordance with our life's area of exploration.

When our choices and decisions align with our soul blueprint, the option of the divine life path comes to the fore. Misaligned choices can still be made, but we will eventually need to weave our way back to the adventure's original plot line. The divine life path then opens up to us as we come into alignment with the truth of our soul's reason for being here. As we stop relying on the rational mind, the 'life plan' gives way to our soul's 'divine life path'.

The future is not set in stone, but our life's lessons and purpose are (the areas of exploration encoded within our blueprint). Our decisions and choices can alter the outcome; our free will can influence the future. Soul signed up for our lessons and purpose, but *how* they unfold is influenced by our free will — and, indeed, the free will of others.

Let's introduce a hypothetical friend, Nora, as an example. Nora's soul agreed to explore self-love in this lifetime. In human form, she makes choices based on the situations she experiences, soon gaining weight. Nora's weight now prompts less-than-loving feelings about herself. She's born, as a female, into a world full of ideas about how her body should look and feel. Taking on outside influence, Nora decides she is unlovable. Here, her soul is able to learn one side of the self-love lesson. Nora might choose to stay in this frame of reference her whole life, thus continuing to explore an absence of self-love. However, in this example, Nora chooses to change her frame of reference. Embarking on an inner journey, Nora rewrites her relationship with herself, her weight and her body. She learns to love and accept herself. Now, her soul has explored the healing journey, but also another aspect of self-love. Soul would have been happy with either (or any other) exploration of the self-love theme. It may have turned up in an abusive relationship, perfectionism, parenting or any other classroom. Nora's free will took her down the body route.

I share this story to highlight the delicate interplay of our choices and our divine life path. There's also a delicate interplay between planning and allowing, and even between our path and someone else's. Another's free will can alter our own path, just as we can alter theirs.

Planning or allowing?

Plans soothe the rational mind. But, as the well-known Woody Allen quote suggests, plans will only make God (or the Universe, or Source) laugh. Our rational mind must instead become the faithful servant of the intuitive mind, so that our logical plans are tasked towards aligning with our divine life path — not detouring from it.

> Fixed plans can place blinkers in your scope of vision, blinding you to all the other wonderful opportunities on the periphery — and that's usually where the Universe is trying to get your attention. With the blinkers off, life serendipitously lines up before us, bringing us the people, opportunities and situations we need in any given moment.

Much like me finally taking that position at the travel company.

Setting goals is OK — in fact, it's an important part of manifesting (which we'll come to in Chapter 21) — and there are obviously certain day-to-day things we must tend to. My kids have to get to school, my calendar must accommodate my clients, my business needs to run like a well-oiled machine. But when this all works in unison with the bigger plan, rather than it *being* the plan, we've found the sweet spot.

The Magic Car

Long before I was cognitively aware of driverless cars, I used to clairvoyantly see a Magic Car in client sessions. This clairvoyant image would pop up whenever I was to communicate to a client how spirit suggests we can balance this interplay of controlling versus allowing life to flow. It's natural to wonder whether we are powerless to these magic forces, or if we do, indeed, exert free will. To illustrate this, imagine an ordinary car with a steering wheel, four wheels, indicators, brakes and so on. Except, it's not so ordinary; it's magic. Just like most things in our lives, we can perceive it as 'ordinary', or trust that it, too, has an element of magic.

You get into the driver's seat with a destination in mind. You can opt to let the magic take you there, or drive the car yourself — much like trusting the serendipitous nature of life to rise to meet you, or to control each facet of your life path. In this instance, you choose the magic, merely telling the car where you want to go. Hearing your request, the Magic Car takes off in that direction.

Inevitably, the car takes a surprise route. Its magic knows the best possible route for you, even if it's not the course your mind wanted to take. Perhaps you have to pick up certain passengers, or drop them (or baggage) off. Perhaps there are roadblocks on your preferred path. Perhaps you've left with plenty of time to spare, so the Magic Car takes the scenic route to keep you entertained while you wait. The magic is aware of far more than our limited human mind, which cannot foresee all the other scenarios beyond what's immediately before us on our pathway.

You can override the magic at any time. You can slam on the brakes, turn the steering wheel and take control. By exercising your free will, you can force the car onto the route you desire, but then, wouldn't it be easier to trust the magic and just enjoy the ride? So it is in navigating this balance point between planning and allowing. As a new life path or direction emerges, we may be too quick to want to course-correct, because our mind can't comprehend the method of the magic at play. Our own life plans are often short-sighted; we don't have the same bird's-eye view of our pathway the magic has. We can exercise our free will to push and pull, sometimes kicking and screaming, to ensure things unfold how our mind wants them to, or we trust that setting the destination is enough, and that the magic will bring us all the twists and turns in due course, to ensure we not only arrive at the destination, but enjoy the ride as well.

CASE STUDY – Maggie

Maggie and I began working together as she felt disconnection and disillusionment creep in after a long career in corporate finance while raising her four children. Over the years, Maggie had balanced her career and busy family life with her passion for yoga, meditation and natural therapies. As her nest emptied, she dreamed of days filled with yoga and meditation, but didn't feel it was time to retire from the big corporations she loved.

Reconnecting to her inner navigation and SST, Maggie realised the new possibilities her 'dreams' signalled aligned with the next phase of her life path. Maggie turned up the navigational volume and course-corrected. Following the same process you're about to learn in this book, Maggie began to see the pieces of her life — the teaching, yoga, meditation and even her corporate experience — in a new way. Before long, Maggie qualified as a yoga and meditation teacher, and brought yoga and meditation into these big corporates.

Her stirrings of remembering came through her disconnect and dissatisfaction, coupled with her dreams of spending her days in tranquillity and peace. Upon reflection, Maggie realised that her expectations of her life contributed to this separation from her divine life path.

Together, we unravelled her expectations from the roles as wife and mother, as daughter and teacher. We explored her ideas for earning money as a natural therapies teacher, and running a business of this nature after her time in corporates, and how it could make financial sense. In Maggie's case, as is true for so many of us, she'd absorbed her expectations from her parents, society, culture, husband and more. This process tested it all.

Through an inner transformation, led by her own intuition and SST, Maggie recognised her breadcrumbs for what they really were: clues to her gifts and her ability to help others — particularly other working mothers and employees in general — connect to themselves through yoga and meditation.

Maggie shared this with friends, going on retreats and weekend workshops, and noticed the difference it brought to her friends (some of whom were colleagues). Maggie's joy returned; the things that lit her up soon outshone her dissatisfaction.

Maggie wasn't off-path while raising her children or working in finance. Her SST soon showed her it was *because* of these experiences she was able to find her calling, not despite them.

Maggie soon combined her business background with yoga and meditation, creating corporate wellness programs, resources and retreats, especially for working mothers.

CHOOSE YOUR ADVENTURE — ARE YOU WILLING?
Usually at this point, the rational mind starts worrying about
losing control. It feels unsafe to step out onto an unclear and
unknown path. But you're not alone! You have your intuition;
you're about to meet your SST. And a whole new pathway will
emerge for you. How willing are you to pioneer a new way? The
journal prompts below will help you consider your willingness.

- How do you feel about letting go of the old ways? Notice any
  emotions, as well as sensations in your body.
- Are you scared? What are you scared of? Which part of you
  is scared?
- Could this be exciting? What are you excitedly anticipating?
  Which part of you is looking forward to a new way?
- What do you need to help ease yourself into a new way?

CHAPTER 4

★

ALL OF LIFE SUPPORTS YOU

I'm not going to lie to you; I don't always glide through life. In case you were under any illusion, I am human. With a human perception, too. While I can certainly access these higher insights and understandings, it's not my default position. You only need to ask Gary, my mum or my beautiful circle of soul-led friends how often I need reminding of the higher viewpoint, too. I have a wonderful physical support team, as well as my SST, Chris (you will gather your own in a few chapters' time if you haven't already). They can help put my circumstances in context within a far bigger picture — one that aligns to my divine life path.

Standing in the eye of a storm, we cannot always see how things are changing. We only see what is swirling around us. If you're in the middle of your own storm, you may not believe what I'm about to tell you, because of your current viewpoint. But our storms — and life in general — is geared in your favour. Our storms, just like our rainbows, always serve us; we must train ourselves to see it this way. Life is always rushing in to take us where we want to go, the storm may just be clearing the way.

Looking back at my story, I was miserable in PR and longed for a new career with meaning. I yearned for a partner and was keen on Chris' vision showing the tall man with dark curly hair. (Had Chris just shown me his face, this would've made spotting Gary *much* easier.) Deep in my human aches and pains, desires and longing, I didn't see how life was bringing me not only what I wanted, but also what I needed to make it happen.

None of this is what my logical mind ever would have created. Instead, when I switch from my human, rational mind by creating more stillness, space and silence, when I follow the breadcrumbs, hear the divine invitations and follow the wisdom of my own intuition and Chris, things have a way of turning out in their own way, and in their own time. If I let it, life comes rushing in.

Life happens for you

Despite the storms and harsh terrain, we haven't arrived in an inhospitable environment. Of course, our rational mind may easily perceive it as such. To be sure, there are lessons and challenges here, but what our logical mind perceives as a setback, our soul sees very differently. Soul sees opportunity where our minds see challenge.

Our life does not happen to us; it happens for us. Our divine life path is unfolding to ensure we experience life's lessons and challenges, as soul desired. Our divine life path unfolds ensuring soul experiences the love, joy, breakthroughs and celebrations it came here to experience. And, our divine life path requires we express and share what our soul came here to offer. Our divine life path unfolds according to our life's manual; life works to ensure we fulfil what our soul came here to do.

Life is really just a classroom for soul to learn, experience and express, rather than a challenging and hostile place our mind can't reconcile. All of this was agreed to ahead of time, before your soul chose this human form, as you now know it. Based on your unique soul blueprint, your soul made many choices that would set up the particular lessons it came here to experience. This can range from choosing relevant aspects of your physical body and aspects of your life, such as your family of origin and culture, through to the soul mate relationships and environments that will encourage you to live out the blueprint. All of life is supporting you on the adventure your soul has chosen, even if your mind doesn't always view it as such.

SPIRIT SPEAK

Soul mate is a term for another soul who is mated or paired with your own, to ensure you each learn what you agreed to learn together, or teach what you promised to teach. Sometimes our soul mates arrive as romantic partners, but they can also be any other relationship. We can have many soul mate relationships in any given lifetime.

CASE STUDY – **Emma**

Emma suffered many health concerns; they started in her teens and culminated with fertility challenges in her thirties. Emma never received the praise and love she craved from her father growing up and often felt second fiddle to her older brothers. Although a high-performing woman, Emma felt unworthy — like nothing she did was ever enough.

In our work together, I explained to Emma that her soul had chosen to explore the balance of masculine and feminine energies, contributing to the family environment she experienced growing up. Emma's SST showed her that her body wasn't against her; it was working *for* her, and reminding her to reclaim her femininity and power as a woman. (In fact, the same could be said for her father and brothers, too, at the soul level. On the flip side of this lesson, they were exploring the reclaiming of femininity by first seeing it in motion.) She'd never been taught to honour her femininity and had shunned her menstruation as an obvious reminder of her differences from her brothers.

Emma used these themes to heal and transform, coming out the other side deeply passionate about women's health. She forgave her father and brothers, but more importantly, she forgave herself. Within this family dynamic, we can see Emma's soul learned and taught through these soul mate relationships. Accepting her femininity started to bring changes in her health, allowing Emma to have two daughters of her own. Her fertility challenge wasn't punishment for being female; it was trying to show her she'd disconnected from her femininity.

What you seek is seeking you

As much as Emma wanted to repair her relationship with her family and to start a family of her own, healing and motherhood also sought her out. In fact, I believe the souls of our unborn children work to prepare us for them, just as our SST is working to prepare us, too. Emma's body communicated with her the only way it knew how, to bring her back into alignment.

Because all of life is happening *for* you, the feelings, lessons, experiences are all also happening to remind you of where you're going. You seek such change because change is seeking you. What you seek is seeking you, too, and it's trying to communicate with you and lure you forward.

What if, like Emma and Maggie, your dreams, desires, feelings and guidance were actually showing you not only what is possible, but also what is *inevitable*? What if the storm arrives to clear the way for what you want? And what if the only thing stopping you is your perception of what's been before you?

Please don't punish yourself over this. It's par for the course. And you're about to learn a new way, to get out of your own way, and allow a new way to support you. We are not alone on our divine life path. Something so much bigger than us is trying to get our attention — if only we would listen and allow it to unfold, just like driving the Magic Car.

Divine timing

A pregnant woman doesn't force her baby's growth. The baby figures out which cell will become a liver, hair follicles, or skin — and when. The mother is not responsible for who is forming within her; she is not managing the how. Instead, she may focus on her health and prepare the space for her baby's arrival. A mother trusts her baby knows how to come into form.

This same magic that is present in a growing baby, tucked into its mother's womb, will support us long after we exit the womb, too. Whatever is at play during that phase is there for the rest of the baby's — and mother's — life, too.

As part of the Process of Forgetting, we seem to also have forgotten this beautiful connectivity to all of life.

We find it in the stillness, space and silence slipping into our lives.

We find it in the serendipity, signs and symbols we begin to notice.

We find it in the messengers who appear, guiding us forward.

And we find it in the remarkable way in which life can organise itself to meet us — when we get out of the way long enough to allow it.

Not only is there a divine life path, but beautiful divine timing at play in our lives. This timing is frustrating to our rational mind, but it's there nonetheless. Syncing up with our life's divine timing, to this wondrous magic underpinning it all, we can rest in the knowledge that we are taken care of. Working with this energy, as you're about to learn, we have the right people appear, opportunities turn up out of nowhere and more and more breadcrumbs arrive, leading us forward.

SPIRIT SPEAK

Energy as referred to in this book is not just your physical get-up-and-go. Rather, this type of energy is your life force.

Beyond our rational mind we can now see a more vast collective consciousness underpinning and orchestrating our lives. Maybe it's magic; maybe it's God, the Universe or Source. I've called it each of these and more, from time to time. No matter what we call it, that power created all of this: our physical world's ecosystems, seasons, galaxies, mysteries and wonder. It set us forth in motion. I believe this power is also big and clever enough to continue guiding and supporting me, and you, among this wonder, don't you?

We are part of something so much greater than our rational minds can perceive.

Web of interconnectivity

Something quite magical is at play in our mother and baby scenario, and again in the Magic Car story. After the thousands of hours spent in communication with the spirit world and beyond, I believe there is something so much bigger than us, something quite magical in its approach, orchestrating things in a way we could not manipulate (let alone fathom) on our own.

Beyond the idea that our soul chose our human form and an experience of life with a certain set of lessons and purpose, is the notion that Earth actually called each soul here to bring through said experience and purpose. Our souls came forth in response to Earth's call.

As each individual remembers what they were called here to do and be, we weave together a glorious interconnected web between heaven and Earth, where we benefit from each other's experiences.

Earth wanted each of us here to benefit from the frequency, gifts, lessons and purpose buried deep within us. As we bring forth that which is inside us, we activate this web of connectivity. You weren't just created the way you are for you — with your skills, assets, talents, interests, passions and also with your 'limitations', challenges and perceived flaws. Oh no! You were called here, to Earth, with your soul's unique programming, to support many other souls, and the Earth herself, in the process.

As we were guided earlier: '*Once you remember, you will set forth with greater clarity and focus to offer your soul's gifts, talents and skills.*

'*A mass Process of Remembering brings the mass rising of soul-led relationships, businesses, healthcare, financial structures. As each individual remembers who they are and the soul-role they play in the greater collective blueprint, then your earthly structures are remodelled. As an individual remembers, so does the collective.*'

We are not just remembering who we are for ourselves;
our remembering creates a chain reaction across the globe.
And as each of us lives out our divine life path, great
soul-led change will ricochet around the world.

We are in the throes of this change right now, and there are many, many beings (physical and non-physical) with a vested interest in our success.

Your team of advisors

Because heaven and Earth knew we'd forget our assignments upon arrival, they assigned each of us a team of advisors, our SST, to help us reboot our programming.

Earth called to soul, enlisting it to the Earth at this time. Soul came forth, with its unique expression, to meet the call. Preparing for its human adventure, soul met with a specific team of advisors, reviewing and agreeing to many of the terms of the mission. These details — our lessons, purpose, soul mates, karma and so on — were recorded in the manual.

Clairvoyantly, this meeting looks to me somewhat like the office of Albus Dumbledore in the *Harry Potter* movie franchise. Within this enchanted room, a specific team of high-level advisors called the blueprint guides meet to confer with the soul ready to reincarnate. All parties agree to what will happen on Earth in this lifetime — not all the finer details, for we have free will — but certainly the top-level themes that will come up on this adventure.

SPIRIT SPEAK

Blueprint guides are a specific type of spirit guide tasked with liaising with souls regarding their blueprints. These guides counsel each soul regarding the agreements, choices and experiences detailed in their blueprint prior to incarnating, as well as record and review amendments to the blueprint once the soul completes its lifetime.

Then, individual teams are assigned to help the soul navigate its time on Earth. This is your SST, made up of the guiding beings that will oversee, from a distance at first, how your soul performs in this lifetime. From time to time, if the soul has completely veered away from the agreement, or there is a sudden need to interject — say an immediate threat to the soul's life — then the SST will intervene to awaken that soul.

Even when it feels like we're all alone here, in an inhospitable environment, we are never alone; there are many guiding beings vested in our time here.

CHOOSE YOUR ADVENTURE –
RECOGNISE YOUR SUPPORT

 Consider how life has been working for you, supporting you, moving you through a timing beyond your own. Below are some journal prompts for you to reflect on how life has led you here, and how it may actually have been conspiring in your favour.

Consider the path you've followed to get where you are today. Looking back over your life ...

- Can you recognise the signposts that led you to where you are right now?
- What were the big, pivotal turning points? How have they helped you?
- Consider the moments you thought should have turned out differently, or that went against you. Can you alter your perception? Could you attach a different meaning to them now?

Consider where you are in your life today.

- Is this where you thought you'd be? Why/why not?
- Is it where the Universe intended you to be? Why/why not?
- What led you here? Were there breadcrumbs pointing you here? Were they pointing you elsewhere?
- What have you learned about yourself along this path? Why might learning this have been important to the path?

Now consider what you desire in your life right now.

- What do you desire? What are you seeking in your life?
- What if this was also seeking you? What would that belief mean to your life?
- If this thing is also seeking you, what might you do differently in your life?

CHAPTER 5

★

YOUR DIVINE INVITATION

Life whispers to us. It vies for our attention, trying to remind us why we're here. My psychic ability first arrived as a divine whisper, asking me to use my talents in a particular way. Admittedly, that whisper needed to become a smack about the head before my ability was channelled into giving readings. Before long, other whispers came, inviting me to create workshops, guided meditations, a deck of oracle cards, online courses, retreats and, more recently, this book. Each required a great deal of processing on my behalf to turn that whisper into form.

Our whispers don't just tell us where to use our talents and gifts, they steer us in other ways, too. Maggie's whisper asked her to share wellness and inner peace. Emma wanted to become a mother. Other clients have been called to leave relationships, improve their health or forgive parts of their past. Whatever the whisper received, each person was guided into the experiences, lessons, karma, relationships and the soul contracts in their manual. Many have gone on to access the manual, too.

Chris has given me various whispers and intuitive instructions, each ensuring I learn my lessons as well as present what my soul has to offer. Chris led me to my work, my marriage and through mothering my children. Each divine whisper prepares us for the next step along our divine life path, to fulfil our calling, which is only possible as we learn, heal and grow. The whispers will guide us through this, too.

Relinquishing the rational mind allows a new whisper, a more intuitive, soul-aligned directive, to reach us. And it's inviting us further along our divine life path and into our lessons and purpose.

Follow your calling

There's a reason, purpose, or mission that has called us into this lifetime — a vocation luring us forward. Our intuition and SST constantly invite us to remember that call and follow the breadcrumbs to be who we came here to be, to fill every corner of our lives with the unique beat pulsing through our heart and soul. Our feelings and intuitive hits invite us deeper into our purpose, which requires us to know, and then be, ourselves. Our vocation is to arrive as we are, offering who we are.

Every invitation, divine whisper and breadcrumb asks us to take the next immediate step towards being *ourselves*. We can no longer be who our rational mind has constructed us to be. Step by step, we are invited deeper and deeper into ourselves and into the secrets of our life path stored within us. But we will only ever receive the immediate next step, not the entire plan our rational mind desires. Not only do the divine whispers guide us, they ask us to move through a tremendous inner transformation, one step at a time.

If we listen and heed each call, we are led through huge inner growth and transformation, unearthing and remembering our truest self. A beautiful by-product of the inner transformation often emerges, birthing not only ourselves, but the very vocation at our core. In my case, this led to an entirely new career path, but it was more a by-product than the intended outcome. Purpose and career are not the same thing. We mustn't confuse the two. Often, our career helps to fund our vocation, and we must be mindful not to put pressure on our calling to also pay our bills.

My purpose now also pays my bills, however this isn't always the case, nor is it the goal. Maggie relied on her career when she began teaching yoga and meditation, and this did eventually replace her corporate salary as her sole income source. Emma's vocation, motherhood, was never at all about an income source; this always came from her career. While accepting that divine invitation is not necessarily a means to a new career ends, I've long joked with my clients that it sure is nice to be paid for being who you are.

A new voice arises

We must trust these gentle taps, whispers and nudges leading us forward. We must follow the breadcrumbs leading the way. We must let go of the rational mind's 'life plan' to allow our soul's divine life path to appear. In doing so, we edge ever closer to our vault and the secrets encoded within. Trust and surrender as you answer the call, knowing you're inviting something else to come rushing in to support you. We will remember not just what we're here to do, but who we were born to be.

Yes, it is possible to live this way — and still feel like you're getting things done — moving forward and achieving. I live this way and still get two children out the door each morning, run a business (and a busy household) and manage a full personal and professional schedule. To be clear, this isn't my forte; I juggle like most people do. I share this more as an indication that my life is perhaps not so different from yours. How I approach it, though, may differ.

Letting go of the rational mind's control isn't about letting go of your life or even letting go of the outcome (assuming your life plan is already aligned with your divine life path); it's about loosening your mind's grip to gain the life you were born to live. We want the rational and intuitive minds, our head and heart, to work in harmony. Our plans need to support the divine invitation we receive.

The next immediate step

I hope you're not expecting your invitation to be accompanied by a detailed road map, with every twist and turn itemised for you. I have found my past invitations to be more vague and somewhat piecemeal. Imagine you stand on one side of a room and want to get to the other side. All that's before you is a grid of tiles. Now imagine a tile in row one lighting up, let's say, to the far right. You step on it, only to see another tile in the next row, now further over on the left, lighting up. You continue on in such a way, stepping from lit tile to lit tile, as they light your way to the other side. So it is with our divine life path. Only the next step will light up, not the entire pathway. It can feel like you jump from place to place, but it all leads you forward. When it's time to take the next immediate step, the next whisper will arrive. We may get a sense of the overarching trajectory, or a pull in a particular direction, but rarely do we see every single step along the way, much to our rational mind's frustration. Instead, we receive a series of instructions preparing us for the next invitation.

For me, after finally acknowledging Cathy's visitation, my immediate next step was to practise giving readings — without placing pressure on them to become my livelihood. In fact, there was a period of time where I practised around my full-time PR job. Eventually, I knew it was time to leave. And that step gave way to more. Rest and meditate. 'Now, make this phone call.' 'Remove this from your diet,' Chris would suggest. The instructions varied in nature.

I followed; more guidance arrived. Each whisper gave way to the next: to leave my job to give readings full-time, to create products, then courses and, eventually, this book. My automatic writing hinted to the destination I was moving towards (it was telling me to use 'technology to disseminate' the messages I received, but I really had no idea what that even meant). I just focused on the step at hand, and I've been doing that ever since. The dots have connected looking back, like yours will one day, too.

The call of the times

Chris ensures the information I need arrives in a form I'm going to notice it in. When books appear on my radar, I tend to pay attention. One such book, *The Great Work of Your Life* by Stephen Cope, came to my attention. In it, Stephen explores vocation in people of all walks of life, from primatologist and anthropologist Jane Goodall and poet Robert Frost to a teacher, nurse and others. Across all these people, he identifies common traits among those who follow their vocation. As Stephen suggested one of these common traits was 'listening for the call of the times' I recognised that's what I'd done. Kind of like standing on a subway platform: you can hear the approaching train before it hurtles past you, and then the sound fades out again. This is the call of the times — it can creep up on you, then you're in the throes of the fast-moving effort, before it subsides once more. I followed the echo of a whisper, until another one came along. And there's always another whisper, another train.

In Maggie's case, the call of her times asked her to focus on her children and corporate career. The call led her to deepen her yoga and meditation practice through qualifications, before the call asked her to share it with colleagues — until she saw the materials and programs she could offer others. For us both, the call of the times was also present in the disconnection and confusion, for this is where the lessons lay. Neither Maggie nor I would have transformed without this impetus. As we'll explore later, it is most valuable to put your gift into service in the moment that you're in; when the moment changes, you follow the call.

More recently, the call of the times led me to writing this very book you're reading. As any author will tell you, I won't put pressure on this book to pay my bills. When asked as a child what I wanted to be when I grew up, I'd say, 'a writer'. This led me into journalism, PR and even blogging, too. Writing has been my passion — no doubt that's why I have 200+ journals from the past decade — but it's never squarely paid my bills. If I hadn't listened to the call of the times to grow my business and online presence, I wouldn't have connected with the people I have, which may have meant this book wouldn't have come into form in the way it did.

Every call is connected. Listening to each and every divine whisper, invitation, breadcrumb and utterance of our intuition and SST will eventually reveal a trail our minds couldn't have constructed on their own. Our job is to listen for the call — then follow where it leads.

Hear the call; notice the breadcrumbs

So much competing noise drowns out the whispers. It's hard for spirit to get our attention when we're driving blindfolded, radio blaring, one hand off the wheel as we clutch our mobile phones — which we stare at, one eye peeking out of the blindfold, concerned with what everyone else is doing on social media, blissfully unaware that we're careening into a ditch, or about to hit a tree. Sometimes it takes us smashing in to that tree for us to awaken to what is really in front of us — and to wish we had a Magic Car.

Sadly, we've lost the ability to trust ourselves, our own ideas and inner voice. Instead, we look to each other to answer our internal questions. Our rational mind and our expectations have concocted false versions of ourselves, based on anything other than who we truly are.

We've disconnected from that truth, our higher guidance
and the magic driving force underpinning our journey.
We're not running our own truth and our own programming,
we're relying on a false sense of self.

We've all constructed a false self from all the stories, beliefs, expectations and meanings our rational mind attaches to our human experiences, without understanding the web of connectivity underpinning it all. Quite different from the false self is our true self, the part of us that already knows why you've been sent forth here, what gifts you have to offer, the lessons you're here to experience and the purpose that can be found by offering this unique blend of who you are to those around you.

SPIRIT SPEAK

False self is a masked sense of self, often hiding behind ego, limiting beliefs, stories and meanings the mind has attached to our life. **True self** is your true nature or essence free from the mind's attachments, and shaped by your unique composition in this lifetime, without the mind's meanings.

Heeding your whispers, you'll be guided into the multi-faceted layers of your self, fostering a deeper relationship with yourself, as well as your intuition and SST. Step by step, your own divine life path emerges as the breadcrumbs lead you into the lessons, relationships and situations that allow your true self to shine.

Chances are, of course, that your relationship with your true self has not been front and centre thus far. Perhaps this feels confronting. For others, perhaps not so much. As I share the tools, techniques and suggestions throughout this book, you'll slowly come to see yourself in new ways, remembering what you've already always known, but had simply forgotten. My sincere hope — and trust — is that you'll come to love who you discover.

In the coming chapters, I'll outline a number of activities to connect you to your intuition and higher guidance, to your vault and manual and the myriad information available to you in any moment. More than anything else, I hope these tools and techniques help you to trust, love and honour yourself. When this becomes the foundation, then the true exploration of your life path will have been lived out. Because (spoiler alert) we're ultimately all here to experience true, unconditional love. And that's really who we are.

CHOOSE YOUR ADVENTURE – YOUR WHISPERS

Use the following journal prompts to reflect in your journal what is whispering to you, right now.

- If you knew you couldn't fail or get it wrong, what's the one thing you'd most like to do with your life?
- Imagine lying on your deathbed. What would you most regret not doing with your life?
- Like Maggie, is there something you dream of doing?
- Do you receive recurring signs, like my friend emailing me to join her workplace?
- What are you called to do? Who is the call asking you to be?

★

CHAPTER 6

STILLNESS. SPACE. SILENCE.

Rest and meditate. Rest and meditate. This was Chris' advice as I established my full-time psychic reading practice — not quite what my mind (or business background) expected. It was, of course, exactly the right advice.

Chris suggested I approach my days a little differently while starting this new phase. As I connected with Chris via meditation and automatic writing, he prompted me to tune in to my inner guidance on seemingly mundane issues such as what to eat, what to wear and what to do each day. Approaching each daily decision, I referred to my intuition before acting. As I progressed, Chris would bring new insights, adding to my own intuitive hunches, like removing meat and alcohol from my diet, drawing away from some relationships but leaning in to others, especially my new relationship with Gary. He would explain much of this via automatic writing, adding context to my own intuitive senses.

What my mind really wanted, though, was answers about my business. I asked Chris why my intuition and his guidance focused elsewhere. He said these steps would set the stage for what was to come. I was intrigued, but still somewhat in the dark on the *how*. Committed to the experiment, I kept going, applying what I could, as best I could. I continued journaling and observing similarities and patterns across client sessions.

After years in high-pressured work environments, driven by deadlines, media requests and client expectations, suddenly being told to rest, meditate, play, wait and relax was discombobulating. I had much to unravel as I began this new phase of my life. Expectations and any pretence of control went out the window. I had to find a new rhythm, a new pace, new practices and a whole new way of being in the world.

What I didn't realise at the time was that this unravelling was also helping me create enough stillness, space and silence to hear more of my whispers and notice more of the breadcrumbs. I was creating the perfect conditions to better, and more frequently, access my intuition and connect with the world of spirit.

Laying the foundations

What follows are the tools and practices Chris led me to as I created more receptive conditions for a relationship with him, and my intuition. Although I seemed to naturally tune in during my client sessions, I needed tools to better connect during my everyday moments too. I still use a combination of these tools, even though life's much busier now with children and a business. No doubt your life is very full, too – good! We don't need to run to the hills like mystics of old; modern life demands we find this in our everyday. (Although, if you're guided to have more solitary time for this process, *listen and honour that need*.)

You can incorporate many of these suggestions in to your existing routine. Chris continued to prompt me when it was time to tweak my lifestyle or routine to accommodate more stillness and space. When we discuss seasons and cycles in Chapter 24, you'll see there are peaks and troughs best suited to certain tools. Allow this to ebb and flow.

Start small. Layer the suggestions into your practice, mastering one before adding another. Notice which of my suggestions you're drawn to, and which ones you're not. Your avoidance and resistance may be a red flag. Observe your preferences with curiosity, and note them in your journal. If your rational mind interjects, this is likely when you need the tools the most.

> Cultivating more stillness, space and silence alleviates the rational mind's grip, giving way to the subtle intuitive whisper just below the surface. In this space, you begin to feel and know your heart and soul.

Stillness, space and silence

In an increasingly busy world, we must remind ourselves of our basic need to rest and recuperate. The popularity of activities such as yoga and meditation is rising. Even our devices now remind us to step away from them. Beyond the more obvious benefits to our physical, mental and emotional health, we can also receive a spiritual benefit.

Various options are available to help you cultivate stillness, space and silence. Watch the ones that come into your awareness now, hammering home their necessity. Please know, it's not the tool that is important, but the time and space you create to focus on the tool.

Meditate
About to protest? I've heard all the excuses before.

'Oh, I tried meditation and it wasn't for me. My mind's just too busy.' This is exactly *why* you need to try meditation, not avoid it!

'I cannot silence my mind.' You're not meant to. We have a rational mind for a reason; we must learn to master it, not let it master us. Meditation helps.

I may be unpopular for saying this, but I don't subscribe to the notion of a formal meditation practice (although I've learned various styles). Formal meditation practice is useful, but when it comes to meditation as a tool to connect to guidance, it's not the only way. Start where you can, with what you can.

Mindfulness can be found in the most mundane and busy moments of our day, too. With two small kids, my daily shower has become an efficient way for me to now meditate.

Meditation, to me, is any activity that allows you to sink beneath the mind-chatter and notice the wisdom waiting there. Perhaps you find this in your creative pursuits, or when reading a good book or out walking your dog. Do what works for you.

Common to most meditation is non-attachment to thoughts. Allow the thoughts to come and go; observe them, without grasping and attaching meaning to them. In the spaces between our thoughts, guidance slips in — it's wise to notice these thoughts!

Meditation is a tool, not a rule. We must be careful not to attach to meditation itself; if we have, we've missed the point. After meditating for twenty minutes, I'm far more interested in what you do in minute twenty-one. If we jump straight back into our old, busy, distracted ways, our meditation hasn't hit its mark. We practise meditation so we can call mindfulness into our everyday — with the kids, in meetings, on public transport, while cooking dinner and so on. Stringing together more and more present moments allows our purpose to rise to the surface, as you'll soon see.

Have fun

Yes, I am actually reminding you to do this! Having fun pulls us into the present moment; in it, we can't ruminate on the past or anticipate the future. Fun opens the door so the whispers can creep in and delight us.

Feeling good sets off an energetic chain reaction, which you'll become more familiar with later in the book. Feeling good is like programming an energetic magnet to bring us more of the same feelings. Being in alignment with our own divine life path feels good, but we can also work to cultivate these feelings more of the time in general.

Have you ever lost track of time when you've done something you love? Or, you've been thinking about a problem, only to go for a walk or wash the dishes (albeit, not that fun!), and realise your solution arrives. This is the kind of non-attachment having fun creates, and it's where wisdom can sneak in.

Where can you have more fun? Can you bring more fun to mundane activities? If you no longer know what you enjoy, experiment and find out. *Have fun* finding out. There's no pressure on an outcome, it's the process that's important.

Observe your response to having fun. Is it comfortable for you? How you feel about having fun hints towards your inner world. We'll explore this idea again in Chapter 15. For now, just note your feelings.

Journal

Regularly writing in my journal was single-handedly the best thing I did to develop a relationship and trust in my guidance. In my 200+ journals I've recorded my own thoughts, feelings and progress, as well as Chris' guidance via automatic writing. Even if you don't channel volumes from your own guides, establishing a journaling practice has other benefits.

Because I date and record all my observations, feelings, questions I ask Chris and his answers, my journals became the tangible proof my logical mind needed. The pages became written evidence my rational mind couldn't argue with. Even when your interpretation of a message or sign is inaccurate, you'll learn to interpret it differently next time.

Patterns and themes also emerge, which, when you move through the inner transformation later in the book, can be incredibly useful to reflect upon.

Oracle cards

Oracle cards are a divination tool, similar to tarot cards, but very different in energy. Each card brings with it a meaning, so you can select the cards to receive higher guidance. Working with oracle cards helped me connect to my SST, especially early on in client readings. Find a deck you are drawn to working with. When I couldn't find that for myself, I followed Chris' advice and made my own deck, The Little Sage Oracle Cards.

✳ *The Little Sage Oracle Cards were channelled through me, from Chris. He advised which cards were needed in the deck, and the meaning each card was to hold — I put these into the deck's reference book. Over the years, as I worked with Chris to channel more of the process now outlined in this book, I realised he'd already laid the groundwork with the specific cards he suggested for the deck. This oracle deck can help you navigate any of the phases from this book. You can find The Little Sage Oracle Cards on my website: helenjacobs.co.*

You can use oracle cards in many ways, but here are my favourites. Connect inward, then simply ask a question and pull an oracle card at random to answer it. Record the question and card meaning in your journal. Be sure to date it and watch your prediction unfold.

Sometimes, when I had an intuitive sense on something, I'd draw cards from the deck to help me better understand this feeling.

In my early readings, I used the cards as a trigger, turning on the tap to Chris. Giving practise readings to willing participants can boost confidence and trust in your abilities. With each reading, you build your own reference library of signs, symbols and additional meanings in your guidance. You'll come back to this reference library of meanings in upcoming chapters.

Connect with nature

Modern Australian living connects us to the outdoors, but this isn't true of all urban areas, and is certainly not true for all countries. If you can't get out into nature, try bringing the outdoors in. Potted plants, fresh flowers, crystals or salt water in your home or office can help. Try meditating in nature. Open your heart to the nature around you. Drop in to sync with its natural rhythms and cycles. Nature is in no rush and holds a wisdom all of its own. There's a good reason people hug trees!

Ground, clear and protect your energy

Think of your body as an electrical conductor. Your energy, like electricity, needs to be grounded or 'earthed', so the conductor doesn't overload. When our energy isn't earthed, we can feel 'off', with scattered focus. We can feel a little frayed.

Some telltale signs your energy isn't grounded include feeling
- physically, mentally, emotionally or energetically drained;
- easily influenced by what's going on around you, especially the moods, energy and feelings of others to the point of overwhelm;
- unfocused;
- irritable or scattered;
- 'spacey' or lightheaded;
- too busy — constantly rushing without being present in the moment;
- clumsy;
- dizzy, or like you're spinning; and
- queasy or nauseous before, during or after meditations, healing or spiritual work.

How to ground your energy:
- Eat fresh, organic (where possible) plant-based foods.
- Stand barefoot on the earth or hug a tree.
- Sit in nature.
- Swim or bathe in salt water (the ocean is ideal).
- Wash your face, hands and/or feet.
- Carry crystals such as smoky quartz and red jasper.
- Use guided meditations designed to ground, balance or protect your energy.

Observe

Think of someone important to you, right now. Notice how you feel in your body. Now, notice your thinking. Which part of you is thinking? Are the thinking and feeling different? And which part of you is noticing? The part of you doing the *noticing* is what I call the observer — tune into this part of you often, especially as you move deeper into this book. Your observer will want to notice the difference between your thinking and feeling. Practise this often. Your observer objectively detects patterns, themes and clues in your mind, body, emotion and spirit that your rational mind may not. Keep recording your observations in your journal.

Self-love and self-care

Your relationship with self will come front and centre. An unconditional love for self must be cultivated — in fact, your guidance will ensure it. Self-care practices will fall in line with levels of self-love. And our love and care for ourself will be interwoven with our divine life path; they are also often the first practices sacrificed when we are out of sync with it.

Low levels of self-care require more time for silence, stillness and space — but may also prevent it, too. Women, in particular, are often far too unfamiliar with dedicating time to themselves in this deeply self-appreciating way, let alone doing it consistently. Your levels of self-love and self-care will be highlighted to you as you continue through the book.

> We cannot trust our intuition if we do not trust ourselves. We cannot love our lives if we do not love ourselves. We cannot listen to and honour our guidance and life path if we do not listen to and honour ourselves.

Coming in closer to our true self, we'll come face-to-face with these inner turmoils, and be led into healing them.

Remembering what you know means remembering how loved, and loving, you are. Our world could remarkably change as we each send forth ripples of love, all born out of a deeper love for ourselves.

Rhythm and ritual

Life is influenced by many natural rhythms and cycles. Our seasons are a perfect example, as is the daily rising and falling of the Sun and Moon. As women, our monthly menstrual cycle provides another natural rhythm to our lives. In order to hear the divine's whispers, we must sync with the divine's rhythms.

In our Western, modern world, we've tried to outsmart and override many of these rhythms. No wonder we're disconnected from their wisdom. Consider how attuned your life is to the array of personal and universal rhythms at play. Contemplate this across your day, week, month and year.

Honour the beautiful transition points in your days, weeks, months and life, and harmonise with the natural points of rest and work, and giving and receiving. Remember back in Chapter 2, when describing the head and heart, I said it's the same as the balance between masculine and feminine? We need both energies in our rhythms; but we have ignored the more feminine, receiving, intuitive, creative moments in our lives. This is where the wisdom is kept.

Within the rhythms, then, we can create rituals that are sacred to us and our individual practice. Many of the tools I've suggested, like journaling and meditation, have become rituals at key points in my natural rhythm. Notice what you're drawn to in different points in your own seasons and cycles, and trust what you discover as you explore.

 ## CHOOSE YOUR ADVENTURE — FIND YOUR RHYTHM

Encouraging more stillness, space and silence in your life, whether through these suggestions or others you're drawn to, switches gears from the rational mind to the intuitive. Our hearts and souls have a chance to speak, and be heard. From an observer's position, we're more likely to spot the breadcrumbs, leading us where our physical eyes weren't looking. Within this stillness, space and silence, more messengers arrive with specific instructions for you. You're about to meet them in the next few chapters.

It's time to layer some of these practices into your routine. Review the suggested activities in this chapter and notice which ones you're drawn to. Why are you drawn to them? Which ones are you less drawn to? Why?

Visualise your ideal day, week, month and year. What is it filled with? How do you feel in those activities? How can you bring more of those feelings into your current reality?

Now put these into your calendar. If you're like me, putting things into your calendar feels like making a commitment — but that's what this may take to begin. Select the activities you're committing to and slot them into your schedule. Identify where you can bring the activities into moments already scheduled, rather than finding more time, if you're time-poor.

A lovely starting point is to review your morning and/or evening routine. Many people have shared with me they use The Little Sage Oracle Cards as part of their morning routine. Why not try turning over a card or two each morning to help set your intention and focus for the day ahead? Making a few intuitive tweaks to your existing routine can make a big difference, opening the way for more intuitive guidance to arrive.

CHAPTER 7

★

LIFE'S MESSENGERS

Guidance finds me in the most unusual places. When Isla was young, I found myself at an impasse with motherhood and my work. Wondering what was next for me, I took Isla out for a walk in her pram, only to wind up at our local library. Along the way, I asked Chris to send me a sign. Meandering the library's shelves, I picked up a random book. Flicking through the pages, a small card fell out. On that card someone had printed a Richard Buckminster Fuller quote, reminding me that when I begin to do what I really want, I will have a very different life. Got the message loud and clear, Chris! I returned to work soon after.

Many people tell me they see repeating numbers, especially 1:11 or 11:11 (it's a positive manifestation sign and gateway). Pay attention to any recurring number pattern and interpret its meaning. Between my PR jobs, while giving psychic readings, I saw 55 everywhere — even carved on a tree in nearby bushland. It's a number signalling great change.

Car number plates often provide signs, too, like the time Gary and I bought our first house together. As I'm self-employed, we had a little trouble securing our home loan, but my spirit guides were on the case. Let's pretend the new home's address was 19 Star Street; well, when a car with the number plate 195TAR pulled in front of me, I knew the house was ours.

One of my all-time favourite stories about signs is from my mum. Mum was desperate to move from our family home, but Dad is a little slower moving in nature. When my parents built that home, Mum planned on being there for a few years. Some twenty years later and Dad still wasn't ready to go. After her mother passed away, Mum was desperate for a sign, let alone a fresh start in her life.

She says she sat at the end of her bed, literally threw her hands up in the air and pleaded out loud: 'Send me a sign!'

Within twenty-four hours there was a knock on the front door. Dad answered the door to find a real estate agent, claiming to have a buyer. My parents' home was not on the market, nor had they contacted any agents; this was a cold-call (or, more accurately, a cold-knock). Dad was closing the door as Mum came flying down the hallway shouting, 'Come in, come in!'

The agent did have a buyer — two in fact. A day later, they'd sold their house for the dream price Mum had wished for. She got both a sign and the means to start afresh.

I have countless examples of these types of moments that sadly are more often than not assigned to mere coincidence. I urge you to look more closely, and to start inviting more of them in.

Who are the messengers?

All this talk of breadcrumbs, whispers, invitations, signs, intuition and spirit! Suffice to say, we each have many messengers bearing many messages — and they're all trying to get our attention.

There are many ways we might receive such messages, reminding us of our life's mission. We receive messages within our own body, through our intuition and the wisdom of our physical, mental, emotional and spiritual layers. We can also receive messages from sources outside of our body, like life supporting us with signs and communication from our SST. Indeed, as my own story highlights, we can receive information from the spirit of loved ones who've passed away, too. There are many layers to the realms of spirit wishing to communicate with us.

My awakening to spirit was rather sudden and dramatic. Rest assured, yours may not be. Opening to my psychic and medium abilities came relatively easily for me, but I had to actively work to understand the other forms of guidance available to me, especially my intuition. Chris has explained to me that I needed to go into the world of spirit so I could understand intuition from spirit's perspective, then come back to teach others how to access their intuition, so they could access spirit. For the past decade, I've worked with Chris in this back-to-front way, dissecting the knowledge in ways my head could understand — and then, figure out just what the heck I was supposed to do with all this information. I hope you may now benefit from my practice.

Most of my clients start by connecting with the messengers of signs and symbols, intuition and feelings — you may, too. From there, you may build up to working with spirit guides or higher guiding beings. Over the years, I've noticed that as people strengthen their intuition, they are naturally, simultaneously allowing more space for their SST to pop in. A relationship (and communication) with spirit becomes stronger and more sustainable over time.

That said, there's no hard and fast rule to it — and, as I've shown, I didn't do it this way, anyway! Follow the path that appears for you without putting pressure on it to be a certain way. We'll take a much deeper look at each of these messengers in the coming chapters, but let's briefly become acquainted with the guidance available.

Signs

Did you notice all the signs in this chapter's opening passage? The quote card falling out of the library book; the angel number signalling great change; the number plate with our new home address; the knock on my parent's front door answering Mum's prayers (and nudging Dad along). Such signs are now commonplace in my days — but they were there long before I recognised them.

Don't expect a neon-flashing sign to fall from the sky and land at your feet; signs are usually far more subtle than that. Sometimes, and especially in the beginning, signs are best recognised from the vantage point of hindsight. Among the more common signs people notice are repeating numbers, songs, feathers, coins, butterflies or dragonflies. These can be quite common calling cards from our loved ones, but can also be used by our SST, too.

Like Usher's song in Cathy's visitation, another song signalled when it was my grandma's time to pass away. For three weeks, our family kept vigil by Granny's hospital bed. Like I had every other day for those weeks, I jumped into my car that morning for my daily hospital trip, only to be caught off-guard by the song playing on the radio. Puff Daddy's 'I'll Be Missing You' blared from the car stereo at the chorus, where Faith Evans sings of the life after death — the life taken and the bond broken, and all that would be missed. Upon hearing the lyrics, I thought I'd missed Granny's departure, but I arrived at the hospital to have another couple of hours with her. She passed later that day.

Who knows why these two ageing Irish women chose Usher and Puff Daddy as their messengers, but they did. I doubt in life they even knew who these people were, but that makes me love these signs even more.

Not everything and anything constitutes a sign, though. It's also better to ask for *a* sign, rather than dictating a *specific* sign. Allow the Universe and your SST to decide how to answer you, then stay open and receptive to what shows up. You'll know it's a sign by how it *feels*.

Because all of life is working to support us, the collective consciousness — the magic — can bring us signs, as can the members of our SST, or as Cathy and Granny showed us, our loved ones. But we have other messengers, too, like our intuition.

Intuition

I like a good pun and word play, so when someone once highlighted that intuition is rather like 'inner-tuition', I remembered it. Our inner tutor is always teaching, helping and guiding. It's our internal navigation system tasked with keeping us moving along our divine life path.

Like a sixth sense, instinct or gut reaction, intuition is a (mostly) broad feeling or hunch; a push or pull in a particular direction that often can't be logically explained. Your intuition may come as an inner sense or a call to move in a particular life direction, without a logical or rational explanation as to why (like, say, leaving a secure and respected PR job to become a psychic reader in your twenties).

Connecting with our intuition requires us to observe our bodies and our feelings. Intuition can be hard to put your finger on. It's intangible and illogical, and what your mind will likely deem irrelevant or 'just a silly feeling'. I hope by now you know it's *not* just a silly feeling; intuition is rich with information. Your job is to interpret it and put it to good use. You're about to learn how.

Spiritual Support Team

If your intuition is your internal navigation system, then your SST is like a group of tour guides you consult with from time to time, or even a fellow passenger (although, my fellow physical passengers aren't always so accurate in their guidance!).

Your SST is the team of advisors preparing you to access your vault. We may not always be aware of them, and that awareness may change at different stages of our life, but our SST is *always* there. This team's guidance builds on your hunches, providing context and specific details and explanations. My conversations with Chris are much like my favourite physical conversations. We banter. I'm often amused, but mostly I'm asking questions and listening intently. In the beginning, many of our conversations would occur while I was in meditation. In this altered state, space was created for impressions to bubble up into my awareness, usually visually in my mind's eye (commonly known as clairvoyance) or auditory in my mind's ear (less commonly known as clairaudience). Deeper conversations have occurred in the pages of my journal, via automatic writing. These are particularly useful conversations, where I can pose a question, then receive Chris' response. However, Chris also reaches me in the middle of my day-to-day activities — it's not unusual for me to be mid-(physical) conversation with someone, and for Chris' impressions to interject. This is also how I run my client sessions: by hearing, seeing and feeling Chris' non-physical impressions, then relaying them via physical communication with my client. As you might imagine, there's a lot going on for me at any given time!

Calling the SST a team naturally implies there is more than one spirit guide, and you'll get to know the specific members of your SST in Chapter 10. This team is comprised of a group of non-physical beings from the realm of spirit; it's a combination of spirit guides, angels, archangels, ascended masters or other light beings. There will be at least one main spirit guide and also one guardian angel — both assigned to you for your entire lifetime. Typically, there's also at least one healing guide, teacher guide, gatekeeper guide and a purpose guide, although there may be more of certain guides at any given time. I've worked with a number of blueprint guides, too. The angel realm works in a similar way, although I tend to focus on spirit guides.

Some spirit guides have a speciality focus, and are more like consultants on our path; they may turn up during important moments, but not stay. I had a particular business guide when I first built my business, and another guide when I became a mother.

Many people feel guided by their loved ones who've passed away. Cathy and, more recently, my maternal grandmother, have played important roles in spirit. However, I don't include them in my SST. I communicate with them from time to time, but I don't believe they are assigned to help me on my life path in quite the same way as my guides and angels are. I see them more as soul mates — other souls assigned to my soul's learning and growth — than spirit guides. (Also, spirit guides rarely incarnate on Earth.)

I love my grandmother dearly, but she's a very mischievous woman in spirit, just as she was in life. While she always has my best interests at heart, she still likes to play games with me! Like the time she gave us the lotto numbers while I channelled her messages to my family — we have all played them religiously since, but alas no win (yet!). So, I take her guidance into account in a slightly different way than I do the main guides in my SST. Our loved ones don't necessarily take on the same role as our spirit guides to nurture our spiritual growth upon leaving their physical bodies, so please don't feel like you have to follow their advice just because now they're in spirit. If you didn't take a loved one's advice in life, there's no need to start when they're in spirit.

Beyond your SST is other, higher guidance, too.

Higher self

While your SST is a wonderful group of high-vibrational counsellors and advisors, they are not the same as your higher self. As we've seen, the members of your SST are non-physical beings who are assigned to your soul's growth and development. Your higher self is quite different. It's not assigned to oversee the growth and development of your soul, but rather to help you attain your highest potential in this particular lifetime. Your higher self is you, from this lifetime, but on a much higher dimension than this earthly plane. I think of my higher self as the highest, truest, purest energetic version of me, without the 'baggage' of the earthly dimension.

Your higher self is not your physical, mental or emotional self nor is it your 'stories', your past, present or future. It is not defined by personality or experience in this lifetime. In fact, it is a higher part of you, unrelated to the humanly 'stuff' of life. You can recognise your higher self as a pure, loving, non-judgmental and unlimited being, quite different to the personality or thinking self, but separate again from the members of your SST and your soul.

Just as your higher self doesn't have the 'baggage' or heavier three-dimensional effects of the human self, it also doesn't carry the karma of accumulated lifetimes, which your soul does. So, there is also a distinction between your higher self and soul. We can think of the higher self as an aspect or expression of the soul, but not the soul itself.

You can communicate directly with your higher self, when the time is right. And as you familiarise with your true self, you're really accessing your higher self.

Soul

The soul is the aspect of us that has incarnated across an extended timeline of lifetimes, linking us to these multiple lifetimes. In contrast, our higher self is linked only to this lifetime. Our soul is the part of us coming to Earth to explore, learn and grow in accordance with the blueprint. Thus, the soul has accumulated lifetimes of experiences, lessons and relationships, as well as gathered many gifts and talents. As the soul incarnates, it chooses which of these will be brought forward into this particular lifetime.

Each of us was sent forth from the same source. We are all born forth from this, yet separate in what we are sent forth to experience in our lives.

Our soul takes on human form, as my soul chose me to be Helen Jacobs. As Helen, I have a higher self — me on a higher dimension — as well as my soul, who has lived through lifetime after lifetime. I've clairvoyantly seen a number of these lifetimes, and the accumulation of the lessons, gifts and experiences that all feed into this particular lifetime, in various ways.

Our SST, then, works to remind the soul of its task this time around. We can work with our SST, our soul and also our higher self to gather information to help us in this human form.

Building a relationship

Our relationship with our inner and higher wisdom will ask us to be present in new ways. It will require us to come in deeper, to trust more, and commit and actively engage in the relationship. This, of course, takes time and practise. But the objective is not just about receiving more guidance; it's also about creating a deeper and more meaningful relationship with your self, and in turn, others.

All too often, I see people turn to their intuition or higher guidance in moments of impending change — as they notice they're careening into a ditch or about to collide with a tree. While we may be able to obtain guidance in those moments, it's a rather ineffectual ongoing strategy.

Consider the last time you were faced with a major life choice. Were you inclined to walk out your front door and ask the first person you saw for advice, let alone take it?

No, probably not.

You may be more likely, however, to turn to people you love and trust, and vice versa, as you value their input into your life (although, they may not actually be privy to your exact divine life path). It's best to turn to someone we know, love and trust, *and* who knows our soul's path and purpose.

If we only ever call on guidance in those big life moments, it can add extra pressure to our choices, as we haven't developed a trusting relationship with our intuition over time. We can't yet decipher the advice — and in a pressure-fuelled situation, that just adds more stress. In those charged moments, as we hurtle towards the crash ahead and brace for impact, it can be far too difficult to clearly and reliably work with our guidance, unless we've taken the time in moments with less 'charge' to understand our guidance's nuances. These big defining moments aren't necessarily the best place to foster trust, which is why I suggest you start with seemingly smaller, more mundane choices.

Clearly, leaving my job to pursue psychic readings was a big life change, and it was all-consuming at the time. I certainly had a baptism by fire in my relationship with spirit — but that was also part of my divine life path. Unless it's part of yours, give yourself some time and space, and start small. If you find yourself in a defining moment, by all means, call on your guidance, but know it may be in the act of working with it that you learn most about it, rather than guaranteeing an outcome.

> To be best prepared in times of crisis and change,
> we must cultivate a relationship with our intuition,
> our SST, and the signs and symbols we receive,
> and nurture that relationship over time.

Imagine if we all learned this as children! Alas, we didn't learn it as children (and I'm surely working harder so my kids learn this from the outset), but we're coming to it later, so please give it time. Don't put pressure on the relationship, especially too early. Remain open and willing, but don't give away your power either. To give your relationship the best chance at success, you must create the right environment for it to thrive.

Yes, even you

Let's clear something up before you ask me: yes, you have the ability to connect with some form of higher guidance, just as I do. Where we may differ is how we use our abilities.

Let's say you and I are in the same room, alongside a piano. Both of us can sit down at the piano, press the keys and make a sound. Technically, we both *can* play the piano. Now, I have no inclination to learn piano, but let's say you do. So you stay on, practising. I've heard it can take 10,000 hours to become an expert in an area — so after you dedicate that amount of time to it, suffice to say you're on par with Mozart, and I'm, well, still mashing keys. Mozart's gifts clearly lay with music, certainly far surpassing my personal musical ability. I suspect this was a deep soul knowledge wired within him. You, me and Mozart can all generate sound from the piano, each with glaringly different results.

When it comes to guidance, I've put in well over 10,000 hours of practise. And while I don't wish to pretend I'm the Mozart of my field, I do feel like I have a strong natural inbuilt ability to do what I do; it's how *my* soul is wired. But that doesn't stop anyone else from also honing their abilities beyond a basic level. In fact, I believe it a darn shame if you don't.

So, yes. Each of us is born with a built-in ability to connect to our guidance.

All of life is supporting *all* of life, not just a select few.

Maybe you have stories of your own — signs you've seen or the spirit visitations you've had. If you haven't, that doesn't mean they haven't occured, you just haven't noticed them yet. But, you're about to!

 ## CHOOSE YOUR ADVENTURE – ACCESS YOUR GUIDANCE
Over the next few chapters, you'll become more familiar with working with signs, intuition and your SST. On the next page is a guided meditation to help you create stillness, space and silence. It is specifically geared towards opening to your SST.

Going higher — Sacred Space visualisation

Your Sacred Space is a beautiful multi-dimensional environment where you can receive guidance and integrate new knowledge and energies. Come to your Sacred Space often to initiate the new information, or to release what comes up for you. Your Sacred Space provides a safe haven, a refuge and an opportunity to connect with your SST, higher self or soul. You can come here for specific enquiries, or simply to spend time in meditation — becoming familiar with the space and the beings that commune there. Trust your intuition here, and interact with the space and any beings who arrive here, as you feel guided to interact. Your Sacred Space may offer you healing when you need it or nourishment when it's required. Any other need can be met here, if you allow it to happen.

Follow these simple steps to transport yourself to your Sacred Space any time you need (and remember to always record your experiences there — your notes may make more sense to you at a later time).

Transporting yourself to your Sacred Space:

1. Create physical time and space for yourself, and invoke the sacred in whatever way feels good to you. This may be through prayer, lighting a candle or incense, playing quiet music in the background, or performing some other ritual you feel drawn to.

2. Take some deep breaths into your belly, letting your belly rise and fall. Don't alter this or force it. Just allow the breath to fill you up, and expel it when ready.

3. Sink into the support beneath you (the bed, chair or floor). Let it take your full weight. Allow all of your muscles to relax and become incredibly heavy — knowing you are supported to fully let go and surrender. Close your eyes and relax.

4. Invite in your SST, just by holding the intention to do so. Call in white light. Invite your soul to join you, or any other guiding being who wishes to work with you.

5. Then, simply hold the intention or make the request to be transported to your Sacred Space. Allow the scenery to form in your mind's eye, without overthinking it or questioning it.

6. Spend as much time here as possible. Notice who turns up, what they offer you, and how your energy feels and changes with each visit. You can come here with a particular question in mind, or to revisit something from one of the guided meditations. Or you can just connect within and with your SST.

7. When today's visit feels complete, give thanks and simply bring your awareness back to your breathing — deep breaths into your belly. Begin to feel your physical body connect with the support beneath you. A few gentle movements may help to bring you back. Then, open your eyes, gently, when you're ready.

8. Remember to record your impressions from today's visit in your journal.

✳ To help you connect to your Sacred Space and spirit guides, check out my full suite of guided meditations at helenjacobs.co.

CHAPTER 8

★

SIGNS & SYMBOLS

One of the most beautiful signs I've ever received came to me via Isla and my grandmother, who died when Isla was six months old. This sign hit me by surprise one afternoon, as an almost three-year-old Isla and I sat on my bedroom floor, rolling a ball back and forth. As we played, Isla said to me, 'Mum, soon there will be a baby in your tummy, it's my sister Rosie, and I wish she'd hurry up because we need to ride our bikes together.'

What Isla didn't know (as best as we could hide it from her) was that I'd just experienced my third miscarriage, which had left me wondering if our second baby would ever turn up. In between our losses, Gary and I often privately discussed baby names; we had earmarked Rose for a girl, in homage to Granny. She loved roses, and often wore tuberose fragrance. Isla's unprompted prediction in and of itself was a remarkable sign — but it doesn't end there.

A month after Isla's prediction, I did indeed fall pregnant again. Due to the miscarriages, I was referred to a new obstetrician working out of a new maternity hospital near our home. I probably wouldn't have chosen that particular hospital if not for the referral — not only had I been happy where I delivered Isla, but this new maternity hospital was actually a recent addition to the very same hospital Granny died in three years earlier. Working with our obstetrician, we soon realised our baby's due date would be the exact anniversary of Granny's death. How's that for divine timing?

As Granny lay in that same hospital all those years before, she knew we would want a sign from her in spirit. In her last conversation with us, Granny told my sisters, my parents and I that she would send us a rose. And it's the most beautiful I've ever seen. She certainly wouldn't smell as sweet by any other name.

Much divine timing was at play to deliver our Rose in such a way. While in the eye of my own private storm with those miscarriages, I truly couldn't see life working for me. But it was. We couldn't have orchestrated that sign, and its timing, any better if we'd tried, which is the nature of such authentic divine signs. No amount of baby planning could have delivered us our Rose to arrive on Granny's anniversary, in the same hospital where she passed away in, if we tried.

Is it a sign?

Signs don't always come from our deceased loved ones; they can come from the magic underpinning all of life, as well as from our spirit guides and angels. They often turn up as confirmation that our hopes and prayers have been heard and answered, much like the car license plate 195TAR confirming we'd get our new home.

As an amusing anecdote, and a true indication of how Chris likes to work with me, here's a story that took place while I was writing this chapter. Unsure if I should include certain anecdotes, I wanted Gary's opinion. He was tidying the kitchen while I worked at the dining table nearby. At the exact same time I asked this question, Gary walked over to me, carrying something. I finished my question as he placed a white feather on the table beside me. Pay attention to your thoughts when such a sign is received, as feathers are often seen as confirmation from spirit guides and angels that they're listening and affirming we are on the right track. It's these kind of serendipitous events that constitute a 'symbolic' sign — and I took the feather as confirmation Chris enjoyed my anecdotal inclusion.

Tasking our observer to spot these signs, synchronicities, 'coincidences' or 'strange' occurrences ensures we'll notice them. They're happening all the time, even when we aren't paying attention. A sign can come in any form, really, but it will come in answer to the question you've been pondering — just like my feather. Not all signs are so obvious. Some signs will repeat until we notice them, like recurring patterns and themes. These are great signs flagging your lessons in life. While the signs to our life path may repeat, it can take quite a lot of energy, particularly for our deceased loved ones, to bring us such signs. I'm sure you'd hate to miss their call.

Genuinely receiving a sign is not the same thing as looking for one. Objectivity is key here. We can't just randomly see things and take them as confirmation we're doing the right thing. This is likely your mind playing tricks, trying to convince you of its preferred way, not soul's. Working with signs works best from a place of observation and curiosity — a healthy scepticism keeps things in check. You can always ask for confirmation of the sign, too, like a quality assurance it was the real deal. Repeating confirmations is a far better sign than a one-off.

You'll know it's a sign by how it *feels*.

Asking for a sign

If you'd like to receive a sign, *ask*. Then, allow it to come to you in whatever way it can. But be sure to look out for its arrival — and believe it when it comes. I've seen people demand guidance rather than politely ask for it. 'Show me a yellow car now if I should quit my job,' someone might say, desperate for a sign. But perhaps they're going about it the wrong way. Rather than specifying the sign, simply ask your messenger to bring you a sign you'll understand. 'Please show me a clear sign this is the right move for me to make,' may get you better results.

Gary asked for and received a great sign recently. For some time, another online travel company (this time a social media app for travellers) had tried to pique Gary's interest in working with them. Had I known this part of the story from the beginning, it would've felt more familiar — but I didn't know it at the time.

Gary and I sat down one night, creating a request of the Universe for Gary's work to give him, and our family, more freedom, flexibility and funds. He actually interviewed for another company soon after — and in between his interviews, he freelanced for the travel app. When he didn't get the job he interviewed for, he finally mentioned this travel app to me, along with their attempts over the past year or so to lure him to their employ. After he missed out on the other job opportunity, the app people finally asked him what it would take for Gary to come and work for them. He was still about to dismiss it, when I explained the bigger picture of this turn of events to him from Chris' point of view. This was actually the Universe delivering what we'd asked for.

Gary met with the app founders and expressed his needs for freedom, flexibility and funds with his potential new employers. They offered him a job with the conditions he desired. Driving home from that meeting, Gary says he asked for a sign if this was the right job to take.

On the fifteen-minute drive home, Gary's phone pinged as an email arrived. He was reading the email as he walked in the door. A recruiter had emailed, telling Gary about an amazing job opportunity he'd be perfect for — the very job he'd just been offered. He took that as confirmation and accepted the job.

✳ *You'll discover the specific process we can use when asking for,
receiving and interpreting signs in Chapter 11.*

Literal or symbolic?

Not every sign is literal; they are usually highly symbolic. I've learned
to tell the difference through trial and error.

Remember when I switched jobs from the PR agency to the online
travel company? I had a six-week break between jobs, coinciding with
the Australian summer. Sadly, I lost my favourite watch the day after
I left the PR agency. I'd pulled my house and car apart trying to find
this watch, to no avail. As it turns out, I didn't really miss it too much
while enjoying my hiatus.

Not long before I was due to start my new job, I was rummaging
in the boot of my car, cleaning out the sand from the holidays. I opened
the latched lid to the spare tyre compartment and saw my shiny silver
watch staring back at me. Intuitively, I felt Chris had shown me it was
better to have lost all track of time than to have been bound by it.
I haven't worn a watch since.

Let's say you kept seeing keys everywhere. It's a sign! But
to what?

A literal explanation could be linked with the actual keys, perhaps
foretelling you're about to get some new keys (a new house, or car?) or
that you need to pay attention so you don't lose them. Symbolically,
keys may signal you're about to 'unlock' a vital piece of information,
or that you're feeling locked out of a situation. When it comes to the
sign our messengers bring us, we must first check if it's a literal or
symbolic message.

Symbolism

Logic loves literalism; soul loves symbolism. We must be able to interpret
both and use them wisely. Literal signs aren't too difficult to decipher,
but the symbolic ones can be. This is often where people run in to

trouble — it's not the message itself that's missed, but the meaning it was trying to convey. We cannot shoot the messenger!

I've already mentioned that feathers are symbolic calling cards from angels, or in my case, Chris. Butterflies and dragonflies signal change and transformation. Keys symbolise unlocking. In the next chapter on intuition, we'll see that our body also signals to us using symbolism, just as we saw earlier in Emma's story of healing her femininity to improve her fertility. Consider the language we use to describe common ailments — a pain in the neck, backbreaking work. How we interpret such signs and sensations is important. We must dig for the hidden meaning (but not expect to find it in everything).

Dreams provided a great learning ground for me when exploring symbolism. We have up to five dreams each night, filled with a wealth of information about our life path and experience of it. Dream interpretation books and websites helped me in the beginning to understand symbolism. I applied many dream interpretations to signs and symbols in my waking life, too. I didn't always intuitively agree with these interpretations, though; I always ran it through my own intuition and Chris, too. I suggest you do the same.

Interpreting signs and symbols

Slowing down, curiously enquiring into our lives and receiving the wisdom is paramount. Before we blindly act on the information we're given, we must be sure we've understood and interpreted the details properly.

For now, as you explore your signs and symbols trailing your breadcrumbs, remember to

- slow down and observe the subtleties and nuanced information (remember to observe, journal, meditate and reflect);
- determine if the message is literal or symbolic (you'll usually have an intuitive hunch one way or the other);

- interpret the message's meaning (if literal, this is straightforward; if symbolic, look to build your reference library through dream interpretation resources);
- ask more questions to round out the meaning (then wait for an intuitive answer, more signs or an answer from your SST); and
- intuitively check in on the response (sit with it for a while and notice how you feel about it).

It's a game of Q&A. Ask and receive an answer. Then, ask and receive an answer again. Continue asking and receiving information from your SST, and life itself — then develop your own reference library. The exercise at the end of this chapter will help. Patient trial and error is key — and recording it all in your journal.

CASE STUDY – Mandy

Mandy recently came to me in tears, worried she'd interpreted her spirit guides' advice incorrectly. For some time, they'd shown her the importance of changing jobs, which she had done. They had also encouraged her to pursue a particular client once she started her new job. Mandy had worked tirelessly to secure that client, despite sometimes feeling uneasy about some of the methods involved in the workplace's pitch and proposed work tactics should they win the client. All was going well, until the client pulled out at the last minute. The deal fell over. Naturally, Mandy thought she'd misinterpreted the guidance.

While I understood Mandy's frustration, for it had been my own many times before, she had not got the guidance wrong. She was indeed right to pursue the client — but her spirit guides weren't as interested in winning the client as Mandy's mind was. Instead, Mandy's spirit guides led her down this path to ensure

Mandy (and arguably her employer, colleagues and the potential client) learned some very valuable lessons about the way they were all conducting business.

Mandy's uneasy feeling is important here, too — we must always refer back to our intuition, and enquire into our feelings. While she may still have pursued the client, she may have had a better understanding of what needed tweaking and adjusting by running the information through her intuition, too.

Our messengers are assigned to lead us into the situations where we'll learn and explore what our soul came here to do. These situations don't always look like our minds expect them to. Our intuition can help steer us through this.

 ## CHOOSE YOUR ADVENTURE —
DEVELOP A REFERENCE LIBRARY

Alongside my journal, I also found an indexed address book to use as a personal symbolism reference library. These kinds of books may be a little harder to find in our technologically driven world, but I encourage you to find one and put it to use.

As you continue to recognise your own signs and symbols, place them into the reference library by sign and meaning. You can already add feathers, keys, butterflies and dragonflies.

Your dreams will also help you rapidly build out your interpretation library. Keep adding to this book as you move through the upcoming chapters.

CHAPTER 9

★

INTUITION

I knew with every fibre of my being we would buy 19 Star Street. The odds seemed stacked against us, though, even with the sign on the license plate. Stumbling upon the online property listing, I gasped and my heart skipped a beat. One cursory glance and my body knew it was our place. Arriving at the first open home, I was daunted by the volume of other house-hunters. As soon as I walked in, it felt like home. I recognised it on a cellular level. I could also sense the energy of the current owners as I wandered through the home — something was up.

Leaving, I stopped to chat with the real estate agent. As soon as he mentioned the owners, a young couple like Gary and me, the spirit of the male owner's deceased father arrived to talk to me. He'd died just a week before. He told me we'd get the house — and the price his son and daughter-in-law wanted.

We put in an offer and secured the home. Entering into a purchase contract on the house, with a clause subject to us securing finance, we tasked our rational minds to support the guidance we'd received.

The banks do not favour self-employment, so we shouldn't have been surprised when our mortgage broker informed us that unless I was willing to find employment, we were unlikely to secure the loan and would therefore lose the property. Heartbroken (and a little confused with the signs), Gary and I held faith that somehow the guidance would come good. Seeking employment wasn't an option for me; I'd committed to my path. We both knew in our hearts and souls this house was meant for us.

We asked for divine intervention.

The next evening, I received a text message from my old boss from the online travel company, where Gary and I first met. My replacement was about to go on maternity leave and they weren't able to find anyone to fill the role — would I be interested? It was a part-time position, three days a week for a few months. I agreed to take that job, provided I received a letter of employment in time to secure the loan from the bank. We fulfilled the finance clause just in time.

Our guidance is always leading us to the lessons, experiences and situations for us to live out our lessons and purpose. For Gary and me, that house was part of our journey together, just as much as it was about us receiving the message that all of life is supporting us.

By the time we bought that house, I'd spent a few years experimenting with the interplay of guidance and creating our lives in accordance with our life plan. In this story, my intuitive hunch promised the house was ours. This wisdom didn't match what the world was trying to tell us, but, by recognising the signs and following the threads before us, we found an outcome, balancing head and heart.

This easily could've gone the other way. So many times, people have told me about their intuitive hunches that haven't worked out. Familiarising yourself with the world of intuition isn't as easy and natural as it may seem, but the results are totally with it.

Impressions and instinct

Intuition is a highly symbolic language we don't readily recognise. Mastering this language reminds us who we really are — why wouldn't we want to become fluent in it?

A multitude of intuitive impressions bombard us daily. Observe some that arrive for you today. For example, pay attention to your impressions of the next person you meet. Not a mental judgement of someone, but the *feeling* you have about them. Ever had butterflies when you've met a new love interest? Or felt the hairs on your arms or neck stand up in foreboding distrust? How do you know these signs? Do you trust them? Are you more likely to trust these but not others?

Back to the discussion on mental judgements. Often, these go against what our body might be telling us. Despite our body saying, 'Don't trust him,' our rational mind counterbalances with, 'Oh, but he looks so trustworthy. There's no logical reason right now not to trust him.' Rational thought wants to override our intuition advising us not to get involved. Trust those feelings!

It's not just impressions of people. Maybe your job makes you sick in the stomach, or you've walked into someone's home and immediately felt at peace — or not! Our body's response to the world around us constantly offers us clues. Are you paying attention?

All this intuitive data adds up, narrating our story over time. That information is invaluable and it passes fleetingly.

Self-reflection: Have you received intuitive impressions before? Perhaps you felt a gut instinct and had a visceral response to a situation? Did you listen? How did things play out? Sometimes ignoring our inner sense teaches us the most. What have you noticed as you've created more stillness, space and silence in your life? What impressions and clues have bubbled to the surface?

Working with intuition

Wisdom is housed in our bodies — and not just our physical bodies, but our mental, emotional and energetic (or spiritual) bodies, too. To access our intuition, we must be accessing all Four Bodies and interpreting what they tell us.

Emma's story reminded us that our body is working for us, not against us. Our Four Bodies (also known as layers) — physical, mental, emotional and spiritual — were designed to relay information to us. The rational mind won't recognise this of course, but our intuitive mind will — and we must be fluent in symbolism to understand what our Four Bodies are trying to tell us.

Logically, there's much we know about our body. I'm not suggesting we don't use this scientific and medical information, too, but we can push beyond the limits of rational thought and draw additional insights to round out our knowledge. Keep this in mind as I introduce you to the symbolic nature of these Four Bodies, rather than the literal layers we are more familiar with.

Four Bodies

Our anatomic, physical body is only one source of our intuitive data. Our awareness must also span our mental, emotional and spiritual (or energetic) bodies, or layers, too.

All four layers are connected; what happens in one layer impacts the others. What ails us in one layer will eventually also show up in the other layers. In Emma's story, the emotions she felt around her upbringing and the stories she'd attached to it about her worth eventually showed up in her anatomical body, in the form of reproductive issues. Digging deeper, we saw the energy of these events stored in her energetic body, and I've shared that all of this was part of her soul's desired exploration. But modern medicine only focused on Emma's fertility challenges.

Each body flags whether it is aligned with its divine life path, or off-kilter. Information is relayed from each layer, signalling what is truth and what is a construct of the false self. Tasking our rational mind, then, to listen to the Four Bodies a little differently starts to guide us deeper into ourselves, uncovering more of our true self. Observing each layer, we can intuit the state of our inner world and identify where we can course-correct to better align with our path.

Your Four Bodies already know what you need in any particular moment — to rest, recover, clear, create, express, wait or begin. Tuning in to each of your Four Bodies will rapidly change the way you interact with the world, and how the world interacts with you.

Let's get to know the intuitive wisdom of your Four Bodies.

Physical Body

The Physical Body is comprised of another four layers. I call these the 4Ps (or 4 Physicals).

1. Physical, anatomical body
2. Possessions
3. Places
4. People

Physical, anatomical body

I've mostly focused on the physical, anatomical body — 'a pain in the neck' or 'a lump in my throat' give a good indication of the symbolic nature of our bodies. Interpreting the symbolism here, a literal pain in the neck may be representing your annoyance and frustration in life. Ever tried not to cry in a sad movie? You'll know the feeling of a lump in your throat, symbolic of unexpressed emotions (you really should cry!).

In readings, Chris will often take me to the root cause of someone's physical ailments, much like Emma's case. Because much of our physical 'dis-ease' stems from long-held beliefs, suppressed emotions or blocked or stagnant energy that needs to be cleared, this is usually where Chris tends to focus. Often, if a client asks about their physical body, Chris will draw my attention to the ailment's underlying issue so I can relay this to the client. While physically communicating with the client, I am also psychically receiving information from Chris. This comes visually, audibly and even through short-term physical symptoms in my own body. I will often actually feel the same symptom as my client in my own body! This is probably more common if a client hasn't raised the question — this way, I know Chris is flagging the symptom as something important to discuss. I've also observed during readings that Chris doesn't always apply the exact same meaning to all physical ailments — they are personal. There's no blanket diagnosis, and there is certainly also a place for doctors and health professionals. If you can diagnose *and* go deeper, I believe the results are deeper, too.

Louise Hay's work in her book *You Can Heal Your Life* is a wonderful starting point for understanding anatomical symbolism. The author and healer includes a wonderful reference table, charting many physical ailments and some of the symbolic connectivity. Use her work as encouragement — but always trust your own interpretation over someone else's. I worked with Chris to develop my own interpretations. Record them in the reference library you started in the last chapter.

Possessions

Everyday items store energy. As someone who is sensitive to such energies, it's possible for me to 'read' the energy of some possessions. I used to ask clients in my early readings to bring a piece of jewellery with them. As I held the piece, I would receive information about the piece and the owners (this is called psychometry).

Antique shops are a minefield for me. I also can't just adopt any recycled or pre-loved item into my home or life. You might find you have intuitive hints about inanimate objects, too. If you start to feel differently about your furniture, clothing, home and so on, pay attention. You may have outgrown its energy, or need to clear it.

Places

Buildings, homes, suburbs, cities and countries all hold an energetic history, too, which, if we attune ourselves well, we can connect to. When my sister, Claire, first started working in a historical building in London, she sent me photos of some of the older parts of the building. From these, I was able to share some psychic insights about its prior use. A little Google search later, and many of the insights were confirmed.

Notice how you feel walking into your neighbour's home, your office block or your local library. Your body will respond, telling you what is imprinted in these places. What energy might you be impressing upon the places you frequent?

People

Each of us leaves an energetic impression; our energy doesn't lie. So, when we interact with others and receive impressions about them, they are receiving energetic impressions about us, too.

In Chapters 15 and 16 we will work more closely with these bodies to understand how to work with them and the impressions they impart.

Mental Body

Witnessing our thinking from the observer position highlights some interesting information that is rich in themes and patterns for exploration.

Much has already been written elsewhere about our inner critic; I don't wish to reinvent the wheel here, but it does deserve a mention. An inner critic constantly fills our minds with chatter, judging our every move. We would never speak to another the way our inner critic speaks to us. However, identifying the inner critic's comments and isolating their origins, and the stories and emotions we've attached to them, can bring significant inner change.

Don't attach to the thoughts you observe — the intuitive mind *beneath* your rational thoughts is where the wisdom resides — nonetheless, thoughts themselves are important flags, signalling inner work to explore. We'll work more closely with this in Chapters 13 and 14.

Emotional Body

Despite our tendency to avoid, squash and ignore our feelings, I see all emotions as equally important. There are no 'good' or 'bad' emotions, just indicators.

Positive emotions like love, joy, happiness, contentment and so on indicate alignment with our soul and life path. Following these good vibes only is tempting, but it is only one side of the equation. Ignoring the other half of our feelings in pursuit of bliss defeats the purpose of the intuitive data at hand.

We must also welcome the less-great feelings, like anger, jealousy, frustration or dissatisfaction. They indicate where something is out of alignment. Emotions like these poke and prod at you, prompting you in deeper so you can understand how they're working for you, not against you. When you allow yourself to actually feel them, they pass, giving way to the more positive feelings once more. The irony in avoiding our feelings is that they poke at us for far longer than they need to.

I'm not an advocate for pain, per se; I want to avoid it as much as the next person. I do, however, advocate recognising every feeling that arises with curiosity, for all emotions come to teach us something. Our emotions are every bit a guide as our SST or intuition, and must be valued as such. Excavate the years of buried emotions, past pains and disappointments to find the jewel buried within — *you*.

Spiritual Body

This layer is not your physical energy, nor the stamina that allows you to run all day long. Instead, it is your spirit, or the life force (energy) running through your being. Each of us has our own energetic imprint, just like the energetic imprint of the soul's blueprint we are working to attune ourselves to. When we can 'read' energy, we receive intuitive data about the wisdom within the imprint.

On the morning of Cathy's visitation, I couldn't see her but I sensed her presence. Maybe you've been at home when a loved one has walked in, and you've felt them before you've seen or heard them? This is energy. Or maybe you've walked into a room after a heated conversation, and can feel the tension in the air. This, too, is energy.

> You are constantly exchanging energy — or life force — with the world around you. There are the more obvious ways of exchanging energy with people, places and nature, but you can also send and absorb energy through your possessions, memories, words, beliefs, thoughts, emotions and actions.

Everything running through our physical, mental and emotional layers leaves an energetic impression in our energy. If you want your life to flow, then your energy has to flow — physically, mentally, emotionally and spiritually. If your life is feeling more stop/start, heavy and blocked, then you no doubt have some stagnant or heavy energy to clear.

 Self-reflection: Have you ever been part of a toxic relationship, work team or group? Maybe you've brightly stepped out to catch up with a friend, only to walk away feeling more drained and down on life than before you met? Are there people in your life you feel very drawn to? Energy may be the answer as to why.

Other people's energy (and that of places, possessions, foods, the past etc.) can affect you long after you've physically parted ways. Vigilance is required to keep our own energy clear, ensuring another's energy isn't adversely affecting us (and vice versa).

It's important to remember we are sovereign, energetic beings — you are not powerless to others. While others may drain or impact our energy, it is our individual responsibility to improve our energetic boundaries (and maybe our physical and emotional ones, too) to prevent such drainage. No one can energetically attack you without your consent — often, we just don't know that we've let the barriers down. Once we know, we can better protect ourselves in the future. I discuss psychic protection further and share a few suggestions for protecting your energy on page 127.

Chakras and auras

No discussion on energy is complete without mentioning our chakras and aura. I prefer to work with chakras over auras, but both contain reams of information. Your main chakras — the seven wheels of energy housed within your body from the base of your spine to the crown of your head — are the energetic equivalent to your digestive system.

These energy centres process, clear and balance your energy, or life force, as it enters, moves through and leaves your energetic body. Your aura does a similar job, but sits around the physical body as an energetic field. Every thought, interaction, behaviour, emotion, decision and desire is processed through these energetic fields, so if we're not taking care of this processing system, we're likely to not only experience blocks within the system, but also their knock-on effects on our emotional, mental and physical bodies. Each of the seven chakras process energy relating to certain themes and life areas. The table on pages 176 and 177 outlines each chakra, its location and theme.

In Emma's case, her sacral chakra (an energy centre connected to feminine energy and located around the womb) had stored many of her beliefs, feelings and emotions from her upbringing in an all-male environment. Both the symbolism and the literal location of the chakra would have impacted her physical ailment.

Daily chakra clearing and balancing creates harmony across all Four Bodies, and also a clear channel for your energy, or life force, to run through. Like brushing your teeth, daily chakra cleaning is beneficial, but from time to time you need a deeper cleanse. For this, I recommend working with local practitioners or remote healers. I work with my clients to understand the type of practitioner or areas to focus on, which you'll learn more about in Chapter 14.

Our chakra health provides psychic information for the rest of our lives, and by intuitively sensing and reading our chakras, we are often given rich data to work with.

✳ *For regular chakra maintenance, you may like the Chakra Balancing meditation on my website.*

 **CHOOSE YOUR ADVENTURE —
SCAN YOUR FOUR BODIES**
In Chapters 15 and 16, you'll learn more techniques for interpreting your intuition and the information in your Four Bodies. For now, let's start by simply scanning these layers and recording what you observe in your journal.

Scan your Four Bodies
Take a few deep breaths; centre yourself in quiet stillness. Start to notice what's happening in each of your Four Bodies. When you feel ready, without overthinking your answers, complete the sentence prompts given on the following pages.

1. **Physical Body**
    This includes what I call the 4Ps:

1. *Physical body* (your tangible body — may link to diet, exercise and sleep)
2. *Possessions* (yours, and those of others in your physical space)
3. *Places* (physical places you frequent — home, work, play, even city and country)
4. *People* (all those physically around you)

Use the following as prompts for self-reflection.
*   My physical, anatomical body feels ...
*   What I sense about my loved ones/others is ...
*   Places/locations I'm drawn to go are ... because ...
*   Places I can't go near are ... because ...
*   Possessions I'm drawn to are ...
*   Possessions I feel no longer reflect me include ...

2. **Mental Body**
    This includes the thoughts, beliefs, perceptions and understanding you have of the world. It is the part of you that is thinking and planning, and, most likely, doubting and fearing.

Use the following as prompts for journaling.
*   My mind and thoughts are ...
*   Repeating stories in my mind are saying ... because ...

3. **Emotional Body**
    This includes your feelings towards situations, people and events, as well as stored emotions from the past and anticipated emotions projected on to the future.

Use the following as a prompt for self-reflection.

* I feel ... about ... because ...

4.   Spiritual Body

This encompasses who you really are — your true self
or spirit; it's pure, spiritual energy. Energy at this level is
quite different from physical energy. It's subtler, and flows
under the busy surface.

Use the following as prompts for journaling.

* My true self feels ...
* It wants to tell me ...

Remember to date your answers and keep them. Complete
this task several times over the coming weeks, perhaps at
the end of each week or fortnight. Compare your answers
over time to track your progress.

CHAPTER 10

★

SPIRITUAL
SUPPORT TEAM

I spent a fair chunk of time wondering if I was crazy. In the beginning, while getting to know Chris (aka all the spirit guides within my SST), I was often unsure just whom I was communicating with, and I questioned myself constantly. When Cathy's spirit visited, I recognised her, but Chris was completely foreign to me. Opening the floodgates, it felt as if the whole damned spirit world arrived at once. I wondered, 'Are you a spirit guide or an angel? Did you turn up yesterday? Have I worked with you before? How do I know who I'm talking with?'

I couldn't rationalise it. Instead, I intended to only work with higher beings of positive intentions. Employing psychic protection tools, like bathing myself in white light, I surrendered to whoever turned up. Not always knowing who arrived actually helped hone my skill. I had to find new ways to recognise who I was working with.

Fortunately, around this time, the tall, thin man in his tails and top hat from my childhood reappeared. I could finally place him — he was a gatekeeper guide. A little like a nightclub bouncer, his role was to protect me from lower frequency beings. I've put him to work ever since.

Other ground rules were implemented. Take a number and get in line! Operating hours were enforced, stopping midnight wake-up calls from the spirit world. I needed boundaries in place; I couldn't be available to spirit all of the time. The spirit world isn't bound by our time and physical realities; they needed reminding of mine. Just as we are spiritual beings having a human experience, spirit is just spirit having a spiritual experience. Our worlds had to meet somewhere in the middle.

I got to know each spirit from my SST that visited, recognising them by *feel*. Like us, each guiding being has a different frequency, presence and resonance. Their messages would come as sound, images, sensations — and I started to notice that different beings used different vocabulary, speed and diction. Chris tends to talk to me, but not in the same way I hear physical voices. Chris sounds the way all my own thoughts sound in my head; his messages kind of pop up between my thoughts. I have to be quick to notice them. In early client readings, messages would sound like people talking at the other end of a tunnel. Wind carried the messages downwind, but I couldn't always make them out.

Some SST members I know intimately; others not so well. A few have revealed their names, although, most haven't. People are often fascinated by the names and forms spirit guides take, but Chris tells me spirit guides will assume names and physical forms so they can present to us humans in ways we can interpret and understand. As non-physical beings, they don't really have these characteristics at all.

Getting to know my SST has been quite the adventure — one you're about to embark upon now.

From intuition to your SST

Intuition is our internal messenger while our SST is a collective of external, or higher messengers from the spirit world. Spirit guides have a different perspective of our experience here — and not always one that is bound by our time frames and physical realities.

Spirit guides may still use symbolism to communicate with us, but I've found their insights typically are more specific and detailed than intuitive impressions. Combining both sources builds up the dossier we are compiling of our divine life path.

A vast gap exists, though, between humans and the world of spirit. Imagine a sliding scale or spectrum, where humans stand at one end and spirit at the other. At the human end, things are quite dense and tangible. For spirit, not so much. Each end operates in different realities and, in fact, in different dimensions. Spirit has to work to lower its vibration to enter into our energy field. Reaching up to higher frequencies is a challenge for us humans. Clearly, it can be done, but it's not often sustained for any length of time. Until now.

Part of the collective Process of Remembering is allowing us humans, both individually and as a group, to slide up the scale, raising our vibrations closer to that of the world of spirit, so we can better (and more frequently) communicate with each other.

Every breadcrumb, sign and symbol, divine whisper and intuitive impression across the Four Bodies, and now your SST, have not just been revealing your individual life path. This guidance also works to increase your vibration, sliding you further up the scale.

All of life supports your ascension up the energetic sliding scale, bringing you closer to the frequencies of the world of spirit. Like these spirit guides, you, too, are a spiritual being, but your current human form has made it harder for you to remember how to operate at this level.

Whispers to change your diet, wardrobe, relationships etc. are all geared towards increasing your vibration and reminding you of your spiritual nature. Increasing our vibration allows us to better receive the frequencies of our spirit guides.

Once I ditched the heavier energies my human self was bogged down with — leaving PR, resting and meditating more, removing meat and alcohol from my diet — the world of spirit came rushing in. Tending to my seven energy centres — my chakras — meant they could process higher energy coming into my body, and the impressions from the spirit world increased. You're about to do the same.

Intuition versus psychic ability

Spirit guides are non-physical beings who will, not surprisingly, want to communicate with us in non-physical ways. Good news — just as you have physical senses, you also have non-physical, or psychic senses, which spirit use to communicate with you. I call these psychic senses the 6Cs, which will make sense as you look at the list below.

1. Clairvoyance (clear seeing)
2. Clairsentience (clear sensing)
3. Clairgustance (clear tasting)
4. Clairailience (clear smelling)
5. Clairaudience (clear hearing)
6. Claircognizance (clear knowing)

Clairsentience, or clear sensing, is very much linked to our intuition. Looking at this list, you may now realise there's far more psychic information available than just *feeling* something. Our mind's eye sees what our physical eyes cannot; cognitive information can drop in without rational knowledge; non-physical smells arrive (Granny often sends me her scents of tuberose or flowering jasmine); we can psychically taste despite not physically eating anything.

Traditionally, clairvoyance is a term used to broadly label all psychics, mediums and channels, but it's grossly inaccurate. Not everyone who has a connection with the spirit world will be clairvoyant; they may be clairaudient or clairsentient, or possess any other psychic sense. My clairvoyance developed with time; clairaudience was strongest at first. You, too, can develop and strengthen your 6Cs. This is no longer something reserved for those labelled psychic; we all have these abilities.

Your SST will use these psychic senses to communicate with you — it's their language. Different guides may 'favour' one type of psychic sense over another, although you may request another sense if you prefer. They'll likely accommodate your request; they want to make contact.

Chakra connections

Each of the 6Cs not only represents your psychic senses, but is also linked to your chakras, or energy centres. Along with the seven main chakras located from the base of your spine to the crown of your head, there are many other chakras, such as those in your hands, feet and ears. Clairvoyance, for example, is linked with your third eye chakra, located at the brow centre, which is also known as your mind's eye. This type of 'seeing' is very different to physical eyesight. Clairaudience is linked to your ear chakras, while claircognizance is associated with your crown chakra, located at the top of your head.

Improving spirit communication relies on strong psychics senses, which can be strengthened by clearing and balancing your chakras. Regularly balance and cleanse your chakras, either with a guided meditation or with a practitioner. Trust that each intuitive nudge across your Four Bodies also changes your energetic make up to improve your connection to the spirit world. Your intuition has been working to open you to spirit all along.

Two-way communication

Hopefully, you employ two-way communication in your relationships with others. A give and take, listen and speak relationship is important with spirit. We must be willing participants in the exchange — asking questions, listening and responding.

Communication with spirit is like using a telephone: you can make a call, or receive one. If you're waiting on a call, do make sure your phone is switched on, volume up. Don't leave it on mute. Incoming calls may initially arrive in emergency situations or at pivotal life points, much like Cathy's surprise wake-up call to me. Typically, though, we want to initiate the calls. Trust me, your guides are eagerly awaiting to hear from you. Be warned, once you invite in this guidance, your phone may start to ring off the hook.

Asking for spirit guidance is often a prerequisite to receiving it. Unless we are in extreme danger or it's part of our soul agreement to be 'interrupted' and reminded of our abilities, our guidance can't interfere with our free will — we often need to invite it in before the floodgates open.

Incoming and outgoing calls can happen in a number of ways, which I'll introduce to you now.

Incoming

Dreams, signs, repeating number patterns and our 6Cs are common incoming calls. If spirit guides can't reach us directly, they often send us physical messengers, too. While contemplating leaving PR, I attended a Buddhist meditation evening. During the break, an older man (a stranger) approached me from the other side of the room. Sitting down, he handed me a book, *Buddhism for Busy People*.

'This book will help you,' he said, before leaving to mingle with other guests. Its author, David Michie, details how Buddhism supported his transition out of a busy corporate communications environment to focus on meditation and spirituality. I enjoyed it thoroughly.

Another time, my sister Liz was searching in a bookstore for a Christmas gift for me. Out of her comfort zone, she says she stood in the self-development and spirituality section, contemplating what I might like. Pleading internally for the perfect book to materialise, a male customer came around the corner into the aisle. He picked up a book and gave it to her, saying 'She might enjoy this one.' That Christmas, I unwrapped *You Are Psychic* by Debra Lynne Katz, and enjoyed working with it that summer holiday between PR jobs as my practise readings took off.

Secretly, I hope my book found you in a similar way.

Chris gets my attention through my physical body, too. My hands used to itch when spirit wanted to talk, although that doesn't tend to happen so much anymore. Rather unglamorously, I tend to sweat and overheat when I channel from spirit. When the heat arrives, I know spirit's ready. Enjoy finding the ways your SST reaches out to you.

Outgoing

Rather than waiting for the phone to ring, we can actively seek guidance from spirit and place a call. Spirit will decide when and if they 'pick up', just as they'll determine what they'll share on the call.

Many of the tools shared thus far provide gateways to spirit. Meditation, particularly guided meditations that are designed to access spirit, is a great starting point. I created my own guided meditations, available on my website, which I worked with Chris to create. I've also included a visualisation at the end of this chapter to help you connect to spirit in meditation.

Oracle cards are another way we can activate communication with higher guidance. In The Little Sage Oracle Card deck I created, I share several ways to use the cards to connect with spirit. They can become a trigger, turning on the tap each time you use them.

Automatic writing is another technique I've long employed to ask questions of Chris. In the beginning, I only received a random word or two, but now I can fill almost an entire journal in one sitting. An early foray into automatic writing long before I was married saw me create a page filled with doodling, and one lone word: Gary. This only ended up making sense to me long after we met. My handwriting in these sessions often doesn't appear like my own. My sisters, Liz and Claire, were gobsmacked the first time I showed them sample pages — I'd written the entire entry back to front!

Prayer also works. Growing up in a religious environment, I had preconceived ideas about what prayer looked and felt like. Loosening my mind's ideas on this, I've come to understand that prayer is simply us offering our attention and intention to our hopes, dreams, gratitude and love. Spirit listens and responds.

Many other divination tools exist. There's a reason clairvoyants are stereotypically depicted with crystal balls and tarot cards — they all help open up the lines of communication. But, as we learned with meditation, they are tools, not the rule.

The most important step in establishing a line of communication is to ask — then be open to, and believe, what comes back.

CHANNELLED GUIDANCE – Spirit's take on spirit guides
The following is an excerpt from channelling I recorded for my students in late 2015, explaining spirit guides.

'We are often so surprised at the level of interest in us. We are light beings. Many have incarnated on Earth before, and yet, for guides at a much higher, higher level, it is some time since we have been on Earth.

'While it is not necessarily a hierarchy in how your minds would connect with that term, there are layers, or levels, of beings. Now, one is not better than the other, but there are layers closer to Earth. Usually this is where you will find the spirit of those who have passed away.

'If by chance you work with a spirit guide who has been on Earth, perhaps it would pay to take caution in ascertaining how far along this particular guide is in their own development. Just because you work with spirit, spirit guides, light beings or any other energetic being or form, you cannot hand your power away.

'And just because you receive guidance doesn't mean you must act on it on Earth.

'You have free will for a reason and we implore you to take into consideration and run through your own intuition, and even your own logic, what is right for you.

'We do not care what you call us and, in truth, we do not really have names. We have vibrations. We are energetic beings. For some, that energy may translate at the same vibration as a name, but we are not physical beings. We may appear in a physical form but that doesn't mean that we actually have a physical form. For many who work with animal guides, or who may see their spirit guides in physical form, it may well be that you are working with a group of guides at a different layer or level of this so-called hierarchy. It does not matter.

'We are delighted that so many wish to connect with their guides. And you can connect with your own. You can invite in guides for particular life areas.

'As a mother may remind her child: Take your time to roll. Take your time to crawl. Take your time to walk before you get up and run, because once you're up and running, there is a marathon ahead and there are lifetimes, and lifetimes in between lifetimes, for us to commune and connect. There is time.'

**CHOOSE YOUR ADVENTURE —
REVISIT YOUR SACRED SPACE**

Dedicate time and space for this practice — you're about to meet, or return to, your SST by entering your Sacred Space. When your guides appear to you, simply notice how it feels, how they appear to you and any messages they may have for you at this time. Simply follow the prompts below.

Transporting yourself to your Sacred Space:

1. Before the meditation, you might like to think about your intentions for meeting your spirit guides, including any particular questions you might like to ask.

2. Create physical time and space for yourself, and invoke the sacred in whatever way feels good to you. This may be through prayer, lighting a candle or incense, playing quiet music in the background or performing some other ritual you feel drawn to.

3. Take some deep breaths into your belly, letting your belly rise and fall. Don't alter this or force it. Just allow the breath to fill you up, and expel it when ready.

4. Sink into the support beneath you (the bed, chair or floor). Let it take your full weight. Allow all your muscles to relax and become incredibly heavy — knowing you are supported to fully let go and relax. Close your eyes and relax.

5. Arrive in your Sacred Space. Call in white light and ask for psychic protection. Then, ask for your spirit guide to step forward to meet you.

6. Spend as much time here as possible. Notice who turns up, what they offer you, how your energy feels and changes with each visit. This is your opportunity to ask any questions you might have about your spirit guide.

7. When today's visit feels complete, give thanks and simply bring your awareness back to your breathing — deep breaths into your belly. Begin to feel your physical body connect with the support beneath you. A few gentle movements help to bring you back. Then, open your eyes, gently, when you're ready.

8. Record your impressions from today's visit in your journal.

* *For a more specific process, you might like my Meet Your Spirit Guide meditation on my website.*

CHAPTER 11

★

WORKING WITH MESSENGERS: A PROCESS

'Surely there's got to be something more than this?' I lamented to a colleague, standing in my office at the PR agency. 'I wish I could go write a book,' I said. 'I just don't know what my story's about yet.' I had no idea how this book-sized nugget of guidance was about to unfold.

In the moment, I'd answered my own question — I just couldn't see it at the time. Instead, I was only at the start of the journey. I was picking up random breadcrumbs that were slowly leading me out of that PR agency, into meeting my soon-to-be husband and into a new, then unfathomable, career. Each answer came in response to the questions I asked.

Those breadcrumbs soon became a torrent of guidance. As more guidance came, more questions followed. Automatic writing filled pages and pages of my journal; a picture of my future was starting to form, including this very book you're now reading. Over the past decade, many of the predictions in those journals have come to fruition; many exciting, beautiful dreams are still yet to arrive. But there's a rhythm and timing to it all far greater than my own desires and understanding. As best I could, I've tried to stay focused on the immediate next step, trusting it will all connect up down the road.

Chris and I now have a deep, committed relationship. He's my most trusted advisor — he's also ensured I found the same love and support in my physical support team, too. Chris is as much a part of my family as Gary, my girls, parents and sisters. By default, they've got to know him, too. So, when Chris arrives with news, we all pay attention.

I believe the key has been the process I'm about to share with you, the *how*. My relationship with Chris has moved beyond the questions and answers — although there's still plenty of that! Our relationship now is one of teacher and student, mentor and mentee. Chris moved beyond offering breadcrumbs and began to guide me through a process of change. Knowing where I was going was not enough; Chris led me there, step by step. Of course, it was *not* the route I expected.

From random questions to specific path

Once our initial human curiosities are allayed, spirit starts focusing our efforts. Committed to this new approach, living from our intuition above all else, the breadcrumbs no longer remain ad hoc stepping stones. Instead, the guidance corrals us through a very specific process of change and transformation. To make the changes we desire, we actually need to *change* — and we'll be guided through the process.

Trust each individual piece of guidance will connect up; we may not see how with our physical eyes, but we will know it in our hearts and soul. Each step — and transformation we undergo — is indeed part of our divine life path, even if we don't know it yet.

It might feel like you've landed smack-bang in the centre of another storm. Keep going! Step by step, the dust settles. As the pathway clears, the obstacles shrink. Even then, you'll really only know the immediate next step to take.

An exciting and exhilarating adventure awaits — are you ready?

A new way of living

Can you feel the resounding *YES!* in your being? Maybe you're not quite there yet, and that's perfectly fine. Fear and doubt are likely to arrive at this point. In fact, it's par for the course. You don't need to know how the adventure will unfold, just be willing. Then practise your stillness, space and silence, and let spirit lead the way. The right supports, teachers and modalities will all arrive to help you through these changes and transitions. You'll land squarely in your lessons and in the moments of great purpose, too.

Deepening your devotion to your mission, your guidance will ask you to move through inner growth and transformation, alchemising or removing what is not aligned with your truth. Your true self emerges — then you must show up in the world as you truly are. The following few chapters will lead you through this.

 Self-reflection: It's time to actively choose this new way forward. Are you at least *willing* to do things differently? Are you *willing* to trust your intuitive hunches, signs and guidance to act on them — even when it feels terrifying, isolating and damn near crazy? Can you commit to yourself, your SST and your soul? You don't need to know how — they already know. For now, you just need to be willing.

Protect yourself

Before we get too much further, let's readdress the importance of psychic protection. If you're about to open your channels of communication, and you're new to this, then we need to ensure you call in reinforcements until you can better protect yourself.

Working with spirit, we don't always know who will turn up. People ask me if they'll invite in lower or negative energies. While it is possible, it hasn't been my experience.

I clearly set my intention to only work with and invite in energies of the light; energies dedicated to the highest vibration and outcomes for the good of all. I have tasked my gatekeeper guide (like my personal bouncer) to hold the energetics for me, so only vibrations of good intent can work with me and enter my energy field and awareness.

Over time, I've worked with my energy field to ensure its sovereignty. In time, you'll do the same. But, until then, call in reinforcements.

Back in my twenties, dabbling with my abilities, I learned this the hard way. A friend and I went out for a few drinks. Sitting at one end of a long table, it wasn't long before another party occupied the empty seats. Talking to one of the guys I'd just met, it quickly became apparent I knew far too much about him relative to the time I knew him. My friend could see what had happened — I'd unintentionally opened to spirit — and she quickly escorted me home. Because we are sovereign energetic beings, I believe we must actively choose to invite spirit into our lives. However, alcohol had weakened my defences, blurring the lines between my cognitive knowledge and my higher knowledge, meaning I'd inadvertently let down the barriers to the spiritual floodgates and tapped into information without permission — not just my own permission, but also the guy's.

Drugs and alcohol not only affect our physical and mental states, but also our energetic state. After that moment, I chose to not drink twenty-four hours prior to a reading (and on Chris' advice, alcohol was soon limited further). Ask for your own guidance on what might work for you. The clearer your system, the clearer your channels — and the less likely lower vibrations are to be drawn to your energy.

I'm not a fan of working with heavier or darker energy. If that's your interest, go in knowingly, and be sure to protect your own energy, as well as anyone else's you're working with.

Disclaimers aside, here's how I protect my energy. I call in my spirit guides; I call on white light from Source, or the highest energy life emerged from, and red light from Mother Earth. I simply hold the intention and belief that this light has been commanded and then I visualise the light surrounding me and the room/building I am in (or as far and wide as you'd like). I visualise everything is bathed in a pure, healing and protective light. I'll also run the energy through my chakras. As the white and red lights swirl, you become bathed in a beautiful pink hue, the colour of unconditional love.

SPIRIT SPEAK

Source can be thought of as the energetic origin from which all life came from — the beginning of all life, abundance, love and creativity.

Over time, I needed this external protection less. Working with the guidance you're about to receive, you'll naturally strengthen your own energy field to withstand lower frequencies.

Crystals like hematite and clear quartz are also useful for protecting energy. Other people visualise an energetic shield psychically warding off negativity. Call on Archangel Michael (a leader and guardian among the angels) to protect you; he'd be honoured to work with you.

Whatever you choose to protect yourself with, please use it regularly before attempting the following suggestions.

⁕ Try the Ground, Clear and Protect Your Energy meditation on my website.

Asking for guidance

Asking for and receiving guidance alone is not enough. Chris has shown me a process to undertake any time we want to go in deeper with our messengers, especially if we're committed to our divine life path and the healing, growth and transformation required along it.

There are six steps to the process:

1. Ask
2. Trust
3. Rhythm and ritual
4. Receive
5. Reflect and interpret
6. Act

By collecting your breadcrumbs, listening for the whispers and noticing the signs and symbols, you may have already been following a similar process. Let's now go a little deeper with your practice.

Ask

It seems simple enough, but we really must ask for what we want, whether guidance or otherwise. Working with a client, I'll often have them refine and reframe their question multiple times so we get to the specifics of what they want to know.

We've seen how to ask for a sign, but how we ask for intuitive guidance and even information from our SST may differ. Intuitive guidance requires we ask a question for our body to respond to. Sometimes I'll do this by offering alternate options and comparing the responses. I may simply ask the question in my mind, and notice my body's response; other times, the question may be written in my journal. For example, I'll think of one course of action or choice I can make and run through the remaining steps of the process. Then, I'll repeat the process with another option.

Our Four Bodies often send signals to things we didn't know needed answering. When all else fails, I'll ask, 'What do I need to know about (insert question)?'

Questions to our SST tend to be a little more specific. Keep them open-ended and focused on growth and healing. For example, 'How will (a particular course of action) support my growth, or the growth of others?' Through trial and error, you'll see what works best for you.

Much of our asking happens at the energetic level. Your vibration, the quality of your energy centres and where you focus your energy and attention naturally asks questions of the Universe in a language it's familiar with, even if you're not.

Trust

Trust your request is heard and answered. Like in Gary's story of asking for a sign, the response was almost immediate. Other times, not so much. Many of the things in my life, this book included, have taken much longer to come to the fore. I trust, despite not logically understanding. You are always heard.

No matter the gap between asking and receiving an answer, hold faith and stay the course. It might appear in the coming days or weeks, or sometimes longer.

There's no point asking a question, believing it won't be heard or answered, and stepping in to answer it yourself anyway. One particular client comes to mind here — I've often joked with her that she's simply too fast-moving. By the time she's asked for guidance and spirit has coordinated an answer, she's already moved on to the next thing (or two or three). Give your guides time!

Rhythm and ritual

Cultivate stillness, space and silence. There's no need to rush to a solution. Instead, slow down and create the stillness and space you need. Come into observer mode so you recognise what answers come.

Trusting life will take care of this for you, because all of life supports you, means you can relax and tend to what's needed while waiting for your answer to arrive. This may mean simply relaxing into your meditation until a response drops in, or it may mean focusing on other things in your day-to-day life for a week or two while a bigger piece of guidance arrives in your awareness. Continuing your practice of rhythm and ritual — creating stillness and space — ensures you'll be ready to take spirit's call, even if you're busy doing other things.

Sometimes, for an answer to arrive, we need to create the space for it. There have been many times when the guidance or awareness I needed was much greater than I was ready for — it needed a bit of time to bring my rational mind into alignment with a higher knowledge. As you'll see in the next chapter, continuing to work with other guidance while waiting for bigger pieces to arrive ensures you're creating the space, and energetic resonance, for this to arrive.

Remember, spirit is working at the other end of the spectrum to our human selves. It can take a bit of time for the human self to access and integrate the energy, let alone make logical sense of it.

Receive

Receive the guidance. Answers don't always come through the mental plane. Guidance might not arrive in an obvious flashing-neon-sign kind of way. Sometimes, it's someone offering you a book, a song on the radio or a chance encounter with a stranger. I cannot tell you the number of times I've had random conversations with people who have used the exact same phrasing for something I've pondered, but never uttered to them.

Stillness, space and silence are critical. Observing helps. Noticing the sensations in our Four Bodies, picking up on the impressions via our 6Cs and journaling through repetitive themes and messages help, too. Used together, these practices will ensure you find your answers.

Be prepared: the answers may not be what you wanted to hear. This in and of itself may take some adjustment and further questioning.

When you expect one thing, you may not notice something else. Stay open and receptive.

Reflect and interpret

Look for literal or symbolic meanings. Interpret any signs, dreams, symbols and messages you receive. Scan your Four Bodies for additional information. Journal or pull oracle cards to support the impressions you receive.

This is also your chance to ask again, or clarify what you received. Go into conversation with your SST, seeking illumination or further information. Give the guidance the head and heart treatment, ensuring your interpretation isn't to bend something to the mind's expectations, or to mitigate something you'd rather not do.

Allow time for the puzzle pieces to fit together, knowing you may not need an entire picture right now. When I left PR, I had enough guidance to know to start giving readings, but not much else.

Act

Only after completing all those phases do I recommend finally acting on the guidance. Often, people rush to this point without undertaking any due diligence on the other stages. Not surprisingly, we can also ask when it's time to act.

Too often, I received clear guidance from Chris but failed to ask about the timing (or I simply let my mind run wild with its own timing). Not all guidance requires immediate action — this book is a case in point. Years passed between my knowing and it coming into form.

Sometimes we receive a simple piece of understanding, a bigger picture, rather than the next immediate step to take. Other times, we'll know with every fibre of our being that we are meant to act. Then again, we can see there are other things required first — just be sure these also come from guidance, not your mind.

You'll know it's time to act when every one of your Four Bodies, every sign and every serendipitous event lines up. There'll be no questions left to ask, it will just be time to *do*.

Am I doing this right?

In just about every live event, workshop and teaching session I've held, someone asks how they will know if it's their guidance or mind communicating with them.

Ultimately, if it is guidance geared towards the highest good for all involved, does it really matter how you got there? To play devil's advocate, it doesn't matter if you're doing it right or not as long as it's creating positive change in your life and the lives of others.

However, I know that's not enough to convince you, so here are a few other things to keep in mind.

Trial and error

Although we crave instant gratification, guidance probably won't offer it. So, when we're trying to figure out if we're communicating right (which is such a head-based question anyway), we may not know straight away. I actually think this is part of the point – spirit wants us to learn, and to make mistakes through imperfection.

This isn't a quick fix, or a new means to an old end. We won't win a battle of wills with spirit! Give this time, and expect mistakes. Your journal and reference library will alleviate some confusion as tangible 'proof' starts to build. Misinterpretation won't happen twice. Perhaps you won't know if you're doing it right until you know what 'wrong' looks like. To soul, it's all data.

Let go of the outcome

Soul lives in the void of the unknown; the mind, not so much. You must become comfortable with the discomfort of the unknown. Risky leaps of faith are easier when you've started small first.

You must believe in order to see, not see in order to believe — and spirit will hold you out on this one. Your relationship with your team of advisors is so important, don't rush or push it. Let go of the idea of this taking you to some place, or any place at all.

Don't give away your power

On the flip side of trust is completely letting go of your power. Yes, I encourage you to develop a relationship with your SST, but not to lose your role within the relationship. All too often I see people become so fixated on their guidance that they become unable to make decisions for themselves anymore. Remember I suggested you have a healthy scepticism? Well, I'd equally suggest a healthy boundary with your guides — we don't want to lose our own desires and decisions to such a point we are merely puppets for something bigger. Being a relationship, you have a say and the final choice. Be a rebel — you don't always have to follow the guidance just as it's been given to you (although, you're bound to figure out your balance point with this soon enough).

Let it be fun

Getting to know your SST can be a fun, magical, wondrous game. I invite you to banter, and stay childlike and curious. *You already know* the answers — so when you're asking, trust yourself, your body, your intuition and your higher guidance, too. Sure, you might get it wrong once in a while — but that can be half the fun, at least to soul. Rather than this being an exploration in perfection, can this just be a wild choose-your-own-adventure game, with no right path or outcome? Can you enjoy the ride?

A word of warning

Fun though this may be, I've seen and experienced my share of pitfalls, too. I dedicate an entire chapter to this later, but here are a few common misperceptions I want to clear up now.

This is not a free pass to easy street
Easy is not where soul learns. Where you are led isn't necessarily always the most pleasant or easiest route. However, it will be the best path for you to learn your soul's lessons, the best time and place to offer your soul's purpose, and, ultimately the path will allow you to create the highest possible good for all involved.

This does not guarantee happy ever after
In fact, it doesn't guarantee outcomes at all. As cliché as it is, this process is more about the journey than the destination. While you may be guided by some beautiful vision or end point, it is *how* you get there that is important. Yup, as you might think, each step must be guided, not just the vision at the end.

This is not to serve the mind
Our mind's a tricky little thing. Time and again it can fool us into using our guidance as a way of serving its own needs. Please always check that the guidance you seek is for the highest good of all involved, not just to serve some desire of the mind. It won't work for long.

This is not a fling
Once you begin accessing and following your guidance, you must be all in — spirit is probably going to hammer this point home to you anyway.

> You can't pick and choose when you follow guidance
> and when you don't. Of course, you do have free
> will and you can actually choose — the point here
> is you either follow all the guidance, or none of it;
> this is not a relationship of convenience.

Sometimes, these lessons need to be learned the hard way. That was certainly true for me. No matter where we are guided, we must trust there is a far greater reason for it, even if we don't yet logically understand it.

Once you've built the foundations for accessing and acting on your guidance, a very specific guided journey begins, leading you deeper into the life you were born to live. When this speeds up, that trust in your relationship will be paramount.

 ### CHOOSE YOUR ADVENTURE – SEEKING GUIDANCE

What guidance would you like right now? Formulate your question and write it in your journal.

 Consider how you might like to make your call — which tool would you like to use? Remember the tools available to you from the list below, or use another tool of your choice.

- Meditation
- Oracle cards
- Journaling
- Automatic writing
- Sacred Space visualisation
- Ask for a sign
- Notice your dreams
- Scan your Four Bodies

What guidance do you receive?
- How do you interpret it?
- Do you need clarification? Ask again.
- Is it time to act? If so, are you ready? If not, seek guidance on what you need to do to prepare yourself to act.

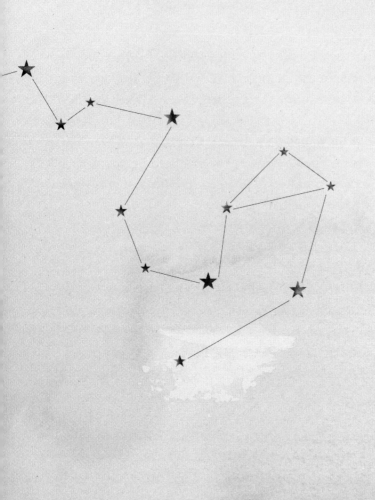

CHAPTER 12

FOLLOW THAT THREAD

I've had a sense of what's ahead for me for some time now, although no idea how it would all come together. Chris even told me in my automatic writing that it would all unfold remarkably differently from how I imagined. Over the years, threads of guidance have emerged. Snippets from some future life often clairvoyantly arrive. Never in chronological order, or with an explanation of how I arrived there — just letting me know that I would. With regards to my work, I knew Chris wanted me to use technology to share a bigger message and that one day, I would write a book (in truth, he's told me there are multiple books). Eight years before this book came to be, Chris even told me what to negotiate into the contract when it arrived; this is dated and recorded in my journal.

This bigger picture was met by smaller, bite-sized pieces. Start a blog. Teach an online course. Produce meditations. Share on social media. I followed each step, doing the best I could with what I had.

Another thread of guidance emerged, too. This guidance stepped me through a series of changes, asking me to let go of the past physically, mentally, emotionally and spiritually. Chris guided me to rebuild myself and see myself anew. He showed me more of the bigger picture, the details of my manual — my understanding and perspective shifted dramatically. Clearing the psychic gunk cleared the path before me.

Similar messages arrived in client sessions, too. Like with Maggie and Emma, spirit would show us what was possible, and the steps to get there — none of it ever resembled what our logical minds expected. My experiment with following my intuition was demonstrating there was a rather predictable pattern and pathway.

Chris confirmed my suspicions. All of life conspires to ensure we remember, heal and emerge as our true selves, guiding us each step of the way. We cannot fail.

Seemingly random, disjointed snippets of guidance are actually far more logically connected than our mind may first perceive. We may not always see the path laid down before us, but we must be willing to take at least the first step before more of the pathway appears. Our guidance will show us the next step, and the next, until we arrive at the very destination we were first intuitively pulled towards — just like the tiles lighting up.

Following the threads of guidance, details from the manual are revealed, while other threads prepare us to receive more. On and on that cycle goes, until we arrive face-to-face with the very manual we've been searching for — and all the riches we've been promised.

Tugging at the strings

There's a beautiful Chinese proverb that suggests soul mates are connected by an invisible thread. The thread cannot break, but it will stretch and tangle, ensuring the two will meet. While this is true of our soul mate relationships, I think it is also true of all the experiences and lessons soul has agreed to explore in this lifetime.

Invisible threads always pull at us, no matter our choices, steering us back to our path. We feel them as intuition, see them as breadcrumbs and hear them as whispers. Our SST prompts us to pay attention, and to unravel the threads.

These threads connect to various points on our body, tugging at us to move in particular directions. Looking down, we may notice the thread tugging at us. Gingerly clasping our hands around the thread, little by little, we edge our way along the thread, unravelling it, climbing in, out and around the obstacles ahead as we move in the direction of the other end of the thread.

Multiple threads connect to our body in this way, each leading us someplace else. According to this clairvoyant image, we need to work our way with each thread in turn, unable to follow one through until the other threads have 'caught up'. We must work our way through each thread, unravelling and untangling them. Progress with each is paced a little differently. Let me introduce you to three such threads.

The three threads

The thread of daily intuitive instruction
This thread helps guide us through day-to-day steps, those basic and somewhat mundane daily decisions. This is what you've been working on these past few chapters — using the daily intuitive instructions and guidance from your SST to make that call, tweak that habit and so on. These intuitive hits are highly practical in-the-moment impressions, geared towards adjustments and adaptations to our everyday living.

Chris initially gave me daily intuitive instructions to rest and meditate more, alter my diet and lean in to some relationships and friendships more than others. Over time, those daily instructions started to shift. More recently, my daily intuitive instructions have been focused on recovering my physical health, juggling school routines and creating space for writing this book.

Review your impressions recorded in your journal to date. How much of them have been this level of day-to-day guidance? Could you seek more of this type of guidance? Continue working with your guidance in this way; follow those breadcrumbs knowing they are part of the overall tapestry being woven together.

The thread of overarching direction

The second thread steers us in the overarching direction of our divine life path. This might be felt as a series of almost elusive impressions, feelings and ideas. Emma wanted children. Maggie wanted to contribute to de-stressing workplaces. I knew there was a book buried inside of me.

The unravelling of this overarching thread may arrive as a faint impression, becoming stronger over time, especially if stillness and space are cultivated to receive these impressions. More of these impressions about our life's purpose are received as we unravel the other two threads (daily intuitive instructions and, as you'll see below, the thread of healing). As we follow the seemingly mundane guidance and journey with our inner healing, we see our life path more clearly. This thread of guidance, hinting at your life's overarching direction, will reveal and unravel at a different pace to the thread of daily intuitive instructions, and is somewhat dependent on our progress unraveling the third thread.

Writing books has long been an overarching thread in my life, while my daily intuitive instructions helped prepare me for this and my healing (third thread) supported this. Continuing to move in this general direction — journalism, PR, blogging, submitting articles, self-publishing, producing course manuals — it all started to add up. This book didn't come to me because I sat down and wrote the book all those years ago; it was quite the opposite!

The thread of healing

This third thread pulls us into an inner journey of healing, transforming us to arrive at this destination. Guidance arrives asking us to clear and heal many things: the past, our false self, and the beliefs, behaviours and stored emotions that are blocking us from our true self. This, too, is guided work, if we let it be.

For me, this began as regular chakra clearing, working with different healing modalities and journaling. At different stages it's looked different; by listening to my Four Bodies and Chris, I've known when it's time to seek new supports. The next few chapters are dedicated to you unravelling this thread.

Simply notice the clues for now, recording them in your journal when you do. This chapter's exercise will help formulate your three threads into something more malleable.

CASE STUDY — Maria

Maria came to see me for a reading after parting ways with the school that employed her as a private music teacher. They couldn't continue to support Maria's creative teaching methods, and Maria wasn't willing to give them up, resulting in her departure from the school. While Maria initially felt hurt by this, I was very excited — her creativity was exactly what she would go on to teach others. This, coupled with her passion for music as a form of self-expression, was moving her towards the perfect opportunity to use musical self-expression to help others.

Compounding her unemployment, Maria's lease on her apartment had almost expired; she now had to find a new home without an income source. Spirit showed me Maria on a smaller property located on someone else's land; she'd work in the garden in return for board. Connection to the earth was another strong message in Maria's reading, so this solution weaved into the overall picture quite nicely. Her own personal music room was filled with plants, as she loved to sing to them.

Among other things in her reading, spirit asked Maria to tend to her physical body. She had a niggling ailment modern medicine couldn't explain, but spirit suggested that it was connected to her expression. Spirit shared that time in nature, creative self-expression and, of course, music would help alleviate her ailment. Maria had recently found a local alternative school and she was drawn to contact them and offer to introduce music to the students in a non-formal, far more expressive way. Spirit confirmed her hunch — this would be enough to cover her bills while the majority of her time could still be focused on her inner healing (largely physical, but also linked to the other bodies). Eventually, Maria would develop her own method for teaching music as a healing modality for others.

Look closely to see the three threads here. Thread one (day-to-day events and instructions) prompted Maria out of her workplace and home to investigate a new job and living arrangement. Thread two asked Maria to heal her beliefs around music and expression; this was also going to alleviate her physical ailment. Thread three gave Maria an overall direction for her path and purpose: to help others heal via creative self-expression through music and nature.

Maria set to work reorganising her life towards this new plan — a plan she didn't logically create for herself, but that she allowed guidance to reveal to her. The third thread would take time to unfold, but she set to work with the job opportunity, healing her health and settling into her new home, knowing all threads would eventually weave together at the right time.

Weaving it together

Cautiously unravel these threads, without letting the rational mind take hold. Temptation exists to see the overall vision and then *mentally* construct a way there. Instead, the way there lies in the other two threads. Following the everyday intuitive instructions and the healing journey creates an Intuitive Action Plan. But this plan needs to be *felt* rather than logically mapped out. We are aligning with our divine life path, not our rational life plan.

Each thread weaves together, creating a tapestry of sorts. A picture emerges, one aligned with our divine life path and, indeed, the manual we've been moving towards. Reviewing your journal thus far, you'll likely identify guidance from each of the three threads. You can also take these insights into your Sacred Space and ask your SST for further insights. The exercise at the end of this chapter will help.

Please don't get caught up on mentally categorising your guidance, though; this isn't an intellectual exercise. Instead, approach this with curiosity, reflecting on and exploring what you already know about where you are going, and how.

Your overarching vision becomes a set point on the horizon, a North Star, to move towards. Feel this in your heart and soul — your core desire, feeling and vision for your own future. Maybe it's not what your mind expected at all. Keep filtering it through your head and heart, and your Four Bodies until you recognise it as your divine life path. Then, your daily intuitive instructions and your inner transformation via your healing journey are the Aligned Action Steps to take you there.

Remain non-attached enough to the outcome, but forever trusting you'll arrive. Then take your next immediate intuitive step.

Follow that thread!

Working with guidance in everyday life

Depending on the thread, some guidance comes in thick and fast, other guidance, not so much. My everyday and healing threads tend to come in almost immediately, while I can spend weeks or months allowing a bigger piece of guidance to settle. My overarching destination unravels far more slowly, with major signposts arriving every so often (journalism, PR, blogging, course creation etc. were all such signposts).

Because so much is unfolding on a timeline all of its own, we rarely have a definitive Intuitive Action Plan mapped out as our minds would prefer. Instead, we set our internal compass to the new North Star, allowing our intuition and divine whispers to navigate the way forward. Continue working with the process from the last chapter to ask for and receive guidance. Here's a quick refresh:

- **Ask** — Be clear about what you're asking for, geared towards where you need to go for growth, expansion and learning.
- **Trust** — Answers will come however and whenever they need to. Your prayers and questions have been heard and will be answered.
- **Rhythm and ritual** — Create an environment of stillness, space and silence to encourage the answers.
- **Receive** — Notice all the ways your questions are answered. Observe and note your impressions.
- **Reflect and interpret** — Is the answer literal? Symbolic? Do you need clarification? Interpret the answers that come.
- **Act** — Is it time to act? Ensure the directive is also coming from your guidance and not your ego, which may have other ideas about when and how to act. Then do it.

Sometimes answers arrive immediately, sometimes more sporadically. You may now start to understand why some pieces of the puzzle arrive more easily than others. Sometimes you need to act on the guidance associated with one thread before you receive the answers from another question via another thread. I recommend recording all of this in your journal, curiously looking for these threads as your mind tries to rationalise it all.

CHOOSE YOUR ADVENTURE – INTUIT YOUR ACTION PLAN

Can you feel the threads tugging at you? Maybe you recognise all three, or maybe just one or two right now. Trust where you are and what you find. Take a clean, separate page in your journal for this exercise. Create three columns on the page, labelling each:

1.　　Day-to-day guidance
2.　　Inner healing guidance
3.　　Overarching path and purpose guidance

Reflect back on your notes so far, contemplating the questions below.

- Can you categorise the guidance you've already received?
- What's your North Star or overarching pull at this time?
- What are the steps you've been given to help you get there? (These are in the healing and day-to-day guidance.)

Now you're going to rewrite this information as you might write a typical to-do list or action plan.

- Title another blank page in your journal 'Intuitive Action Plan'.
- On the next line, write the overarching vision or destination.
- Now create a section called 'Aligned Action Steps'. Under this heading, list out all the information from the other columns. Observe your mind here — does it wish to interject?

What you've now got on your page is a new soul-aligned Intuitive Action Plan that will lead you deeper into your divine life path. Add to this over the coming chapters, as you receive more guidance on the healing journey and your life purpose.

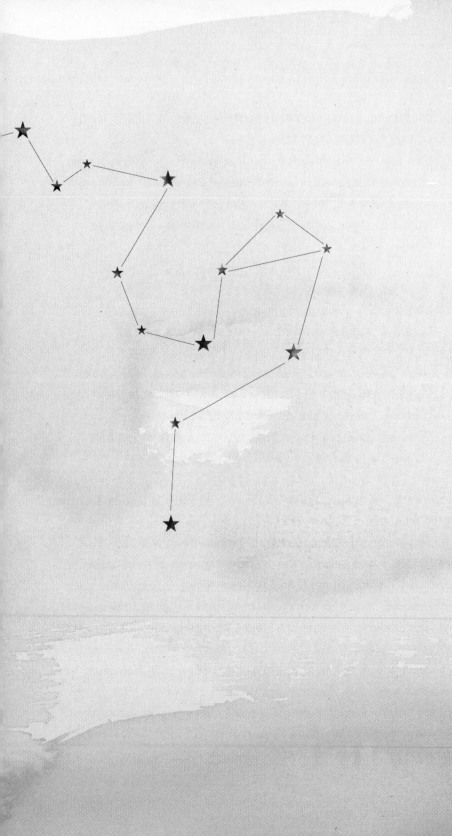

CHAPTER 13

★

INNER TRANSFORMATION

'Mum, that's the man I see in our living room,' I said, innocently pointing to a photograph Mum's sister (another one of my aunts) had just shown her. By the look on Mum's face, at least from my childish perspective, my words caused her a great deal of confusion and pain.

The man in the photograph was Mum's father, my grandfather. He died when Mum was just sixteen — eleven years before I was born. Grief-stricken, Granny destroyed all photographs of him long before my birth and, to my knowledge, no other family member had ever shared one. Until then, I never knew who this man from my living room was.

This was bittersweet for me. Finally, I knew who'd joined me for all those years in our family room. But it came with a gut-wrenching side of anguish, as I'd upset my mother. Unknowingly, I internalised that feeling and attached it to my psychic abilities for many, many years.

Mum says she doesn't remember that specific moment, but it was one of my life's most pivotal. Not that I knew it at the time. This memory only came back to me as an adult, long after Cathy's visitation, when Chris' healing thread led me through my inner transformation.

Given this moment was buried deep within me, I didn't just wake up one day feeling totally OK leaving my PR job to work as a psychic. There was quite a process I moved through — and continued to move through. In that moment, as a child, I absorbed the message that the non-physical things I saw and felt caused great pain and discomfort for others. I believed it was better for everyone if I just kept these experiences to myself.

Mum never said that to me, of course; in fact, she's now one of my biggest, most vocal supporters. But, as a self-centric child, I thought her response was about *me*. Never wanting to upset her, or anyone, again, I buried my psychic abilities — and we all know how that turned out.

Herein lay one of my life's biggest lessons. The culmination of this childhood moment, Mum and Cathy's treatment of psychics and readers in the past, my religious upbringing and Cathy's visitation itself all set the scene for deep inner-healing work as my soul's path and psychic gifts revealed themselves to me.

No doubt you have your own pivotal moment buried within you. We each have core wounding (as well as wounding from our past lives, too) and other tender pains we must now mend. Following our healing thread, we unravel our inner world physically, mentally, emotionally and spiritually to unearth what has been buried, hidden and locked away.

Typically, our early years set up our life's lesson, in accordance with our soul's blueprint; they contribute to our purpose. Such conditions influence our beliefs, behaviours and perceptions; changing them changes our lives. This is the work of soul, and none of this is by chance.

Our soul chose our family and early circumstances for a reason. Placing me into a religious family (with an atheist father) where psychics were scoffed at was the perfect classroom for this psychic kid, ensuring

I'd question myself and my life path. *That's* where my transformation was — ensuring my purpose would reveal itself.

Many similar wounds and experiences have since been reviewed as I follow my thread of healing, from this lifetime and previous ones. This is continuous, dedicated work. Like our relationship with guidance, we must be willing to go all in.

This is where the real change and transformation begins — it's also where the rational mind is likely to fight the hardest.

Bridging here and there

I could lie and sugar-coat this, but you're seeking truth, so I'll give it to you straight: this is the messy middle. Forewarned is forearmed. Knowing this ahead of time would have better prepared me. My lesson needn't be yours.

Excavating all that was buried within — that my rational mind had spent most of my life ignoring — made me want to run. Chris systematically led me into all the 'stuff' in my inner world — all the beliefs, stories and attachments my mind assigned to every pivotal event, the associated emotions I'd bottled up and the energy I'd stored in my system. Everything was up for review.

Healing began when I moved from PR to a psychic reader, but it continued and deepened over the next decade, the past ten years. Whole chunks of my life fell by the wayside. My career had changed. Friendships abruptly ended; others petered out. New friends eventually arrived. Habits and behaviours reorganised. Gary and I fell in love. We test each other constantly, as do the two strong girls we're raising. We moved house seven times in nine years. Three miscarriages shaped us. My business cyclically expands and contracts. Some change has occurred through deliberate design; some of it life surprisingly served up. All of it prompted deep inner work.

Your rational mind will fight you hard at this point. My mind didn't particularly like Chris, anymore. Could I trust him? After building our relationship, it felt like the honeymoon was definitely over. Welcome to the eye of your own storm — but, lucky for you, you know this eventually works out in your favour. This is happening *for* you.

When I asked Chris why he led me here, into this mess, he said: 'Soul didn't lead you here to only lead you here.'

> Unravelling our threads and following our guidance isn't a pass to easy street, but a guarantee we will arrive in the very situations, circumstances and relationships required for us to learn our lessons — and integrate them. Life delivers opportunities to see things differently. Arriving in such moments provides the ingredients for soul growth and transformation, if we let the intuitive mind stay at the helm.

If the rational mind creeps in, we become stuck.

Chris handed me a magnifying glass, showed me the haystack of my life and then asked me to dismantle, it strand by strand, to reveal the needle within. I made peace with Cathy's visitation and the moment I recognised my deceased grandfather. Now my own boss, I unravelled my beliefs around 'hard work' after years in pressurised workplaces. I opened up to Gary, trusting I could be psychic and loved. Sadly, I farewelled many friends, for one reason or another. I grieved the devastating loss of those three children and the hopes and dreams accompanying them.

No amount of Chris' guidance could alleviate the suffering of my very raw human experience, but my trust in him saw me through. Trawling through our inner landscape, we untangle the threads guiding us forward while simultaneously unravelling our inner blocks, snarls and wounds, finally arriving in the open expanse of our true self.

Chris assured me, as I will assure you: Don't give up when you hit this point! *This is not the breakdown, but the breakthrough.* Healing is the bridge between where we are and where we're going. But a bridge is neither here, nor there. Suspended between the past and future, our mind would rather be anywhere but *here*. The discomfort of the present requires our full attention. Such discomfort brings us wisdom, if we know where to look.

Into the chrysalis

Like the metamorphosis of a caterpillar into a butterfly, we, too, must enter a darkened chrysalis to change form. You cannot stay the old you. Transformation awaits, so you can emerge anew. Into the chrysalis we go.

Symbolically, going into the chrysalis represents the unknown, the void, the womb, the inner world or the darkened room. It's a place logic doesn't like. Yet, from this unknown place, all life is born, including the new you. Here, our trust in our guidance is put through its paces; your mind won't like the process.

This transformational stage of the journey is akin to standing in a darkened room with the lights out, blinds drawn. Blindfolded. The room has been torn up; the furniture is overturned and the floor is littered with obstacles. Spun around three times, off-balance and directionless, we are now asked to make our way across the room, towards the exit, and not injure ourselves in the process.

You have a choice: do you remember your guidance, or forget it? Forgetting, we flood with panic. Remembering, we are filled with trust. Soul didn't lead you here to only lead you here, nor did your SST. You've arrived here for a reason, and your internal navigation system and three threads of guidance will lead you out. Once you emerge, you'll never be the same.

Everything outside the room also shifts and changes in response to the happenings inside the room. Of course, we have no idea; we're in the dark! We don't yet realise that every step made inside influences what's happening outside, too.

Now, bear with me on this analogy as I weave in a story I shared earlier. Outside the darkened room, a storm is raging. Don't peek outside the darkened room to see what's spiralling — and definitely don't reach out to hang on to the debris that's swirling. Stay inside until the storm subsides. The storm subsides as you progress through the room. Emerging, *now* you can review what you want to keep, fix or discard. But don't rush out of the darkened room to tend to the outer world; stay the course inside. Tend to the outer world once your new form takes hold. The outside world is preparing for your emergence based on who you are becoming inside.

Inside, keep following the healing thread, navigating the inner, darkened hurdles. You're guided through this process. You were guided here to transform, not to stay stuck.

Process of change — the Guidance Cycle

Inside the room, following the healing thread, we are led over and under the obstacles via a very specific process of clearing, healing and restoring. What happens inside the room, or chrysalis, influences what's happening outside of it; the outer world changes in response to our inner work. Inner transformation influences outer world manifestation; it can only come in response to the clearing, healing and restoring taking place.

This is the Guidance Cycle. Our transformation occurs as we follow our guidance through four phases of change. This Guidance Cycle, then, is comprised of our Clearing, Healing, Restoring and Manifesting phases.

The first three phases prepare us to receive the manual, altering and changing our energetic state so it's a match for the energetic imprint of the manual we want to receive. Because all of life is working for us, and responding to our energetic state, our energetic transformation is mirrored on the outside of the chrysalis. Inner transformation commands the outer, material world to match our new energetic form. Life suddenly brings us everything encoded in our manual to ensure we can live out our purpose.

Let's look at the four steps of the Guidance Cycle in a little more detail:

Clearing

This step is rather like clearing out a container of dirt and debris. If you're the container, the Clearing requires a review of the accumulated dirt and debris across your physical, mental, emotional and spiritual bodies. Systematically, you'll remove the old thinking, behaviours, relationships, emotions and energy of the old false self, allowing the new true self to emerge.

Clearing may be reactive or proactive, although it typically starts as a reactive response to our lives and situations. Earlier in my journey, I responded to what wasn't working in my life — PR, singledom and feeling disconnected, for example. Further along, this process became more proactive — creating products, moving house, ending friendships, for example. There is a natural point in the Guidance Cycle where we move from reactive to proactive steps. Just keep following your guidance for now.

Healing

Once the container is cleared, its condition becomes more obvious. Repairs may be needed, like patching holes or leaks, or the container may need strengthening and reinforcing. Depending on the burden the container has carried, it may simply need to recover before it is used again.

Healing happens physically, mentally, emotionally and spiritually. Listening to our Four Bodies, following the signs and divine whispers, we will begin to see what each body needs to heal, and when.

We can proactively tend to our healing, but it cannot be rushed or forced; it has a timing all of its own. There's not much for us to do, per se, except *allow* the healing to occur. Quite often, we will receive signs, symbols and messengers helping us heal what we may not have even realised needed repairing. Keep paying attention to who and what shows up.

Healing is very closely linked to Restoring — the next phase in the process. While Healing will repair the container, Restoring is more about what the container can now hold.

Restoring

Perhaps you're familiar with the adage, 'You have to fill your own cup before you can fill someone else's.' This is certainly one model of restoring — to fill our own cup, or container, before we give to others. Constantly filling and depleting our own cup, though, is also unsustainable. We need to plug ourselves into a bountiful Source, sending a never-ending and overflowing surplus through our own container and onwards to others. Don't just fill your cup to give to others. Fill it for you first, then share the overflowing surplus.

Restoring, then, not only brings you back to full, but also to a state of overflowing surplus — a state of abundant flow. And when your energy supply is abundantly spilling over, the outside world must respond and mirror the same overflowing abundance.

Most of us start this journey depleted, disconnected, empty and disenchanted, or something similar. Spending time in stillness, space and silence helps to refill the cup; connecting to the energy itself (explained more in Chapter 15) ensures a connection to Source. Perhaps you can now see this within my story, and also in Maggie's and Emma's.

Picture a pyramid of stacked champagne glasses, like what you may see at a wedding. Each flute is stacked on top of the other in such a way that there is one glass at the top and many underneath it, just waiting to be filled.

Now, imagine there is a never-ending bottle of champagne pouring into the top glass. Eventually it cannot hold any more champagne, and the overflow pours into the glasses beneath it, and eventually into the glasses beneath those, and so on and so forth, until every glass is in a state of constant overflow. This is the Restoring phase.

Manifesting

Wouldn't you be drawn to a never-ending flow of champagne? Abundant overflow (especially of champagne) is sure to draw a crowd. The Manifesting stage of the Guidance Cycle is no different.

You constantly draw to you what matches your vibration. So, when you have Cleared, Healed and Restored yourself to a place of overflowing surplus (physically, mentally, emotionally and spiritually), you are likely to draw far more to you than when your container was depleted, dirty and empty. But this isn't just about giving what you have — manifesting is far more than this, as you'll see in Chapter 21.

Your inner world creates your outer world or, more precisely, your current inner world draws to you your future outer world. The Guidance Cycle constantly improves and upgrades your inner world, which means you are proactively moving in the direction of an improved outer world before you've consciously begun creating it.

As you clear, heal and restore your inner world, you allow more of your soul's frequency and your manual's energy to enter into your body. And when you begin to vibrate from this frequency, you attract to you what is a match for your soul, and then you begin to live from there.

Following your healing thread through the Guidance Cycle is preparing you for bigger and better things. Keep going.

You have to go through it

My daughters love the classic storybook, *We're Going on a Bear Hunt*, by Michael Rosen. A family is out on a bear hunt, but they constantly encounter challenges — long grass, mud, a river, a snow storm. They repeatedly remind themselves that they can't go over the obstacle and they can't go under it — they have to go *through* it.

So it is with the Guidance Cycle. A caterpillar cannot become a butterfly until the inner work is complete. A baby won't exit the womb until it's time (says this mother of a once 'overdue' baby). And you cannot come out the other side of your transformation without actually having changed form. You can't hide. You can't run. You can't avoid. Well, you can try. But sooner or later, in this lifetime or the next, you have to go through it. At least now you have a tour guide!

CASE STUDY – EMMA

Remember Emma? When it was time for her inner transformation, she saw her relationship with her dad and brothers as the gateway within, showing her where to start her exploration.

Systematically, she worked through her Four Bodies, unearthing and discovering buried nuggets to turn to gold. Where needed, Emma worked with other practitioners to support herself physically, mentally, emotionally and spiritually. She turned to alternative medicine to better understand her hormones and fertility; she supported her chakras with regular reiki and we used soul-level healing to understand the soul contracts in place with her family of origin.

Emma said things felt like they got worse before they got better. Our inner transformation is the equivalent of stirring up a glass of dirty water: the stirring encourages the dirt to float around. The risk here is in thinking things have gotten worse — after all, there's muddy water where it was settled before! Stay the course. Visible dirt is easier to siphon out. With the clear water remaining, you're better placed to see your way forward. Until then, trust.

Untangling the healing thread brought all of Emma's 'dirt' to the surface — the hurt, the feelings of unworthiness, the shame she felt in her femininity. By feeling everything and staying the course, Emma allowed all the past hurts and pains to make their way out. Once cleared, Emma could see more clearly than she ever had before.

 ## CHOOSE YOUR ADVENTURE – TAKING AN INVENTORY AND MAPPING YOUR JOURNEY

In the next chapter, we'll explore the tools and processes to support you during each phase of the Guidance Cycle. For now, return to the Scan your Four Bodies exercise from page 109. This time, scan your Four Bodies again, enquiring into whether that particular body may be Clearing, Healing, Restoring or Manifesting.

Table 1, below, may help you see which phase you're in, based on the activities you've been guided to.

Table 1 — Phases and focus of the Guidance Cycle

CLEARING	HEALING	RESTORING	MANIFESTING
Letting go	Acceptance	Slowing down	Creating
Releasing	Forgiveness	Grounding	Birthing
Ending/	Self-love	Self-care	Beginning
completing	Unconditional	Time in nature	Change
Shedding	love	Nourishment	Transition
	Compassion		Transformation

In your journal, spend some time reflecting on the following prompts:

- Where are you in the Guidance Cycle? What are the clues signalling this point in the cycle?
- What is happening in each of your Four Bodies?
- How is the Guidance Cycle moving you through your Four Bodies, and what's shifting and changing?
- What's happening in your chakras? What do you feel you need to help support them?

Visit your Sacred Space and ask for specific guidance on your process with the Guidance Cycle and your Four Bodies. Ask what may need to be cleared, healed, restored and manifested in your life. My oracle cards, The Little Sage Oracle Cards, share this message of our Four Bodies and the Guidance Cycle — you may like to work with them to see exactly where you are in the process.

✳ *Work with The Little Sage Oracle Cards for guidance on your Four Bodies.*

Stay open to any additional signs and symbols, dreams and other messages, and see how else you are led into your healing.

At the end of the next chapter, you'll build on what you learn here.

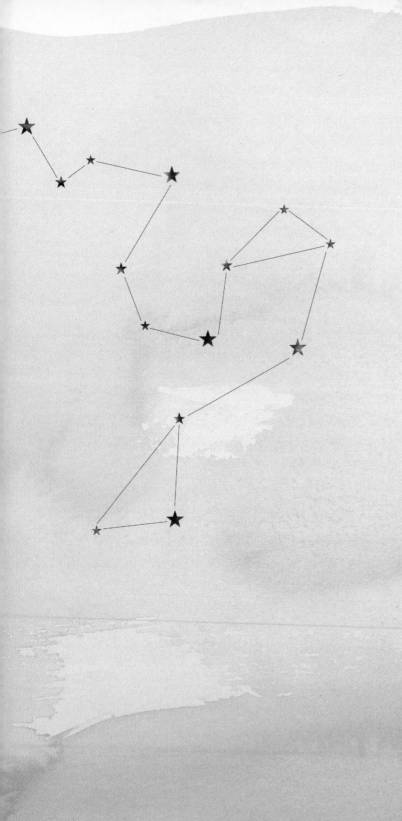

CHAPTER 14

★

HEALING TOOLKIT

Back at the PR agency, I became increasingly frustrated with some of the senior management. I felt the expectations kept increasing, the goal posts kept moving and no matter how much effort and how many hours I put in, it was simply never enough. Now, this may or may not have been true, but it was certainly my perception at the time.

Chris helped me shift that perspective by teaching me the Mirror Technique. Chris suggested I look at this situation — and all outer world circumstances for that matter — as if it were a mirror, reflecting back to me what I needed to see in myself, positive or negative.

'What if this had nothing to do with the senior management, but everything to do with my internal world?' I now wondered. What was my outer world pointing me to, within?

Although a tough pill to swallow (and one I preferred management swallow at the time), this question made me consider where I held

163

unrealistic expectations of myself — and not just of myself at work, but across my life as a whole. What were the benchmarks I was holding myself to? Why did I move my own goal posts? Was it possible I thought I was not enough, period?

By applying this mirror technique, answering these questions helped me process my decision to leave that environment. Loosening my grip, I relaxed my timelines and expectations of myself — and I suspect this is also why my watch was 'misplaced' the summer I was between PR jobs. Forgiving my bosses, the environment and the industry itself came when I went within to ultimately forgive myself. Letting go of the expectations, beliefs and behaviours meant I could also let go of my unrealistic life plan — allowing my divine life path to emerge. PR wasn't soul's plan for me. It was just a classroom to learn my lesson. As I course-corrected internally, so, too, did my external world.

The Mirror Technique tasks us with seeing the symbolism in our life's events and circumstances, reflecting what we must see inside ourselves for transformation to occur. In doing so, we clear, heal and restore our inner world so our outer world can now manifest — but in alignment with our true self and divine life path.

To identify what needs attention, we apply the Guidance Cycle steps. As we do, we will develop a healing toolkit of supports and techniques, which our guidance has likely been serving up to us already.

The Mirror Technique

Take a look now at your outer world and consider it through the Mirror Technique. Your feelings are a mirror. Your jobs, relationships and money are all mirrors. Your Four Bodies — more mirrors. They are all highlighting the core of who you are, and pointing to where to clear, heal or restore to come back into alignment with your true self.

All of life reflects to you where to look internally, every layer bringing you deeper and deeper within, until you process this energetically.

Transforming your energy will transform your life; when your energy is at its most clear, you'll become a clear match for the energy of your soul and manual to imprint upon you. They are one and the same — and you've been guided to create the resonance all along.

Using outer world events and situations as mirrors, you might see that feeling stuck in your job might mirror a 'stuckness' inside. Hurting in your relationships mirrors hurt in your relationship with self. When money (or any thing in your outer world for that matter) doesn't flow, it shows where your inner world isn't flowing. And your own life force, or energy, supports it all. Here, we begin to apply our symbolism anew, looking at all of life in new ways.

Once we know where to look, we can reach for the appropriate tool to help clear, heal or restore what we find there, knowing something marvellous will appear in the outer world in time. Our SST will likely be illuminating this for us, but with this process, we can more proactively move through our healing, too.

Here are the steps for the Mirror Technique:

1. Identify
2. Reflect
3. Toolkit
4. Act

Identify

Identify what's triggering or challenging you. What's the real problem here? Journaling may help highlight your feelings, repeating themes and patterns. What comes up for you? How do you currently see your world? Home in on the core issue.

In my case, I felt frustrated and trapped by pressures, expectations and demands, reflected to me via my bosses and workplace. Emma felt unworthy and uncomfortable with her femininity. This was reflected in her relationships with her father and brothers. Maria enquired into her creativity, self-expression and her feelings, as she'd been told how these ought to be delivered in the world. You may face something different — health issues, relationship drama, insufficient funds. Whatever your outer world shows you, come within to find the root cause.

Reflect

How you see your outer world hints at the beliefs, emotions or energy within (or about) yourself. Uncovering blind spots can be tricky. Your SST can help, but this may also be where a physical support team can help. Clients will often spend a great deal of time in this phase, excavating and uncovering fresh perspectives, physically and psychically, and I share more tools for this in my courses and programs. Ask for further insights and guidance if you need it here, and seek out professionals to support you (or watch who serendipitously turns up).

Your emotions and feelings highlight what's off-kilter physically, mentally, emotionally or spiritually. The mirror will point to one of your Four Bodies, before taking you in deeper. Perhaps it's not a belief at all, but an old emotion buried within, or an energetic cord tying you to the past. Keep digging until you find it. Remember, each of the Four Bodies are connected; what you unearth in one layer has a deeper root elsewhere, and energy is the baseline.

Toolkit

Once you know your inner landscape, you can determine the supports required to heal. Just as you can't mend a broken arm with a Band-Aid, you can't fix an emotional block with thinking or an energetic drain with yoga. The tool employed needs to fit the task. Similarly, there's no point focusing on restoring before you've done the clearing and healing, or vice versa.

Table 1 (*'Phases and focus of the Guidance Cycle'*) in the previous chapter can help suggest which tools may help when — but *always* follow your own intuition. The sample toolkit in Table 2 (*'Supports during the Guidance Cycle'*) of this chapter also suggests specific processes to investigate.

More recently, I've struggled with some health concerns. Naturally, my default is to go straight to the energetic layer — but this is in good shape. I couldn't understand what was causing my physical discomfort. Australian author and nutritional biochemist Dr Libby Weaver's work serendipitously turned up in my world (she provides wonderful materials on the mind-body-emotion connection, if you're interested). My answer came where I wasn't looking, but guidance ensured I found it — better late than never. By making a few tweaks, namely removing caffeine from my diet, my Four Bodies harmonised again. They simply hadn't caught up to much of the energetic work I'd recently done.

Apply the tool, healing modality or other technique you're guided to in order to clear, heal or restore whatever's come to light. Chris has often hinted at a modality for some time, before I recognise why I've needed it. Nudges to go back to your yoga practice or to try reiki or similar practices should be acknowledged. I had long felt it was time to ditch caffeine, but I had to wait for my body to truly enforce that one!

Act

Like all guidance, we must know when to act on the healing required. There's no point knowing you can process old pains and hurts, but never tending to them. Some pains are so ingrained we don't know they're there. Others we simply never want to poke at again; there's a reason we've buried them. You don't have to do it alone — and it may just be that the tool you choose to work with includes turning to qualified practitioners to support you where needed.

Go on the bear hunt, and *go through* whatever is waiting for you.

Mirror Technique meets Guidance Cycle

We can have all the advice in the world, but it's what we do with it that counts. Mirrors will only show you what needs transformation — but then you need to get to work. Spirit can't do this for you, but they'll support you throughout.

A physical support team will be invaluable at this point. If you don't yet have one, *ask,* then watch who turns up. They may be teachers, mentors, healers and practitioners, or a community of other soul-led people. You don't need to do this alone; all of life does really support you, if you let it.

Summarising what I've found in years of private client and group work, I've created the table opposite, highlighting some common challenges during the inner transformation, and the tools, practices and modalities that may support you through them. Part of my work now is helping clients understand where are they in this transformation, and what is really required at that time.

Table 2 — Supports during the Guidance Cycle (sample toolkit)

	CLEARING	HEALING
PHYSICAL	Detoxing diet and body Letting go/ending/completing (jobs, relationships, friendships, etc.) Culling furniture, files, clothing, cupboards, etc. Moving, renovating, redecorating, relocating	Rest, recovery, stillness, gentle activity Practitioner support — doctors, natural therapies, etc. Relationship counselling
MENTAL	Reset mindsets, beliefs, attachments, stories Journaling, self-reflection, meditation	Reframing and re-creating beliefs and perceptions Writing new stories and life scripts
EMOTIONAL	Emotional embodiment (sit in discomfort with all feelings until the sensations pass) Self-expression Physical release — writing, boxing class, dancing, etc.	Forgiveness Acceptance Self-love Unconditional love Compassion
SPIRITUAL/ENERGETIC (FOCUS ON CHAKRAS)	Individual chakra clearing (white light, red light, crystals, sound, reiki, kinesiology) Cutting energy/psychic cords	Balance chakras with one another (white light, crystals, sound, reiki, kinesiology) Protecting boundaries

Table 2 — continued

	RESTORING	MANIFESTING
PHYSICAL	Improving diet, sleep and exercise, increasing nutrients New relationships, supports, jobs, homes, etc. Repairing/buying new items Re-energising your spaces	Beginning/creating anew People/supports Establishing a new routine, diet, etc. Receiving new opportunities
MENTAL	Positive affirmations Meditation White space	Living from new perspectives as your new normal See the new beliefs in the outer world
EMOTIONAL	Receiving Opening Loving Giving	Balance shifts to more positive emotions as the baseline
SPIRITUAL/ENERGETIC (FOCUS ON CHAKRAS)	Grounding and protecting energy Flooding chakras with white and red light, transmitting surplus	Balanced and vital chakras Free-flowing energy (life force) in inner and outer world 'In the flow' Outer world matches inner world

Working with the Four Bodies

Now the Four Bodies meet the Guidance Cycle. It's time to systematically clear, heal and restore across your physical, mental, emotional and spiritual bodies — and manifest the outer world to match. This process does not always unfold in that order, and not always one at a time! Let's look at what we are working with in each of the Four Bodies.

Physical

Remember the 4Ps of the Physical Body from Chapter 9? Here's a recap:

1. Physical, anatomical body
2. Possessions
3. Places
4. People

Intuitive nudges throughout the Guidance Cycle will prompt us to address anything within our Four Bodies, and the 4Ps of the Four Bodies, that is no longer a match for who we are becoming. We'll clear, heal and restore whatever arises.

Physical, anatomical body

People often detox just as breakthroughs arrive. Just before Emma's doctors addressed her fertility concerns, she'd already begun purging her household, and even her diet. She couldn't immediately see the connection, but with her new knowledge she could.

Physically clearing your body may prompt upgrades to diet, sleep and general wellbeing. Healing requires repair, rebuilding or revisiting our health, daily practices, rhythm and rituals. Restoration would encourage us to choose more healthful activities, and increase our fun by seeking new stimuli, people, places, ideas and creativity to truly fill our cup to surplus.

Possessions

Because we're energetic beings, everything we touch bears our energetic imprint. What we touch more frequently stores more energy. Possessions hold much energy and information about the owners.

Culling, then, not only clears the physical clutter but the energetic clutter too. We can also energetically clear our possessions using sage, crystals, sound baths, salt water or essential oils — not everything has to be discarded. We may repair and restore items we wish to keep, or replenish our supplies.

Places

Just like our possessions, environments and buildings can hold energy. Pooling energy in your home, workplace and car may symbolically mirror your internal energy flow. Similarly, stagnant, 'stuck' energy may symbolise stagnation in your energy centres.

Create more flowing, peaceful, inspired spaces by considering the energy of the space, and the possessions within it. Sage, fresh flowers, crystals, salt water, sound/music or aromatherapy can help shift energy. The Chinese practice of feng shui — balancing the energy within a space — may provide insights for the particular flow of energy in your home or office.

Sometimes a space (home, suburb, city or country) reflects the collective energetic imprint. Travelling to different locations around the world, I feel the space I'm in. While visiting sites such as Ground Zero in New York City, Stonehenge in England and even walking through the Colosseum in Rome, I have been flooded with intuitive hits and the energy of the site's history (and multitudes of tourists) within them. Suffice to say, I don't like crowds much.

People

Relationships provide our greatest mirrors. What we see in others must exist within us — but it's not all bad! What we love, admire and appreciate in others can only be seen because we possess this, too.

Look more closely at your relationships. Applying the Mirror Technique, what do you now see differently? Could it be possible that the people challenging you the most are actually your biggest teachers, and therefore the greatest soul gifts you've encountered?

Relationships may end or alter here, even improve, depending on the phase of the Guidance Cycle you're in.

Mental

Monitoring our thoughts, mental loops, stories and chatter on repeat allows us to observe the truth of our self-perceptions, and therefore how we see and interact with our life.

The Guidance Cycle will ask us to clear out these old beliefs and limitations we've placed on ourselves and our communities. Of course, I'm not suggesting we live in a lawless society. There are basic, fundamental rules to live by, but when those rules and laws suppress you, or entire groups, we need to question them. We are certainly moving through an exciting — and excruciating — period of history as we question these ideas en masse and collectively course-correct.

Stumbling upon an old story or belief, ask yourself, 'What if this had another meaning?'

What if I'd applied a different meaning in that moment I recognised my grandfather in that photo? How might things have turned out if I'd subsequently lived governed by a different belief? Of course, it all turned out as it needed to — but if there's an alternative meaning to your stories, you can dislodge their hold from your life, too.

Emotional

Emotional mirrors reflect your alignment with your life force and soul. Stored feelings and emotions from the past must make their way out, and as they leave, we must *feel* them, which of course, we've been trying to avoid. You may want support for this process.

Aligned to Source and soul, our emotions feel more light and positive. Heavier and negative feelings indicate where we are closed off to Source and soul, and therefore misaligned with our divine life path. Heavier feelings are clues to clear, heal or restore something physically, mentally, emotionally or spiritually. By clearing and healing, we open to feeling more positive once more, thus raising our vibration higher.

While not an exhaustive rule, below are some of the less-positive feelings and possible meanings and interpretations for them. Run this list through your intuition and SST, and if you find a new meaning, place it in your reference journal.

- *Anger* — highlights what we haven't said or done, but wanted to; the boundaries that need enforcing, or choices or commitments we must make; where our passions lie.
- *Jealousy* — indicates lack mentality, a belief we cannot have what we want/what others have.
- *Pain* — disconnect from our truth and Source, holding on to the past longer than needed.
- *Shame* — the ideals and standards we want to uphold.
- *Guilt* — not putting our needs and desires first. Living out expectations, not truth.
- *Fear* — not seeing the expansive possibility before us. We need to change our perspective.
- *Frustration* — expectations interfering, distrust of life and the moment you're in. Can't see the lesson, yet.
- *Anxiety* — distrust of life, desire to control and understand from the rational mind.

With clients, I'll often ask them to connect with their emotions and ask the emotion itself what it wants the client to know. It's another guide, after all. This can produce some very insightful results. Be sure to also ask the emotion what it needs in order to transform.

Spiritual/Energetic

Intuition might prompt you into the Guidance Cycle through any one of the Four Bodies, but they'll wind up as the same thing: energy. Our energy systems, chakras and aura store data on every interaction, thought and emotion. Clearing, healing and restoring across our Four Bodies is automatically impacting our energetic health; we've begun dislodging old, stagnant energy by working across any of the other bodies.

Each of the main seven chakras is responsible for processing energy associated with our thoughts, emotions and interactions on particular themes. Thus, when we know a particular belief has come up for exploration, it's a mirror pointing us straight to the corresponding chakra to work with.

Similarly, the location of a physical, mental or emotional ailment will have links with the chakras — inward we go again. Suffice to say, each of the other three bodies is pointing you to your chakras and energy flow. See Table 3 on pages 176 and 177 for an overview of the chakras.

Eventually, you'll work with this layer and observe the effects in the other three. All symptoms mirror your energy — your personal energetic imprint needs to match the manual's energetic imprint. In the next chapter, you'll actively work on your chakras and energy to cause a ripple effect on your emotions, thoughts, physical body and, indeed, to create change in your outer world, too.

As the Guidance Cycle dictates, we must work with our chakras and aura to clear, heal and restore them. We can do this through chakra balancing meditations and working with practitioners of reiki, crystal therapy or kinesiology. Aromatherapy, crystals and working with the corresponding colour of the chakras can also all help us clear, heal and restore them. Individual yoga poses are designed to work with individual chakras, too.

Chakras

Table 3 — Seven Main Chakras

CHAKRA	LOCATION	COLOUR	REPRESENTS
BASE CHAKRA	First chakra at base of the spine	Red	Basic survival and belonging. Material, physical world. Security: physical, financial, career, etc. Sense of grounding and connection to earth.
SACRAL CHAKRA	Second chakra, between the navel and base of the spine	Orange	Inter-relational. Emotions, power and sex. Cravings for physical pleasures, addictions, obsessions. Control and manipulation. Creativity. Feminine energy.
SOLAR PLEXUS CHAKRA	Third chakra, behind the navel	Yellow	Self-image, esteem, power and worth. Confidence. Inner strength.

CHAKRA	LOCATION	COLOUR	REPRESENTS
HEART CHAKRA	Fourth chakra, in the centre of the chest	Green	First of more spiritual chakras. Love, giving and receiving, emotional processing, attachments, forgiveness and compassion.
THROAT CHAKRA	Fifth chakra, in the neck	Blue	Speaking your truth, expressing, asking. Choice and commitment. Transmitting.
THIRD EYE CHAKRA	Sixth chakra, between the eyebrows/ between the eyes	Purple	Clear seeing; past, present and future; seeing within and outward. Spirit and spirituality.
CROWN CHAKRA	Seventh chakra, at the top of the head	White or golden	Clear knowing; connection to the divine or collective mind. Also affected by thoughts on God, religion or spirituality, divine guidance and trust.

**CHOOSE YOUR ADVENTURE –
DEVELOP YOUR HEALING TOOLKIT**
Intuit where you are in the Guidance Cycle and take an
inventory of what is occurring in your Four Bodies and chakras
using this exercise and Table 4 on pages 180 and 181.

1. **Where are you in the Guidance Cycle?**
     Meet with your SST in your Sacred Space and ask about your
    own Guidance Cycle. Record what comes up in your journal.
    Review Table 1 on page 159 and intuitively feel what you're
    working through. Does it match your SST's advice?

2. **What's happening in your Four Bodies?**
    Revisit the Scan your Four Bodies exercise from Chapter 9.
    Now that you notice how you feel about each body, use
    Table 4 on pages 180 and 181 to support your enquiry.

3. **Take a closer look at the chakras**
    Scan and feel into each of your chakras, either self-guided,
    or with a guided meditation or a practitioner.

    *   Do any chakras feel dull, small, sluggish or slow?
    *   Are any oversized or over-energised?
    *   Which chakras need attention?
    *   What are the themes of this chakra (see the 'represents'
        column in Table 3 on pages 176 and 177)?
    *   What does the theme(s) tell you?

If you are unfamiliar with your chakras, you can always go into your Sacred Space and simply ask to be guided through them, or to receive whatever information you need at this time regarding them. Make note of the experience in your journal.

4.   **What does it all mean?**
    Look for patterns and connections between where you are in your Guidance Cycle, which of the Four Bodies you're working with and what's happening in your energy and chakras. You may intuitively get a sense of what's required to work with and through to help you up-level your energy and Clear, Heal, Restore and Manifest. Again, you can go into your Sacred Space and ask for the connections to be made clear to you. Or, use the sample toolkit from Table 2, on page 169.

✳ *Try my Chakra Balancing Meditation on my website.*

Table 4 — Supporting your Four Bodies

PHYSICAL	MENTAL	EMOTIONAL	SPIRITUAL/ ENERGETIC
Anatomical Diet, sleep, exercise, flexibility, strength, wellbeing, health	Beliefs Perceptions Stories and attachments	Primary emotions felt in response to an event (fear, joy)	Your own life force Chakras
Possessions Clothing, furniture, cars, files		Secondary emotions felt in response to the first emotion (e.g. shame, guilt, frustration)	Aura Astrological/ lunar Universal/ collective
Places Home, office, hang-outs, classes, frequently visited locations			Psychic cords Grounding Protecting
People Relationships, family, friendships, children, colleagues			

Table 4 — continued

CLUES THIS BODY NEEDS ATTENTION			
PHYSICAL	**MENTAL**	**EMOTIONAL**	**SPIRITUAL/ ENERGETIC**
Physical sensations (tingles, tense, tight) Ailments and illness Relationship challenges Hoarding/lack mentality Sense of dread about people, places, situations	Noise and constant mind chatter Negative thoughts on repeat Stories you tell yourself Lack mentality Victim mentality Imposter syndrome Strict life rules	Emotional overwhelm Feeling disconnected, numb, unsure Depression, anxiety	Stagnation in particular life areas Feeling 'off in the clouds' and ungrounded None of the 'doors' you're trying to open will open Preoccupied, energetically consumed by others, events or situations

CHAPTER 15

★

IN THE FLOW

In my early days of self-employment, an internal misalignment was typically signalled by a series of clients all cancelling or postponing at once. Usually, once my internal state shifted, an influx of clients would arrive again. Clients often book seeking a particular type of guidance in a particular life area just as I experience the same lessons and struggles. Chris' teachings via automatic writing are frequently reinforced as several clients turn up, unknowingly needing the very thing Chris just gave me.

Using the Mirror Technique, the outer world is a litmus test for what occurs inside. Still tending to all my Four Bodies, I quickly found the best results working at the energetic level, supporting my chakras, because it's the baseline for the other three bodies. As you're familiarising with your energy, please know that any work on the other bodies will also influence the energetic layer, too.

Working with my chakras and energy expedited the transformation process. Clearing, healing and restoring our chakras allows more life force to flow through us — and when I was clean and clear, my body was a clear container allowing an abundant overflow of energy. Seeing this mirrored in my work, finances, opportunities and relationships, I was buoyed to continue.

Clearer chakras and energy flow also increase and clarify spirit's communication. My overarching thread began to tug a little harder; I edged a little bit closer to the vault and its secrets for me. As my own personal energetic imprint refreshed, it was able to receive more of the energetic imprint of my manual. The Guidance Cycle continued to spin, more information came to me and things began to gather momentum. None of which were the result of force in my outer world; it began to flow in response to the efforts focused within. Magic now ran the show.

Life won't always be so serendipitous, but when it is, we know our inner world is clean and clear. When it's not, we must unkink the hose to let the flow, well ... flow.

Being in the flow

At the surface level, being 'in the flow' might imply things are humming along nicely and everything's working out without force — not an obstacle in sight. Sometimes, this phrase is used to describe being in the mental zone, where our cognitive skill is on point. But, because we're more than our physical, mental and emotional bodies, being in the flow has far more to do with our energetic state. For our outer world to be in flow, our inner world must be, too.

Energy must easily flow through our energetic digestive system, without blockages or backing up. Blockages can arise within the chakras themselves, or because of what's stored across the Four Bodies. Working with the Four Bodies alone is not enough; we must focus our efforts on the energy underpinning them.

When our energy is 'in the flow', we've cleared the debris and psychic gunk stored in the chakras (and Four Bodies). Such a clear energetic flow allows us to align with soul's slipstream, and move into the unique essence and frequency of our divine life path. Clear and balanced chakras allow our own life force to move through the system with ease — and ease within creates ease without. To clear and balance our chakras, we tend to the Four Bodies, and to the energy flow itself. We are constantly guided in this process as we follow our intuition and seek guidance from our SST.

What we notice in our Four Bodies and what we perceive in our outer world are a reflection of the quality and vitality of the energy running through our chakras. We've experienced this firsthand working with the Mirror Technique and Guidance Cycle. It's as if our Four Bodies become a sort of interface, linking our energy and our outer world. Just as our SST helps us move through our lessons and identify our purpose, it also ensures we Clear, Heal or Restore this interface, our energy and the Four Bodies, so we're able to Manifest once more. Ultimately, it's *energy* we need to work with.

Sadly, most of us are not utilising our energy to its full potential. Instead, our rational minds identify a problem in our jobs, relationships, bank balance and so on, and attempt to fix it through *thinking*. Everything outside of us is outside our control, so this effort is futile. Sure, you may have had some success to date, but as you begin to open up spiritually, the old ways no longer work. And spirit will now hold you accountable to the choices of this new path.

Where does the flow, flow?

Human trajectory focuses on moving in one linear, forward motion, with an occasional reference to the past and consideration for the future. Energy is far less linear and more cyclical. Energy flows in multiple directions at once, in a sort of spiral motion. Energy flows to us from above, below, in and out. The chakras, our energetic digestive system, must process flows from all directions. The image below helps illustrate these energy circuits.

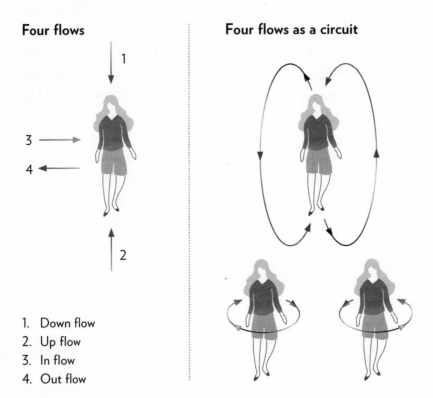

Four flows

1. Down flow
2. Up flow
3. In flow
4. Out flow

Four flows as a circuit

I call these flows of energy the In and Out Flow and the Up and Down Flow. Essentially, what flows in and out of our chakras is the result of our inner state. On the inward flow, we receive from the world around us — from the people, places, possessions, thoughts, food and emotions we engage with. All this energy comes in to each of our chakras for processing, before cycling back out again. Now, what we send out on the outward flow is a reflection of what is happening on the inside. We send out a frequency, or vibration, that is greatly influenced by the quality of our chakras (and all we've cleared, healed and restored here). What we send out into the world via our transmission, expression, offerings and giving has an energetic vibration. Thus, we're in constant exchange with the world around us.

Every single interaction keeps our chakras in a state of flux, thus they need constant care and attention. Daily chakra maintenance is just as important as our daily tooth brushing, yet I hazard a guess that it is far less implemented. And, just as we frequent dentists for a check-up and deeper cleanse, we may need to work with practitioners to help us fine tune our energy centres.

Our Up and Down flow is important too. Receiving a constant flow of energy from the Earth fuels us with energetic nourishment and nutrients. We receive a flow from the heavens, too, of our own life force and a wisdom and knowledge of the higher realms (and our higher self). Flooding our chakras more often with these high-vibrational frequencies can naturally work to clear, heal and restore our chakras. When these forces are also present, they begin to feed in to our out flow, sending out into the world far higher frequencies than our human self, alone. Imagine a world when we are all radiating these higher frequencies.

Being in the flow, then, is not just about allowing ourselves to have our outer world humming, but allowing all the forces of life to fill us up (to surplus), open us to our full capacity to receive and give as the multi-dimensional beings we are. We cannot simply operate from our minds.

Just like we had to become aware of not just one body, but four, we also need to broaden our awareness of our Four Flows — human, spirit, soul and earth — and how our Four Bodies allow us to be in the slipstream when all is in harmony.

In and Out Flow

We are constantly responding to our outer world as it flows in towards us. We can only view the outer world through the lens of our internal world. How we process our experiences is based on the quality of the filter we run it through (our chakras). When that filter is murky, dirty, stagnant or not working properly, we cloud our interpretation of what life is showing us. If we haven't cleared, healed and restored our beliefs, emotions, energy and behaviours from some past event — say, being hurt as a child — we have a filter that now may perceive that all of life is going to hurt us. This is the lens through which we see life.

Because we are all energetic beings, we also receive the inflow of energy from the outer world, from the relationships and situations we find ourselves in. Every thought and action holds an energy, too, all stored in the chakras. Energetic bonds and cords form, tying us to other people, the past, old events and even the future. Clearing the energetic ties, or psychic cords, can energetically free us from the past.

Just imagine for a minute having ended a romantic relationship. You've physically parted ways. Mentally, you understand and have processed the downfall of the relationship. Emotionally, you've cried more tears than you may have wished to. And yet you find yourself still anchored to that person, despite your best efforts. An energetic cord may still connect you. It'll be difficult to move on without cutting it.

What we send out into the world is also run through that filter. In our example of being hurt, if we anticipate being hurt, what we send out into the world may try to prevent pain. This is not a true and full expression of our truth, but instead an expression marred by the filter we haven't cleared, healed or restored. The energetic quality and intention of our give and take with the world is far more potent than what we're actually giving or taking. Energy underpins it all.

When we are guided back into ourselves to heal, we no longer see life as a hard, bad place, and we begin to open up to love again. When we approach life from that place, we have a very different response. We are now in alignment with our own soul's path and purpose.

Increasing our vibration through our chakras allows us to build energetic boundaries and protection. By strengthening our chakras and energy field, we can no longer receive negative energy or psychic attachments from others related to our past or anticipated futures. Working with this energetic circuit, we naturally clear unwanted psychic debris, heal any holes or energy leaks, and strengthen our energetic containers so that we can be flooded with energy from Source to fuel us and return us to overflowing surplus. When we reach this phase, we no longer need to rely on the external psychic protection; we'll have repaired and rebuilt our own.

Up and Down Flow

We constantly receive information from the heavens, the collective mind and, of course, our soul via our SST. This information doesn't come mentally, but energetically. So, if we have a blocked and dysfunctional energy system, the energy from above cannot penetrate, and if it does, it gets jumbled on its descent. Or, we believe there is no higher guidance because we energetically cannot let it in to our system. We also know that working on our chakras can improve our psychic senses, or 6Cs, so we can receive more insights.

Earth also sends energy in the form of love, stability, connection, nutrients and energetic sustenance. But, again, if we are energetically closed off, we can't receive it. Nor can we send our energy back. Failing to receive this nourishment energetically means we will fail to receive it physically, mentally or emotionally, too.

Our body is more than this fleshy form; it's a channel, a vehicle, between heaven and Earth. As all Four Flows run up and down, in and out, our body is not only fuelled but also connected and aligned to our soul's mission.

And, because we have this flow, when we all amplify it, we create a collective web of energy. Our individual journey benefits us personally, of course, but when we all do this en masse, we create new energetic grid works on our planet.

CASE STUDY – Alice

Alice came to me asking about the changes I foresaw in her relationship with her girlfriend, Cassie. Although this was the prompt for her appointment, it was one of the last things we spoke about. First, spirit had me talk about her creativity, her work (where she was not able to express herself creatively and felt very stifled), as well as her living arrangements, then her chakras — mainly her throat and sacral chakras.

Spirit suggested Alice look to unblock her expression through her throat chakra — it was time to admit she hated her job and wanted to work in a far more creative environment. Then, spirit suggested she work on her sacral chakra, the centre for creativity. This chakra was being impacted by the stifled expression, but also by Alice's view of her femininity. Because these two chakras were blocked, it was having a knock-on effect on her life. In effect, Alice had two kinks in her hose and energy was pooling between them, but not flowing through in any direction.

Over time, Alice and I worked with these energy centres. Guiding Alice through her inner transformation, she cleared, healed and restored her past, especially her thoughts, beliefs and feelings around her creativity and femininity. She drew on various tools in her toolkit, helping her to express more creatively and clearly in her life, especially to Cassie. As the energy began to flow through her chakras, we then began to work on Alice's heart chakra. She had so much love to give, especially to Cassie, and as things came back into flow in all

---

four directions, Alice and Cassie's relationship also came back into flow.

To illustrate, I suggested Alice imagine a river flowing through a number of different suburbs or areas. Each suburb is like another life area — in Alice's case, her job, relationship, creative self-expression, health and so on. Although Alice came in asking about her relationship, this was somewhat 'downstream', and the blockage was being felt in the other areas first. We needed to clear that kink, or dam wall, so the energy, or river, could flow freely again.

 ## CHOOSE YOUR ADVENTURE — ACTIVATE YOUR ENERGY

The Energy Activation Visualisation below will help you activate the flow of energy through your chakras. Working with your chakras in such a way will not only help you to clear and balance them, but also connect you with them, building your ability to 'read' and perceive the data stored in them.

Energy Activation Visualisation

Sit in a comfortable position, ready to receive whatever unfolds.

Take a few moments to centre yourself, slowing your thoughts and creating stillness, space and silence within.

Call in your spirit guides, angels, archangels, ascended masters and any beings of light that wish to join you in your Sacred Space.

Hold the intention you wish to raise your vibration. Then, call in white light from the heavens and feel it moving down through your chakras.

Feel it coming in through your crown chakra, your third eye chakra, your throat chakra and down into your heart chakra, then through your solar plexus chakra, down into the sacral and base chakras. Feel it connect into the Earth, just underneath your feet.

Notice yourself filled with this pure, vital energy. This light holds you safe and protected. It also holds all the details of your life blueprint and your connection to the heavens, to the greater cosmos — the whole Universe — and to the collective consciousness. Allow this energy to move through your Four Bodies, through your chakras.

Now call on the healing and grounding energy of Mother Earth, a brilliant red light. Draw it up from the Earth, through your body, into your base chakra, sacral chakra, and the chakras in the solar plexus, the heart, the throat, and the third eye and up to your crown chakra. Draw it up above your head, sending it back up into the heavens. Feel yourself connected through the richness of Mother Earth, plugged into the Earth's blueprint.

See yourself as a channel between heaven and Earth. Each time you connect with this energy you open more and more to cosmic intelligence and the details of your blueprint.

Stay in this energy and meditation as long as you wish, allowing new knowledge and awareness to enter your energy field; it may not come through your mental awareness.

When you are ready, give thanks to the energy you have activated as well as the spirit guides, angels, archangels, ascended masters and light beings who have gathered in your Sacred Space today.

Remember that this knowledge will integrate in the coming hours, days or even weeks.

Slowly come back to the room and record any impressions in your journal, noting progress each time you complete the visualisation.

✳ *An extended audio version of this meditation is available on my website.*

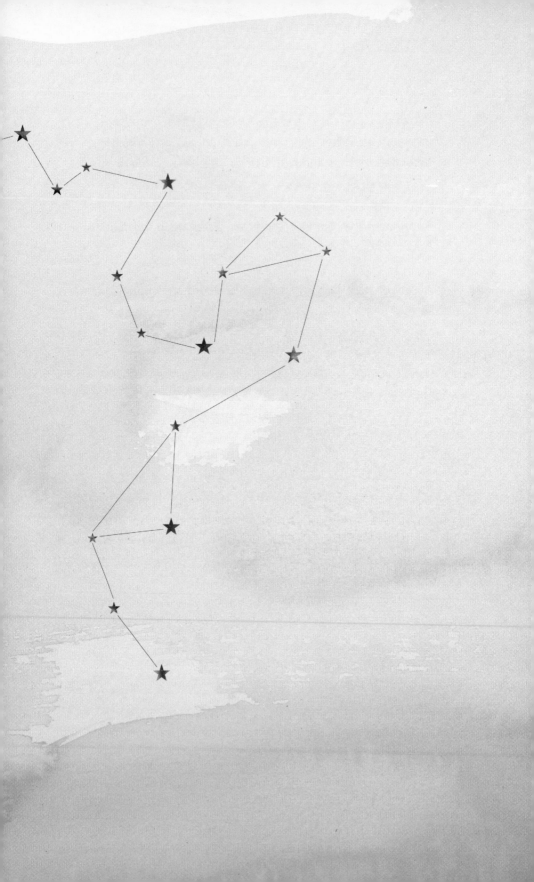

CHAPTER 16

★

THE MANUAL

Upgrading my energetic state subsequently upgraded my understanding of myself and my path. By this stage, I'd built my business beyond giving readings. I was now running an online shop with support tools and products; teaching programs, mentoring and events; and managing a team behind the business. I felt on-path and on-purpose.

With new guidance came new lessons and inner transformations. Without them, I wouldn't have been able to express in physical form the energy I received from soul.

I didn't just receive a business or life plan. Instead, I received waves of energetic imprints, which, once the energy settled across my emotional, mental and physical bodies, I could bring into form. Along the way, Chris showed me the gifts buried within me and the soul contracts made with other souls so we could learn from one another. These contracts and agreements enable your soul to progress through this lifetime via specific lessons and experiences with others.

SPIRIT SPEAK
Soul contracts are the significant, and somewhat binding, agreements our soul enters into in order to learn and teach. Typically, contracts are made with other souls, who then appear in key, impactful relationships in our lives. A soul agreement may not be as binding as a contract, but it's similar in nature, nonetheless. It's more an informal agreement to learn and teach than a soul contract.

Some of my most beautiful introductions to soul contracts came while I was pregnant with each of my daughters. Towards the later stages of each pregnancy, I channelled in my journals specific details about the girls being sent to Gary and me. I had a sense of what they'd be like, what they'd agreed to learn in their lifetimes, and how they would teach and shape me. I even had visual snippets of their physical appearance, like Isla's facial features and Rose's mop of dark, curly hair. My life's biggest joy is the unfolding of them as individuals. I am totally open to them never fulfilling their prophecies. I have no intention of making them fit. Instead, I try and approach my girls from a very human perspective — although, perhaps some psychic insight may be more useful in their teenage years.

Other such agreements have been revealed, too, including my relationship with Gary. I've seen many of the past lives we've shared together and the lessons we've agreed to learn in this one. That doesn't always make it easier; in fact, we've had our share of difficult times. But we both know these challenges are serving our greater purpose and time together.

I've come to understand my work in such a way, too. Just as individuals have an energy and soul, I believe our soul's work is an entity of its own, wanting to be born through us. This book, as much as your own soul-led projects, visions and businesses, also has agreements with the other souls it's here to connect with. You're not reading this by chance. This has certainly turned my marketing background on its head; there is something so much bigger than a publicity plan orchestrating the destiny of our work.

Your manual will ask you, just as mine has asked me, to take what life gives you, process and transform it, understand how it has supported your soul's growth, then send it back out into the world, your lessons and purpose renewed.

The manual

People often quip we aren't born with an instruction manual for life, but I beg to differ. I believe we are born with such a manual *and* an in-built navigation system leading us towards this very manual. It's just that neither of these look like our minds expect them to. As we've seen, mental expectations and life's conditioning block the instruction manual from us and silence our internal navigation, which, just like our modern voice-assisted GPS devices, is constantly guiding us along our life path (although, many of us need to turn the volume up). As I see it, the problem is not that we don't have an instruction manual, it's that we *believe* we haven't got one.

This instruction manual doesn't look like any ordinary document. Your eyes can't see it and you certainly can't pick it up to read cover to cover. Instead, this manual is more of an 'energetic imprint' — something you feel deep inside you but on a subtle level. This manual holds the secrets of your life path. All the wisdom and answers you seek, but in a form your eyes and mind can't perceive. It's totally possible to decode this energetic imprint — and therefore, the secrets of your life path.

The good news is you've already been preparing to receive the energetic imprint of your life's instruction manual. Of course, *how* we receive it may not be what our mind is expecting. You might recall this manual is an energetic imprint containing the agreements our soul committed to in this lifetime. Because spirit and soul aren't truly in physical form, this is not really a physical document, but rather agreements encoded in energetic form. This imprint of energy is what we've been guided to transform and upgrade our human energy flows for to become a match for our manual.

Remember the meeting in our Dumbledore-esque office, where soul met with the blueprint guides to consider the upcoming lifetime? In consultation, a plan was developed, highlighting the lessons our soul would explore, the purpose soul would offer, the soul mates it would work with in order to learn and teach as agreed, and the gifts soul would incarnate with, to help with the quest.

Before we move on, let's explore the concept of soul mates. Often, this term is used to denote our romantic partners, but soul mates can appear within any relationship dynamic — parents, siblings or colleagues. I also don't subscribe to the Hollywood version of soul mates — we may not like our soul mates once in human form. Just like in school, there were teachers I loved, others not so much, but they taught me all the same. So it is with soul mates. A soul mate is another soul mated or paired with our own to ensure both souls learn what they came to life to learn. This isn't always easy.

SPIRIT SPEAK

A **soul mate** is the pairing of two souls, ensuring each can teach and learn from the other. A soul mate relationship needn't only materialise in romantic partnerships, it can exist within any type of impactful relationship.

Now, back to the agreements and discussions. Once all the details are agreed upon — the parameters of the adventure laid down — the soul blueprint is created and an SST is assigned. In time, the soul makes its way into human form, bringing with it a connection to this manual, our soul's blueprint.

Multiple templates

While we don't receive the manual as a physical document, I often clairvoyantly see the blueprints like a blueprint or architectural plans for a building, often in multiple pages or layers. I call these layers Templates, and when each of the Templates stack upon one another, we can see rich data weave together.

There are four templates to the blueprint:

1. Lifetime Template
2. Soul Template
3. Earth Template
4. Spirit Template

Not surprisingly, we don't receive all the templates all at once. Of the templates we're given access to, the details still arrive as breadcrumbs. Spirit and soul will direct the level of detail we can access directly while in human form.

Typically, it's the Lifetime Template we receive first. This details the agreements for this particular lifetime. Mine, for example, details the parameters of this adventure as Helen Jacobs and the lessons, purpose and gifts I'll bring forth in this lifetime. As we're working with our inner transformation, all our clearing, healing and restoring, we're working largely with this lifetime and its events, circumstances and relationships.

A Soul Template details this across all the lifetimes our soul has incarnated into — it's a rich history of our previous lifetimes. While a Lifetime Template focuses on this lifetime, a Soul Template is a culmination of all the many lifetimes, and their templates. Any pertinent information for this lifetime may also be accessed in the beginning.

At the time of writing, I haven't spent much time in either the Earth or Spirit Templates. The Earth Template contains all the relevant material, tangible resources and supports we'll encounter in this lifetime to not only support us, but also to support us in completing the soul mission, or purpose, we've come here to uphold. There's a very specific bounty waiting here for you. The Spirit Template, then, includes details of your multidimensional nature, the hierarchy of your energy across the dimensions from your human self to your higher self.

Alone, each template may not mean much, but overlay them with each other and things start to connect up in new ways. At this stage in the journey, we're most likely to receive details from the Lifetime Template and perhaps snippets from the Soul Template. Trust that whatever arrives is exactly what you need at this point in time.

Energetic imprint

Non-physical beings communicate with one another via energy. Despite now being in physical form, we receive the details of the manual as an energetic imprint upon our awareness, or energy field. It cannot materialise in physical form; we must shift our physical form to accommodate it. We must open our own energetic channels (like clearing our chakras) so we can receive the energy of our manual into our own energetic field. Then, this energetic information can make its way across our emotional, mental and physical understandings. To receive this imprint, we've cleared, healed and restored our energy flows in and out, up and down. This has been the focus of the previous chapters, for good reason.

Receiving energetic imprints, then, is how we've also received our intuitive hits, divine whispers and psychic information. We've been interpreting energy all along! Gaining access direct from the blueprint — rather than just following the threads of information — can now add context and depth to our guidance thus far.

Because our SST oversees our access to this data, we can ask them to help us, particularly our blueprint guides.

Meet your blueprint guides

Blueprint guides are members of your SST specifically charged with helping you remember, access and decode your own life manual, or soul blueprint. These beings were present when your soul made the very agreements detailed within the blueprint. Working with the blueprint guides, you begin to receive pertinent, detailed information from your blueprint, far beyond hunches and threads pulling you forward. Larger snippets of the blueprint arrive. To me, this feels like a 'divine download'. It hovers around my head, energy moving through my body, energy field and awareness, without any real knowledge of what's happening.

CHANNELLED GUIDANCE – blueprint guides
Here is another excerpt from my automatic writing from
18 October 2015.

Soul agreements arise from, *'A process entered into before birth with a series of guides and masters. At any point you can begin to reconvene with these particular guides and masters to understand the depth and intricacies of the blueprint. These guides and masters will work with you at your request. Of course, this may not be as easy as it sounds. And, in fact, these guides and masters are just a few of the many beings on the spiritual planes that will work with your soul for its development.*

'Enter your Spiritual Support Team. There are various beings assigned to various roles to assist you with your soul's experience or "journey" on Earth. There is your main guide, as well as others who turn up at various junctures, or those like the blueprint guides, who can be accessed for finer details of your life.

'The guides and masters of the blueprint are "higher" guides — they may be harder to reach off the bat. And so, for many only

---

now beginning to awaken to their souls, you may begin to be led by other guides, or even your own intuition. All will serve for the same purpose: to bring you into alignment, the personality, the ego with your true self and soul.

'In this way, many find it easier to work with intuition than rising through the levels of spirit to with whom to communicate. You may wish to only work with your intuition, however, as you become fully awake and begin to ascend, the level of beings you reach are higher. To say this in another way, the higher your own energy, the higher the beings you can sustain communication with.'

Receiving the imprint

Good news: you've already received much detail from your blueprint. First, it's received via snippets of intuitive data, hunches, dreams, feelings and desires. This initial focus prepares us to receive more intuitive data, encouraging us into an inner transformation first, so we're better placed to receive more of the manual. Slowly, more pieces of the puzzle arrive.

As we advance in our journey, and we're energetically able to reach them, we can work directly with our blueprint guides, who hold the details of our blueprint and the keys to the room where it's stored. Our blueprint guides, the broader SST and our intuition all bring us details of the blueprint in different ways. We don't just receive a tangible blueprint as a physical document, we also receive a frequency, knowledge and awareness. All of these have to be able to make their way into our body and being.

This Process of Remembering may arrive in stages. Sometimes, there's an intellectual remembrance, which comes to us as ideas, memories or thoughts of who we are — but if you're also listening and remembering with your body, you'll know these messages as truth because of how they feel. Of course, if you are unsure, this is also where guidance from our SST may give us specific clues as to our blueprint. In the first instance, we receive the blueprint as a *memory of who we are*, in this lifetime. This memory of who we are can be likened to the notion of finding our calling or purpose in life. It's aligning who we are with how we want to show up in the world. This is certainly true as we receive the Lifetime Template.

As the imprint arrives, it may feel more like a yearning or a greater sense of truth washing over us. The *calling* arrives. Here, we start to receive more of the blueprint as an energetic document before it makes its way into our mental awareness. We continue to *feel* it. These frequencies cause new ideas and understandings to bubble up within us, shifting us from an overarching call or direction, to an awakened full force of the mission we are here to live out. At first, my soul calling led me to share higher guidance with the world, which initially came through giving readings, but this has certainly evolved and grown over time. In this way, we receive the blueprint as a *memory of who we are called to be* in this lifetime. We must follow the call of the times.

Energy will make its way to us, as we're primed to receive it. We can commune with the blueprint guides and ask for information, too.

 ## CHOOSE YOUR ADVENTURE – MEET YOUR BLUEPRINT GUIDES

This guided meditation will introduce you to your blueprint guides. You can also do this within your Sacred Space (using the guide on page 85). Each time you work with them, observe which layers of the blueprint you receive.

Meet your blueprint guides visualisation
Sit in a comfortable position, centred and ready to receive whatever unfolds.

Call in your spirit guides and angels, archangels, ascended masters and any other beings of light that wish to work with you today. In particular, extend an invitation to the blueprint guides who are ready to step forward and work with you, according to your blueprint and where you are at this point in time.

Now, imagine yourself surrounded by a beautiful golden shimmering white light. Draw all that light around your body like a column connecting you with heaven and Earth. You are safe and protected in this light. You can stay here in this space for as long as you wish.

When you are ready to proceed, imagine yourself arriving in a beautiful chamber. This is a room that stores your blueprint; you may see this room, you may sense it or you may not necessarily feel anything at all. Just allow this to unfold in whatever way it unfolds. Ask your blueprint guides to step forward and help guide you through this process according to whatever is relevant to your soul's work at this point in time.

Take as much time as you need to truly arrive in this space. You get a sense of the guide, light being or master who is joining you today. Perhaps you get a sense of them physically; perhaps there are physical sensations in your body. Perhaps there is an emotional response or perhaps you aren't aware of anything, but that is not to say it is not happening.

When you feel ready, you may pose a question to this guide in relation to your soul's work. You can take as much time as you like to pose this question, remembering, of course, that you may be exploring your own soul lessons.

You may wish to ask your guide what these lessons are, how they're showing up, how you can surrender or how you can learn them.

You may be more interested at this point to open a dialogue about your soul's purpose. Enquire about the soul gifts you have to offer and how you can be of service to each and every other soul you encounter.

Perhaps you are interested to know about your soul mate relationships. About the relationships current and present in your life right now, to relationships which have naturally run their course, or indeed how to open to these types of relationships in the future.

You may even wish to ask particular questions about the nature of your blueprint, such as how to open up to a blueprint, how to connect with its energy, its teachings and its message. Take a deep breath in, open and hold the space you've created and allow any information to come into your awareness in whatever way it wishes to come in.

This may unfold for you right now; it may unfold after a series of sittings with your blueprint guides. It may come by writing down any impressions you have in your journal. Stay in this space, posing questions and opening to receive whatever answers come through.

When you've received all you have to receive, give thanks to your blueprint guides for today's guidance and slowly make your way back to your waking life.

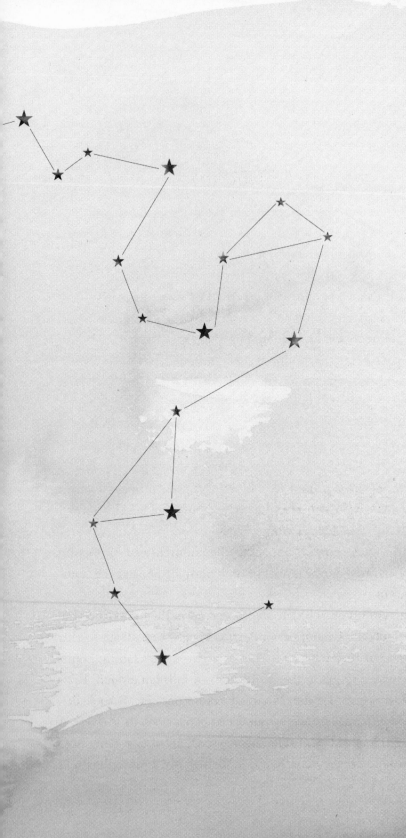

CHAPTER 17

★

LESSONS

Chris pushes my trust in him to the limit. One such lesson in trust unfolded as I followed Chris' advice on securing our family's forever home, where we've ended up (long after Star Street). For many years, visions and insights came to me about the children waiting to turn up for Gary and me, our beautiful future family home, and the home life, awaiting us.

I also had visions of us beachside, tucked up in the hinterland, and even living abroad for periods of our lives, although these all felt further away. One vision that felt closer was of a two-storey family home, where Gary would tinker in the shed while our kids ran around. I saw a dedicated workspace for me, French doors on one side, a bookshelf on the other (with one of my own published books upon its shelves). A golden retriever lounged by my feet. I could see Gary also working from home, in a studio off the main house. Clairvoyantly, I saw animations on his computer screen, but didn't know what they were (Gary is now in app development).

This vision has always been interwoven with my work — I always felt one would support the other, and vice versa, creating a very different lifestyle for our family.

After living in Star Street until Isla was about eighteen months old, I intuitively felt it was time to sell. It was time to expand my work and find our forever home while we wait for more children to arrive. I thought we'd find our forever home in no time.

Five years, four house moves, three miscarriages and one child later, we arrived in our home. I'm writing by the French doors now (although, my book is not on the shelf yet, and the dog is not here, just begged for by my children).

The constant moving (and miscarriages) tested my trust in Chris to the limit.

Given the time and heartache involved, I'm surprised we didn't give up. Sadly, many people do give up, rationalising if it was meant to happen it would have happened *by now*. Sometimes we do need to let go and move on, but when it comes to the thread of overarching direction, we cannot.

Herein lies my life's lesson in trust. This lesson is woven into almost every fibre, of every fabric, of my life. From a small child, I've had to trust that it was safe for me to see, sense and feel what others do not. I've had to trust my own instincts over anyone else's. I must still remind myself I can be who I am and still belong. It is safe for me to be me, and to be seen as such.

Trust has come up in other ways: who I can trust, in spirit and in life; how willing my soul is to trust my human form (and vice versa); how much I can trust this illogical process of opening to something bigger; how much I trust my belief in living life this way; how willing I am to *always* trust my inner voice over anyone else's outer voice. In committing these words to print, I've had to trust it is safe for me to share so much of what I know may be difficult for some people to receive and believe. Most of all, this lifetime is teaching me to trust *myself.*

Your lessons will push you to the limit, too — but the stretch in these classrooms gives way for our divine life path, and purpose, to come to the fore.

The lessons are the path

Lessons provide the chrysalis, pointing us inward for growth. As each interwoven lesson connects up to the next, our divine life path emerges. Lessons always turn up but we might think they arrive because we made some wrong turn, or they're a sign to change direction, or worse — that we *deserved* the heartache and pain. The lessons turn up because they *are* the path, as opposed to signs suggesting we're off it.

Knowing life supports us by serving up a series of classrooms for soul helps us understand our life path from a new perspective, one aligned with who we are and why we are really here. It takes us from being in a reactive state to one of curiosity and, hopefully, light-heartedness — it's all happening *for* us, not against us.

Guidance ensures we arrive squarely in the lessons, then asks us to explore them through every lens possible, so that our choices are not just a means to a soul-aligned end. We will always land in the lesson, no matter the choices we make; it's just *how* we learn them — the classroom, if you will — that changes.

School of Life, Earth Campus

Earth provides soul classrooms it couldn't access in the spirit realms. Earth is rich with duality: light and shadow, masculine and feminine, good and bad, love and fear. These contrasts allow soul to experience and experiment, thus learning in a way it wouldn't ordinarily be able to outside of a physical body. The Earth Campus provides a multitude of classrooms, lecture halls, seminars and smaller tutorials for soul to move in and out of.

Relationships, namely motherhood, my marriage to Gary and my partnership with Chris, have all provided classrooms for major life lessons for me. Other life situations can provide classrooms, too, like business, creative pursuits, health, finances or anything else we turn ourselves to. The Mirror Technique reminds us that our classrooms prompt us within, to see what causes that reflection.

Many classrooms could teach the same lesson; free will determines which classroom (relationship, career, environment) we enter. But the lessons were agreed to. Just like at university, when I majored in PR and marketing, I had to learn the prerequisite subjects but could pick and choose from the timetable which lectures and tutorials suited me best. The lessons fit the major, no matter the classroom I chose.

Some of the teachers were agreed to ahead of time. Soul chooses our parents, family of origin, our culture, generation and so on before incarnating, thus setting the scene for the perfect lesson exploration. Soul mates, the other souls we agree to work with, help us learn and grow; or we may be their teacher. Like in my degree, soul can elect major and minor study areas (life lessons) for this lifetime, as well as choosing the gifts, skills and talents you'll bring with you (life purpose).

Our rational mind, then, is kind of like the big kid on campus. You know the type — they promise to show you around, introduce you to the cool kids, and show you the ropes and shortcuts to getting a passing mark and fitting in. The big kid is bound to get you into trouble if you follow them exclusively. Sooner or later (I hope!), you ditch the big kid on campus and remember your own internal navigation system.

Soul is in no rush to complete the lesson, although your mind might be. Soul doesn't need to complete a lesson by next Tuesday at 10 a.m. — but your head may want you to! True advancement comes when you're ready to go deep, to truly absorb the lesson, heal and release. This is why our guidance is always prompting us to go deeper and deeper, and, ultimately, move beyond the mental constructs of our lessons and life path.

Who's marking these lessons?

Spirit often gives impressions that don't really have an equivalent word or phrase in the English language. Explaining lessons is one such instance where the word isn't a true representation of what spirit means. Terms like lessons, tests and learning imply that someone grades and judges the performance. In these higher realms, there is no judgement. Our mind categorises good or bad, pass or fail. From a higher perspective, it's all data. No matter what we learn, it's all good.

Despite my Catholic upbringing, a decade of working with spirit has changed my beliefs around God, Source, or whatever you'd like to call this higher power. I now believe our maker is not so interested in our earthly ideas of perfection, but rather will always hold us in unconditional love and compassion. This is perhaps the ultimate universal lesson we must each reach for ourselves. We weren't sent here to fail; in fact, I think it's quite the opposite.

Life is to be lived, explored, embraced and *felt* — all of it, the perceived good and bad — for this is how we learn.

Trial and error, curiosity and childlike wonder will take us further than pleasing some perceived superior Source. We came from Source and Source continues to create through us. We are Source in motion, exploring this dense realm of duality via physical form, and acting on Source's behalf.

Recognising your lessons

Wondering what your lessons are? Clues lie in your path through life so far. As all these moments add up, you're likely to see not only your 'minor' areas of study, but also your life's 'major' lessons, too. As you'll soon see, you have lessons for this lifetime but also lessons across your soul's entire timeline. The more present we are in each and every moment, the more visible and obvious the lessons are.

Life lessons

A life lesson is the area of exploration soul agreed to in this particular lifetime. Life lessons are for life. You'll explore them from every angle possible. You'll easily spot them with hindsight, identifying the themes, topics and teachings that frequently repeat. Welcome to your life's 'major' study area.

Trust, as I've mentioned, is one such lifetime theme for me. The more I trust, though, the more my purpose has been fulfilled. Your own lessons and purpose will marry up, too. The exercise at the end of this chapter will help you recognise your life's lessons.

Soul lessons

All these lifetimes add up — lifetime after lifetime. Across soul's timeline of lifetimes, then, an overarching soul lesson emerges. A soul lesson may be different to a particular life lesson, but it could weave across several of soul's lifetimes.

For example, because I have psychically accessed many of my previous lifetimes, I know my soul has explored leadership across a number of lifetimes. Despite (or because of) this leadership not going well in previous lifetimes, my soul chose to explore leadership again in this lifetime. But I'm a little reluctant to trust it. Leadership is more of a minor lesson in this lifetime, but it's woven in as my soul hasn't completed this lesson from other lifetimes.

Lessons that spill over from other lifetimes are often referred to as karma. Soul agrees to explore these lessons again, perhaps from a new perspective or different side of the coin. I've psychically read for clients who once lived as perpetrators only to find themselves the victim in this lifetime. Same lesson; very different classrooms.

In any given lifetime, the soul's purpose is to live out what it came here to explore.

Shared lessons

Aren't we all, then, just learning the same thing? In some ways we are. The very nature of the duality on the Earth Campus means there are universal lessons we're all exploring here. Such universal lessons are the common lessons to us all — unconditional love, forgiveness, acceptance and compassion, for example, would fall into this category. No matter what our major, these are the sort of prerequisite subject areas we will all explore in some shape or form.

While pregnant with my first daughter, Isla, Chris told me she would come in to explore love. Indeed, we are all exploring love, so not only will she explore the base — the ABCs — as we all will, she will also choose to major in it and most likely complete the equivalent of a PhD. After seven years of mothering her, I can see this already proving to be true.

As a universal lesson, I, too, am taking a refresher course on love, from time to time. Isla may brush up on trust from time to time, but we will never explore the themes to the same depth as one another. But, as I believe she is also one of my soul mates, her learnings shape mine, and vice versa. Our agreement allows us to share our learnings, and indeed, for us to teach each other how to trust and love.

There are people in your life playing this role for you, too. What a blessing they are.

Why choose difficulty?

Understandably, in a discussion on lessons, I'm often asked why soul chooses difficulty. We don't always see our teachers and challenges as blessings from the human perspective. Lessons don't always feel great (but we know that's mirroring something within). Before we can achieve soul-level healing, we must experience it in our outer world, so we know to go within, to the level of soul, to heal it. It will be mirrored to us in our human experience first.

Generally speaking, I don't believe soul specifically signs up for the big, awful things that may happen to us in this lifetime. I don't think our soul signs up for abuse, poverty, marginalisation or segregation, for example. Certainly it is difficult for the human mind to conceive why our soul might ever choose that for us, but through the lens of lessons in an earthly classroom providing duality, we may see it differently.

I also don't believe our earthly circumstances are born out of what we deserve. Quite the contrary; soul often chooses hardship because of what can be born out of it. It is often the depth of a lesson from which great growth comes.

For example, in Nora's story in Chapter 3, her soul explored self-love by experiencing weight and body-image issues. Certainly, this lesson could be learned in any number of different environments, but, to the soul, the depth of that exploration would be different if it was an exploration born out of some other circumstance.

Let's say soul chooses to explore the theme of expression, but incarnates with circumstances ranging from a physical inability to speak, through to segregation or marginalisation. Same lesson, different classrooms and different flavours to the lesson. The growth in this case is seeing the challenge as the fertile soil from which true healing comes.

I share these hypothetical examples to highlight why there are conditions, inflictions and situations in this lifetime that are less than ideal to our human judgements. I hope this may also further reinforce a point I made earlier; that our mind sees our life here in a particular way, while our soul does, indeed, see it differently. If we only ever stay in the one, human perception of our life, we can continue to miss the depth of the lesson at play.

This does not mean we choose to be treated badly, that we deserve to suffer injustice, abuse, poverty and negativity. We are not responsible for other people's behaviour and I am not making excuses for that behaviour. Ever. What I aim to highlight, however, is that our souls do choose to explore things that to our human mind and logic might not make immediate sense. I am hard-pressed to think of any movement or change in our world that was born out of comfort zones.

Not set in stone

How we learn our lessons is not set in stone. Free will and choice greatly influence how, where and when we learn a lesson — if at all. Soul may have elected the area of study, but our human self will determine if we turn up to class, if we are a fastidious student or if we prefer to play truant.

Soul can ride it out — it has lifetimes — but our mind often prefers we avoid, resist, defer or ignore the area of exploration before us. Often, this *is* the lesson! Whether we explore or we don't, we learn. We may not end up learning what our soul intended, but we've ultimately wound up in some other avenue of exploration.

This isn't permission to avoid your lessons, just more reassurance that the lesson will continue to arise in one form or another until it is learned — don't beat yourself up over it.

The gift in the challenge

One of the greatest joys I've experienced in my client work over the years is witnessing the moment a client moves from seeing people in their lives as enemies to seeing them as loving soul mates and teachers.

While many of the experiences in our lives can be hard to forgive, when we can reach beyond the human interaction and attempt to move into a state of seeing the true self of the other person behind the experience, we can come to see them in a whole new light.

What if the person who hurt you did so out of love?
What if their soul loved you so much, they agreed to take on the role of teacher in this lifetime? What if their soul honoured your own soul's agreement that it was willing to cause you pain, so you could remember love?

When we can move beyond our mind's judgments into a place of seeing the gifts in our challenges, our entire world begins to shift and change. Not just at the human level, but right across our entire soul timeline, reweaving the narrative of eons of lifetimes.

This is truly learning and integrating a lesson, and it can create karmic waves of healing right across our planet.

 ## CHOOSE YOUR ADVENTURE — WHAT ARE YOUR LESSONS?

Naturally, you may want to know what your lessons are. A simple reflection over your life thus far will likely start to draw you towards the themes and repeating patterns in your life. Keep attracting the same kind of partner? Are you always (insert your habit here)? If you use the Mirror Technique again, what might these themes and patterns be drawing you in deeper towards?

Hindsight is a wonderful tool; through the lens of hindsight, you can recognise recurring themes — or lessons. You can try journaling to identify what themes and patterns are present across your life.

While hindsight is handy, the ultimate goal is to begin recognising the themes as they arise, so you can work in the moment to clear, heal and move forward. To do this, you can work with your SST, particularly your blueprint guides, to ask for information about your lessons in this lifetime and your previous ones.

To connect with your blueprint guides, go into your Sacred Space (using the technique on page 85).

As you arrive, ask your blueprint guides to join you. In this meeting you're going to ask them about your lessons. Opposite is a list of suggested questions to ask as they arrive in your visualisation.

- What are my lessons in this lifetime?
- What are my lessons from previous lifetimes? How do they influence this lifetime?
- How can I best learn my lessons? What will help me grow?
- Who are my teachers (and what are they teaching me)?
- What am I teaching others?
- Who are my soul mates?
- Are there still more soul mates to enter my life?
- What will/do my soul mates teach me?
- What else do I need to know right now?

 Record any impressions and observations in your journal.

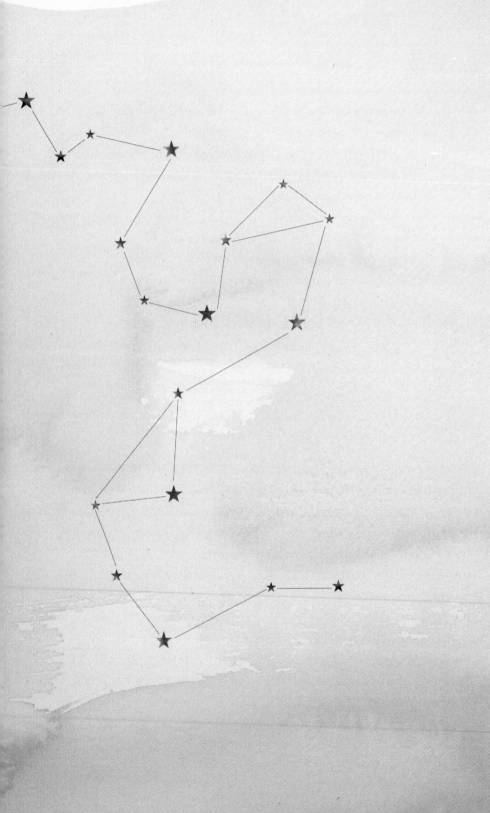

CHAPTER 18

★

PURPOSE

Pivoting from my life's plan to my divine life path, I got a sense of my overarching life purpose. But this vision didn't just land in one piece, just as my blueprint and lessons didn't. Instead, I followed each divine whisper, the overarching thread, step by step, unravelling how I could be of service in each and every moment. As I faced up to my lessons, my purpose emerged. A pattern emerged across the accumulated moments. And as life continues to unfold, so, too, does my purpose.

Let's take this book as an example. It's a large part of my life's purpose to share my experiences and what I've learned about trusting guidance. When asked what I wanted to be when I grew up, I'd often answer, 'A writer'. Working in PR, I knew I wanted to write a book, if only I knew what it would be about. Giving readings, running my intuitive experiment and observing the patterns and themes, I even tried a few times to start this very book. I knew this was part of my purpose, but divine timing was also at play.

On maternity leave with my second daughter, Rose, I sat down again to write this book. I had no plans for publishing it, I just had to get it out. As I typed, something else entirely began to move through me. I began to channel a higher group of beings, called the High Council of Sages. This council is like another SST, but not specifically assigned to me. Instead, the High Council of Sages tell me they are assigned to the entire group of people on Earth now remembering who they really are. Their insights were beyond anything Chris had ever shown me — certainly beyond anything I anticipated when I initially sat down to write the book.

I spent almost two years channelling their core guidance on more advanced topics, then was guided into spending another two years mentoring smaller groups of people through the advance trainings. I continue to work with them as my understanding of their teachings evolves. The same process of observation, sharing and applying came into play. During this time, I stopped all my other work, and closed down the online shop, resources and courses. A new purpose, in the moment, arrived.

Life took more twists and turns, but after a few years, I was no longer squarely focused on the book. My own personal detour added depth to my own development, showing me what this book *really* wanted to be. Once again, life unfolded in a way my mind did not expect but ultimately it met Chris' brief.

During those years spent channelling and sharing the advanced teachings, I struggled to make sense of where I was. Did I get it wrong? Why was I guided to shut it all down? Where had Chris' original vision — the one showing me I was to create this business to begin with, alongside images of writing books, touring, teaching and connecting with people — gone?

In truth, the opportunity to publish this book came while I was busy doing other things. I almost missed the serendipitous meeting. I already knew I was destined to write books; I didn't have to *make* it happen. Unlike many authors, this book didn't come because I sent my work to many publishers. Instead, it was a chance meeting and a genuine conversation that got the ball rolling. Life, once again, had other plans for me. Roman philosopher Seneca said: 'Luck is what happens when preparation meets opportunity.' Being dedicated to following my guidance, and acting on it step by step, prepared me for this moment. None of it came from a logical, mapped-out approach.

Without several attempts at the book, and the journey with the advanced teachings, this book would have been something very different indeed. Without every other step to build my business, it would never have come to fruition. My purpose almost took on a life of its own, and all of life was working to bring it to me.

Share who you are, on purpose

Exploring lessons and undergoing an inner transformation means you've peeled back layers of the false self, as a true self emerges. Remembering who you are at your core, what you've always known of yourself, is one half of your purpose; the other is to live it.

Your true self is your unique composition in this human form, in this life. The unique lessons and experiences that have shaped you, and the interests, talents, passions and skills you possess all point to your life's purpose, even if you can't see it yet. In my story, I've always had an interest in writing, business, speaking, mentoring and communicating — with spirit, or otherwise.

Slowly, as I listened to each divine whisper and followed each of the Three Threads of Guidance, these began to weave together a clearer picture. Showing up in each moment helped me to pull it all together. Through learning my lessons, the healing around my spirit

...munication landed me squarely in my purpose: teaching others how to also trust their guidance.

I didn't know that in the beginning, although I had a sense of it. Instead, I just turned up in each moment, offering what I had to offer. At first that was readings, and then those morphed into resources, courses, events and so on. It's not the form our purpose takes that's important, but that we bring it to the fore at all.

> Honouring your current state — physically, mentally, emotionally and spiritually — in each moment is to honour your soul and where you are on your path right now.

In this way, you are called to offer what you have to offer in this moment, and in each and every moment. Sometimes my purpose has been very inward, and not shared at all.

> Continuing to follow intuitive insights and impressions in every moment gives clear directives on how to offer what you have in each moment. Life puts you squarely in front of the people, situations and events to ensure you're exactly where you need to be.

Even in the less-desirable moments, *turn up anyway*. You've drawn this present moment into your experience and awareness for a reason. Reach for gratitude for this moment, even if it's not where you want to be. Trust it serves you, if only as a reminder to clean up and move forward, manifesting where you do want to be. And if you're not sure what you can offer in this moment, simply start by offering yourself and others unconditional love.

Each moment is of purpose; not everything needs to be on a grand scale, or even known to anyone other than you.

Purpose is found in the small moments, as well as
the large; not everyone is here to save the world or
lead large groups. Purpose can come in the way you
teach your children or welcome in your neighbours,
or lovingly let go of someone from your life.

Life always brings you your teachers, and ensures you're teaching, too.

What's your purpose?

Leaving PR, giving psychic readings, mentoring, teaching and even writing this book were all steps taken by following the divine whisper in each moment. My life's purpose evolves as I turn up in each moment, offering what I have to offer. Like our lessons, these moments accumulate to reveal our overarching purpose.

My purpose isn't always to offer my psychic abilities — this is just one of my soul gifts. Instead, my purpose is to offer *who I am* in each moment, calling upon whatever gifts and energy are at my disposal there and then. Perhaps that's a psychic insight, or simply a frequency to radiate, words to say or truth to own. Sometimes it's as simple as giving a smile and listening. Yes, it can be that simple.

The more wisdom we recall through our Process of Remembering, the more cognitive understanding of our purpose we gain.

Purpose isn't 'discovered', but revealed and remembered. Our purpose is to reveal ourselves, then radiate that to the world. By recognising and honouring our true self, and showing up in the world as such, we have fulfilled the soul's purpose. Our life's purpose, then, is to ensure this true self arrives in each moment it is needed.

Life purpose

Remembering who we are and why we're here is common to us all. Our life's purpose then becomes about expressing the unique assignment we were tasked with. To do so, we must face our lessons and transform within, allowing our true self to emerge. Remembering who we are is only one half of the equation; the other is expressing it to the world. Chapter 22 focuses on the second half of that equation.

Purpose is born out of lessons and inner growth; we cannot plan our purpose. We cannot map its path with our minds; we must feel it through our hearts and souls.

Purpose is not the same thing as a job or career. But it is certainly wonderful when we can also be paid for being who we are! I would just as soon do this work for free (and at various times, I have), because it has to move through me. If I'm not expressing who I am, all else falls apart. Your purpose is the thing you would do for free, the thing that fuels your fire. It's time to stoke its flames.

 Self-reflection: What are you often called upon to do? What are you passionate about? What ticks you off? What are you against? What topics are you drawn to and often read about or pursue? What did you love as a kid? Look for patterns across your answers. Could you group everything under one heading? Advice? Cheerleading? Healing? Counselling? Love? Teaching? Motivating? Creating? Entertaining? An overarching theme or pattern will no doubt emerge — this is an important clue to your life's purpose — the expression of your soul in this lifetime. Explore these ideas in your journal to recall your purpose.

My purpose was not to give psychic readings, although it's one of my gifts. Nor was it to pursue PR, run a business, mentor or write this book, per se. But when all these moments string together, they've shown that my life's work is to *express a message to trust guidance.* This is my life's purpose, and I follow the call of each moment to bring it to the fore.

When you are fully present in this moment, bringing forth your full presence in each and every moment and noticing what adds up, your life's purpose will emerge.

As purposeful as it is to give, we must also recognise the importance in receiving. We must receive what this life has to give us; we must feel it, enjoy it and savour it. It's just as purposeful to receive the gifts of others as it is to share our own. Receiving what another soul has to offer is incredibly powerful and purposeful.

Soul purpose

The purpose of each lifetime also adds up for soul. In each lifetime, soul chooses to incarnate, inhabit a human body and experience life here. This is our purpose: to truly be here, in this body, feeling, experiencing and appreciating this life. We are here to be human in all its messy glory. We are here to remember to enjoy this amazing planet, to enjoy each other, to love and give and receive. Soul wants to have a glorious adventure here, even with the lessons.

At our core, we each have the same soul purpose: to fully experience life on earth, to explore, embody and express ourselves here.

Themes play out for soul, lifetime after lifetime. Many of our soul gifts are born out of this. Psychically visiting many of my past lives, I've certainly used my psychic abilities in many, but I've also explored leadership and expression in many, too. These may contribute to my human-level interest in these topics.

Unearthing your gifts

Soul's accumulated lifetimes present us with many gifts, talents and interests in this lifetime. Soul will weave them together in unique ways in this particular lifetime, creating our life's purpose.

Such gifts are also encoded into our manual. Remember the templates from Chapter 16? When we see these layers together, we can see the gifts emerge. Energetically receiving the manual, we activate many of the gifts within us that may have lain dormant for some time. Now, they suddenly awaken.

Many souls now incarnating on our planet have far clearer parameters for their purpose. As a mother, I am continually frustrated by the idea that children should be all-rounders when, at the soul level, they aren't supposed to be. None of us are.

> Education is important, but our planet changes as our mass spiritual evolution continues. Encouraging children (and adults for that matter) to pursue the areas where they excel, rather than ensure they excel across the board, may be a simple way to support and nurture purpose from the outset.

You can also work with your SST and, in particular, your blueprint guides, to discover the gifts, passions and accumulated experiences (and therefore soul-level expertise) you have incarnated with. If you work to integrate these into your being, they will set you and the world on fire.

Your unique composition

Earlier, I posed some questions for self-reflection in your journal. Your answers will be different from mine and any other reader, too. Your composition is unique to you. It is the perfect combination of interests, skills, dislikes and so on, to assist you in your life's work — to live your truth, your purpose and path. Earth needs you just the way you are in order to experience life the way only you authentically can.

Even if someone answered those questions in a similar way to me, we'd still express our essence differently because of the accumulated gifts and wisdom across our soul's multiple past lives. None of us can bring through the exact same frequency and vibration.

Yet, our minds may wish to change this unique composition — shape it, improve it, ignore it or dull its shine. But this unique composition must be unearthed, honoured, valued, heard and shared in the way only you can share it. I'm not the only person who will write a book on this topic, but I am the only one with my unique life experiences — in this life and past lives — so the energetic imprint I impart here, in these words and pages, is most unlike any other author's work. No matter your purpose, no one will bring it forth in the same way as you.

And, because we each have soul contracts with the other souls we are here to learn from and share with, my work will reach those souls who have a contract with mine. Just as there are souls waiting to hear from you, because you agreed to bring forth your expression to serve them, and vice versa. There is an audience for us all.

My deep hope for you is that you discover your uniqueness, value it and recognise that your unique composition is required on Earth at this time. You're the only person who can provide this to the world, in the way that your soul can. To put our purpose to use, we must celebrate how amazing we really are — and when the call of the times leads us somewhere new, know you are just as purposeful and needed there, too.

Purpose cannot be measured

When it comes to purpose, we must be careful not to place too much emphasis on what we do, what we give, what we contribute and how others might view it. We are purposeful in every moment, not only in the ones in which we produce something. Resting, playing and receiving are all purposeful, too.

Similarly, we must be careful not to compare our purpose to others. At a recent live event, a woman — let's call her Jane — asked me about her purpose and I channelled guidance specifically for her that suggested her purpose in this lifetime was to heal herself. After the event, Jane approached me to clarify — wondering if that guidance meant she was meant to *do* something with her healing. Jane wondered how her healing would help others; was she meant to heal others, too?

Jane raised her children, worked at a job and contributed to her local community — she had *done* plenty! But because our rational minds judge the process, she worried her life's purpose wasn't very grand, outward or even serving anybody other than herself. To soul, it was incredibly purposeful, to dedicate an entire lifetime to healing the wounds of past lifetimes; to the mind, though, it didn't seem as impressive as, say, being on stage, or contributing to world peace or environmental activism.

Purpose also cannot be confused with our worth. Over the years, many clients have expressed fears that their life is not meaningful unless they logically know and understand their life and soul's purpose. Of course, we want to remember — I've written a whole book encouraging it! But it doesn't mean life isn't valid until the moment of remembering.

If you haven't remembered yet, you're still on purpose.

Remembering is only one half of the purpose equation. If you remember, but aren't yet expressing your truth, you're still on purpose. Learning to express our purpose is a process, too, one that deserves its own chapter.

And, if you've arrived fully expressed and actualised in the full depth and wisdom of your soul, there is purpose here, too. But it's no more important than any other phase of the journey.

Lessons are purposeful. Transformation is purposeful. Our humanness is purposeful. Our spiritual nature is purposeful. Every phase of the Guidance Cycle is purposeful. No one place is better than the other. Everything and everyone is purposeful to soul.

CHOOSE YOUR ADVENTURE – EXPLORE YOUR PURPOSE

Go into your Sacred Space (using the technique on page 85) and ask your blueprint guides to join you. Today's exercise is to ask about your purpose. Included below are some suggested questions to ask during your meditation. Be sure to record their messages in your journal.

Suggested questions for your blueprint guides:

- What is my purpose in this lifetime?
- What was my purpose in past lives? How do they contribute to my purpose in this lifetime?
- How can I best offer my purpose? How does it wish to be expressed right now?
- How do my lessons feed into my purpose?
- What are my unique skills, gifts and talents in this lifetime? How may I best use them?
- What gifts, talents, skills and interest areas has soul accumulated over my lifetimes? How do they contribute to this lifetime?
- Where do I need to focus my purpose now — what form does it need to take in this moment? What is the call of the times?
- What else do I need to know right now?

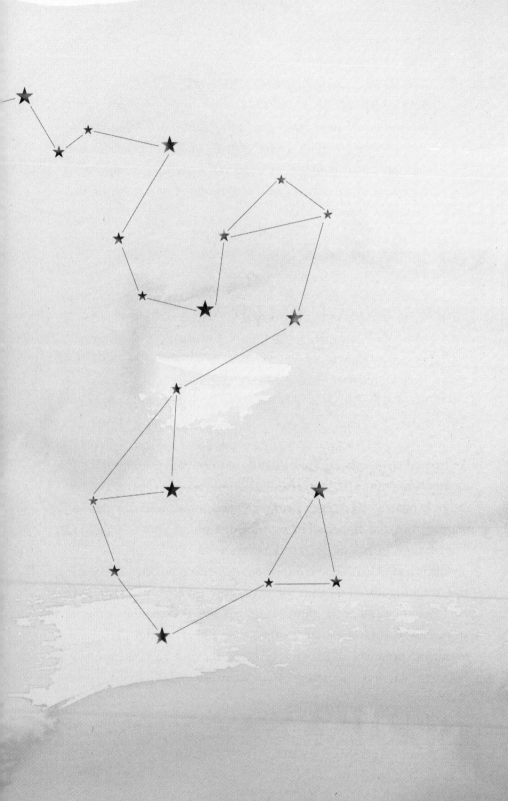

CHAPTER *19*

★

ALCHEMY

As I try to write this chapter, Chris says to me, 'You can lead a horse to water, but you can't make it drink.' Our advisors and messengers can only take us so far; they can provide insights to our own paths and purpose, or parts thereof, but it means nothing if we don't choose it. They cannot fulfil our purpose for us.

Chris had always shown me visions of writing books, and speaking and teaching on this topic of connecting with and trusting our guidance. The call of the times suggested how this could be expressed at various points along my path — readings, mentoring, courses, resources, products. Each time I asked for and received guidance, I had to act, but the acting itself set about a new chain reaction of events.

At first, I took the guidance and defaulted to my rational mind alone to make it happen. It didn't work. Our rational mind must indeed become the faithful servant, but we must also understand how to work with the magic life force supporting all of life.

Like the Magic Car introduced in Chapter 3, I had to actively choose the destination, and then figure out how to work with the magic along the way. It wasn't enough to ask the Magic Car to set the destination for me; I had to program it. Knowing what's possible isn't enough to make it happen. I couldn't force, plot and plan my purpose into fruition. I had to learn a new way of interacting with the world that allowed the magic to play its part, while I still played mine.

Knowing isn't living

Ask any first-time mother if it's what she expected and you're likely to hear a resounding 'No!' Even if she's been told of the steep learning curve ahead, actually experiencing it is quite different from knowing it.

Ask that same mother *how* she settled into her new normal, and you'll soon realise there is an inner transformation happening all of its own accord, without too much interference (and hopefully not too much avoidance) from the mother herself. With the arrival of her baby, a new normal kicks in with force — but this can't happen simply by *thinking* about the baby's arrival. Ask that same mother about six-to-eight weeks into motherhood how she's feeling and, if you've held her awake long enough, she'll likely tell you she rapidly adjusted to accommodate life with a newborn, even if she can't explain how.

Clearly, knowing something isn't the same as actually living it. Knowing our path, purpose, lessons and soul agreements because our messengers told us isn't enough to make them happen. We are the ones who must live these out.

And, just because you have a hunch about where you're going, it doesn't mean it'll *feel* like you expect it to once you're there.

Since I was a young child, I knew I'd be an author. Not just that I wanted to be one, but that I would be one, and a published one at that. I've written plenty over the years (including several attempts at this very manuscript) and even self-published various works before, but I still knew I would one day write something published by a publishing house.

Chris often told me of the books I'll write. Journal entries from 2010 and 2011 specified details of the book deal I'd be offered and what to negotiate into it. Fast forward to 2018, talking to Murdoch Books about this very book you're now reading, and I knew in my soul this was what I'd long been waiting for; my human self, though, was unconvinced. My current lived experience and the potential making its way to me were worlds apart.

Imagine what our grandparents would have thought as children if a time-traveller came to them from 2019. Unfathomable! This is how it may feel to our other bodies, even if our mental body has a heads up of the life that's ahead for us.

After signing the book deal — and even with every other choice I've made to live out my purpose, such as the readings, the business, the products and courses — I needed to bring all Four Bodies up to speed, to ensure all of me knew. And, as we're energetic beings at the core, it's the energy here that matters.

Choice. Commitment. Conviction

We direct our energy, task it, channel it and intend it where we wish it to go. Our power lies in harnessing our energy, our own life force, which is capable of creating far more than our physical, mental and emotional bodies alone.

This is not a book on energetic theory, but I want to share with you the basics to get you started. The more you move through the Guidance Cycle with your Four Bodies, especially your chakras, the more strong and vital your energy flow becomes. Cultivating a strong flow of life force through your system will make the following easier to enact. Just keep following the steps so far; over time this will build.

Our SST can only show us what's possible. We can ask, receive and interpret guidance as much as we like, but if we fail to act and play our part, things may not turn out the way we anticipate. First, we must actively *choose* to participate in the path and purpose revealed to us.

Choice

Choosing the vision, the direction and the purpose — even the lessons, the soul mates and the challenges — at the human level is the first step to commanding our energy to go where we want it to go. We need to confirm soul's choice as our own. Over and over, I have chosen my path and purpose, and allowed it to take whatever form it needed to in each moment. Each time you follow the next step on your own path, you're choosing and intending.

Choosing may present problems. I'm yet to see someone recognise their potential and feel entirely ready to honour it. Instead, another inner transformation arises, one asking us to believe we are worthy, ready and capable of living out what we came here to do. We'll cross these hurdles more specifically in the next chapter. The first round of inner transformation cleared and healed the false self, restoring us with the true self and all it wants to create. Now, as we realise there's a very new life ahead, we must strengthen our resolve to live it. We need to do the very thing our soul agreed to do here — and choose it.

Over and over I chose this book. I actively followed the thread where it led, even when it led me away from the book and into other purposeful moments. When the opportunity arose to publish it, I chose that, too. You, too, will be asked to choose again and again.

Commitment

Choosing it is not enough; we must commit to the information we're given from spirit. Your willingness to follow your guidance, learn lessons and undertake your healing all led you here. This has come into form through every choice you've made, the commitment you've shown to your path and the conviction you have to see it through.

Signing the contract and realising the vision of becoming a published author required commitment to delivering a manuscript. To be fair, having a legal agreement and deadline in place kept me accountable, but perhaps that was the commitment I needed. Committing to the purpose before us requires us to stay the course, to see it through.

At this stage, the healing is in the doing, and in allowing the doing to be guided, too.

Conviction

Anyone willing to do this inner work and follow the beat of their own soul is an incredibly resilient, brave, courageous and tenacious being. Choosing and committing to this path feels risky and terrifying, but it's also an incredible act of self-love — doing what you know is the best thing for you (and others), even when you'd rather not.

Conviction requires us to go all-in on our vision and believe in the destination without having a flipping clue how we're going to get there, just knowing that we will. We must be so sure, deep in our bones, of the truth within us that nothing will deter us from the path (or at least, not for long). And when we are detoured, our conviction holds true that we're not off-path, but gaining what we need in order to arrive at the next location.

Upon reflection, I've held conviction since I was young I'd be an author. I've held conviction for each and every one of the snippets Chris has given me — even when they've been delayed, detoured or disguised.

My choice, and commitment and conviction to that choice, catalysed an energetic chain reaction that allowed me to move from knowing something to living it.

THE SWEET SPOT OF CO-CREATION

Let's imagine we're observing a friend, Mary. In the coming three scenarios, she will show us how to find the sweet spot of co-creation. In the first scenario, Mary is sitting on her couch; she wants a new job.

'Spirit, help me find a new job,' Mary says.

'Alright,' says her SST. 'Leave it with us, and keep following your threads.'

Instead, Mary just sits on the couch. She doesn't leave the house at all, nor she does she proactively assist in her own job search. Instead, Mary reclines comfortably on the couch, waiting for spirit to bring her the job. It's out of her hands. There's no active choice, commitment or conviction on Mary's part. She hasn't followed any thread anywhere.

In the second scenario, Mary again sits on the couch, asking the same question.

'Spirit, help me find a new job,' Mary says.

'Alright,' says her SST. 'Leave it with us, and keep following your threads.'

This time, Mary leaves her house, but she's not convinced spirit is able to answer her prayers the way she desires. She walks out the front door wearing a jumper printed with her résumé. Mary hands out business cards left and right, asking everyone she encounters if they have a job for her. But Mary's distrust in the process blocks her progress; her energy is off-kilter.

In the final scenario, Mary again asks spirit to guide her in her quest.

'Spirit, help me find a new job,' Mary says.

'Alright,' says her SST. 'Leave it with us, and keep following your threads.'

Now, Mary goes about her day as she always does. She has chosen and committed to getting a job, just as much as she has chosen and committed to working with spirit. Mary keeps an open eye, heart and mind throughout her day, spotting opportunities as they arrive — the sign in the local shop window, the friend suggesting she calls an old colleague. But, Mary also holds faith in spirit; she knows the perfect job will appear at exactly the right time. Her job is to do all she can — follow the leads, prepare her résumé, make the phone calls, but to also trust the magic underpinning her job search.

By following the leads and working with spirit, Mary lands a perfect position. It comes about from her choice, commitment and conviction in the co-creation, and from her playing her part to respond to each breadcrumb and actively pursue it.

An alchemical process

Guidance brings us possibilities but we must make them real. All Four Bodies need to be committed to the vision, starting with our energy. Choosing, committing and acting with conviction is the equivalent of creating an energetic set point in our bodies — a magnet, if you will. Effectively, we are commanding the life force within us to set to the frequency of the purpose, vision and lesson we've received from our manual.

Our internal state creates the new level for the outer world to meet. Like being in the darkened room, the outer world will start to shift and move in accordance with what's taking place inside. Except this time, we're not focused on the healing; we're focused on making manifest what is encoded in our manual.

We've become an energetic match for our own manual's energetic imprint. Like will find like and harmoniously meet and merge. Bringing the manual's energetic imprint inside your body, into your energy centres and across your Four Bodies ensures you weave the manual into your being.

In doing so, you've moved through the following stages:

1. **Guidance** — Receiving insights, visions and hunches from your messengers that exist 'out there' or in some future state. You know something you didn't before, through your guidance, but it may not yet be a physical, tangible, lived reality.

2. **Integration** — Recalibrating your internal energetic wiring to match the manual's energetic imprint, drawing it into your energy field and Four Bodies. Following the Guidance Cycle, a constant upgrade occurs, recirculating new frequencies through your body and out into the world.

3. **Realisation** — After energetically alchemising the guidance and energy, and actioning each step to bring your guidance into physical form, your dream or vision is now fully realised. You must now live in that new state.

The manual's energetic imprint has worked through your own, alchemising your inner world so you now see the outer world differently; it now responds accordingly. It's time to go and live out the guidance you've been given. Your SST starts to work with you in a very new and different way.

Call it into your body

To set an internal magnet to draw towards us the vibrational alignment matched to our manual, we must first hold the frequency of it within our bodies. When I left PR to give readings, I had to hold the feeling of it in my body. I didn't realise that's what I was doing at the time, but that's what happened.

Sitting down to write this book — some years after I started giving readings — I knew this was what I was doing, and I actively set my magnet to the resonance I felt of the book. But this book didn't just feel like a book, it felt like *truth* to me. So, I held truth in my body, the feeling of truth.

 Self-reflection: Think of someone you love. Notice how you feel about them. Where do you feel it? How long can you hold that feeling in your body? Now, imagine what $100 might feel like in your body. Again, where do you feel it? How long can you hold that feeling? What happens as you incrementally increase the amount — what does $1000 feel like? $10,000? $100,000? $1,000,000? What's something you'd love to have in your life right now? How does it feel? Can you practise holding this in your body more often?

Soul visions don't come into form by planning them, but by *feeling* them. The more often we feel these within, the more we are influencing the outer world to reflect that inner state.

Recall your impressions about your purpose from the last chapter. How would you describe it? How does it feel? For example, if your purpose is to entertain, then when you are on stage, how does it feel in your body? Like joy? Ecstasy? Then that's your set point. Maybe your purpose is to teach. How does that feel? Like pride? Confidence? Wisdom? Service? Then that's your set point.

Now we need to attune each of our Four Bodies to this feeling and focus our thoughts and beliefs on it so our habits and behaviours are aligned with it. As we call this frequency into our body, we will quickly recognise anything that is not a match for it. We will quickly be prompted to again clear, heal and restore anything that is out of vibrational alignment.

A new chain reaction is ignited. The exercise below will help you home in on the energy of what you want and then how to set your internal magnet to it. Then we'll move on to explore what happens next.

 **CHOOSE YOUR ADVENTURE –
CHOOSE YOUR SET POINT**

Time to put this chapter into practice. Follow the steps below to help you bring this into form.

1. **Know what you want**

   Your desires must be soul-aligned, not just from the rational mind. What guidance have you received? What new truths have you unearthed about yourself? What purpose, passion or project is bubbling up, asking for your attention? Reflect on this in your journal.

2. **Identify how it feels**

   Sit in quiet meditation and feel this vision, intuitive instruction or purpose in your body.

   What does this guidance feel like? How would you describe the feeling? Where do you feel it in your body? How does your body move in response — do you sit up taller? Does your body want to move in new ways? Identifying the feeling helps you understand who you need to become.

3. **Choose it**

    Are you willing to actively choose not only this destination, but this feeling, too? How committed are you to feeling this way — not just when you arrive at the destination, but on the way there, too? Can you trust that choosing this feeling and destination, over and over, is enough to create a strong ripple effect and task your outer world to shift to this new set point? You may need to start smaller while you get the hang of this.

4. **Commit and live it with conviction**

    Holding this new feeling in your body, you must now make choices from this set point. How will you live when you feel this way? Can you make small, day-to-day decisions from this place? Can you still choose it when the storm starts to swirl?

    Just play with this concept for now — we're going to build on it in the next few chapters.

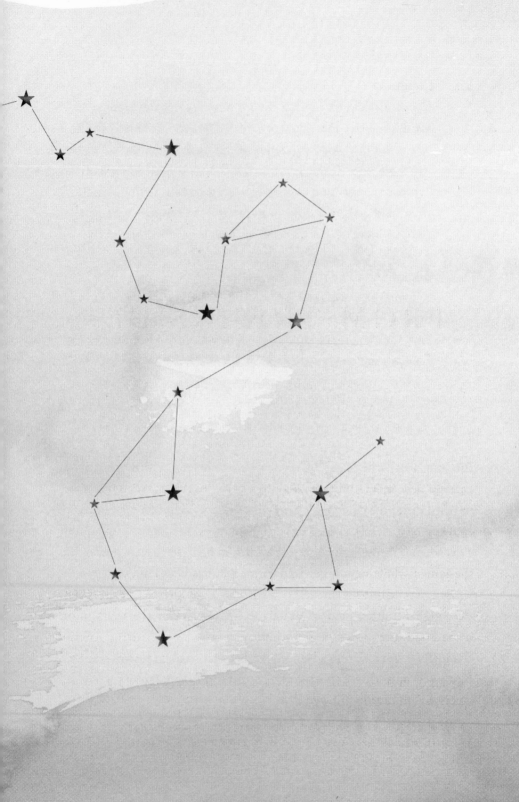

CHAPTER 20

★

FROM THE INSIDE, OUT

Birthing forth the seeds of my soul germinating within created an entirely new inner transformation. Coming out of the psychic closet terrified me to the core, but it was only in leaping that I strengthened my conviction in myself, and received the bountiful life awaiting me. Now, a decade on, through writing this book and bringing a new purpose to the fore, a whole new inner transformation has been catalysed.

My serendipitous meeting with the publisher came in 2018. Although I'd attempted to write the manuscript in the years prior, it had led me down a different pathway — resulting in me channelling and teaching advanced methods for small groups of students. I can see now this detour was preparation. Opportunity knocked when divine timing allowed.

Beginning discussions with my publisher, Kelly, my heart and soul knew this book deal was mine. Before I'd even spoken to her, I was on a flight back home from Sydney, where the initial introduction was offered to me. Tears streamed down my face as the plane took off; a knowing washed over me. It was finally time for my book. Rationally, however, I needed more convincing — in fact, many friends and family kept asking me if I was even excited by the prospect. My mind couldn't yet entertain what my body and soul already knew.

Discussions continued for some months in the background while a familiar dissatisfaction snuck into my awareness. I felt unsure and disconnected to the direction of my work once more. My physical body sent clues. Chris was surprisingly quiet, but my intuition was tuned in. Something was brewing. Logically, it made no sense — my courses and client load were full, business was good. And yet, I knew change was here.

Before securing a book deal, I had to submit the early chapters of the book. My energy was already commanding a new magnetic set point, catalysing a chain reaction. My outer world rapidly began responding to the new inner set point. Rationally, it felt like everything was falling apart. A new external storm swirled. In the midst of my own darkened room, with a very silent Chris, I knew everything was shifting and changing outside. It took all my strength not to grab at what was moving.

In the midst of all of this, while channelling on a live webinar in front of a couple of hundred people, Chris stepped into my awareness, mid-channelling-stream to my audience, to clairaudiently inform me, 'Step back from the business and rest.' The very next day, I enforced that advice, which came about a month before I signed on to write this very book you're reading. Chris knew it was coming before my mind did, and my mind was fighting for dear life. Chris instructed me to close down the advanced teachings and shift all my energy to the book. Effectively, this halted all outward business activity. My head rebelled. I grieved. In fact, I had a tantrum on the floor in a display rivalling my toddler Rose.

All business activities were paused for what I thought would be a month. Three months later, I was still unsure what I'd do with my business. I just kept writing the book. Instead of making plans and tending to my business, life upgraded itself to where my energy was now tasked. Chris brought me full circle, back where I started all those years ago. I opened up my calendar for psychic readings, which naturally built out a full calendar of other mentoring and client work. I was suddenly busier than I'd been in a long while. There was no outer marketing, no Instagramming. Just a focus on my truth and an allowance for life to bring me what I needed to support me in that call of the time. Inadvertently, Chris reminded me of my *truth* and purpose. A new call of the times emerged.

Another wave of transformation occurred, but different from the last. This time, the work itself — the process of bringing through the iterations of the book and materials — cleared, healed and restored me anew. What I didn't realise at the time was that the choice to commit to the book, and whatever else unfolded in between, was now the energetic set point to which my inner and outer world was recalibrated as I brought forth what was buried within me, now from the inside out.

Out of the chrysalis

Up until this point, we've used the Mirror Technique to bring the outside, in. The healing toolkit has been focused on the clearing, healing and restoring work as we've peeled back layers of the false self. Guided, we've increased our vibration and received relevant information from our manual. We know who we're being called to be, and what we've been asked to bring through. No matter what we're now guided to do with what we've remembered about ourselves, we need to exit the chrysalis.

Emerging and unveiling ourselves through a process of metamorphosis as the new, beautiful butterfly — we then promptly panic.

'I've never been a butterfly before. How the hell do I this?' we might wonder.

No longer a caterpillar, we can't go back to the old way of being. We can't deny the transformation. But your new reality — life as a butterfly — brings new questions and fears. Again, you're asked to choose and commit to yourself and your truth. It's time to live what you've already known and remembered of the life you were born to live. Now, we can take the lead from the truth and energetic set point we've arrived with. We must let this jewel buried deep within us make its way from the inside, out.

Showing up as the new you

Have you ever had someone else do your makeup, and not recognise yourself when they've finished? Or maybe tried on a new, beautiful outfit that doesn't quite feel like your style? Welcome to this portion of the journey. You're not yet sure of your new butterfly wings, the colour and vibrancy you now possess, but life is already beginning to respond to this new you, whether you immediately notice it or not.

A long-buried true self is now asked to come out to play, after being kept in the dark, hidden. Naturally, it's reluctant to come out. Our true self can appear a little awkward and clunky at first. We might not recognise ourselves, let alone anyone else. Putting ourselves out into the world in this new way is likely to feel uncomfortable, scary and reckless; our rational mind has long told us this was unsafe. Give this time. Compassionately and lovingly, go gently with yourself.

You're not alone; you're still guided. And again, you must choose, with commitment and conviction. But this time, you're choosing *yourself*. Putting yourself, your truth, your very essence front and centre will require cultivated levels of self-love. Lessons may be revisited here, especially around forgiveness, compassion and acceptance, as we apply everything we learned while in the chrysalis.

This process restores us. Moving this energy, project, idea or purpose through us and out into the world demands we become who we are meant to be in the process. Looping through the In and Out, Up and

Down Flows, we're clearing out any dormant beliefs about ourselves, our path and our purpose, as we now transmit to the world our new truth. The manual's energetic imprint (or at least what you've just received of it) has been embodied and integrated. It's time to now transmit this new frequency to the world around you, causing a new manifestation to occur in accordance with your blueprint. And manifestation comes outwardly when we recalibrate internally.

Loving who you find

New lessons appear here, the predominant one being about loving who you've discovered hidden within. Previously ignoring, shutting down and dimming our light may have arisen from judgments, believing who we were in those previous moments was not loveable or enough. Announcing to the world I was going to work as a psychic (and yes, it literally was announced; a story of my career change was syndicated in newspapers nationally), I quickly had to recalibrate internally to back myself and my decisions. I had to come to peace with who I once thought I was. Restored, filled with the new truth, we must now trust who we are and why we're here — and see a power bigger than us asking us to bring it forth. To ignore it denies us all.

Earth called you here. Soul chose its lessons and took on your magnificent physical form. None of this was by chance. You are a very deliberate creation, and what you are creating now becomes one, too.

Wishing you were someone or something else denies the magic that is you. We need you. You feed into the web of interconnectivity. You must play your part to weave these new energies on our planet. Your self-love and commitment to your purpose is not just self-serving, it helps us all. Simply by being you, you are of wonderful, meaningful service to the world.

Our faith, commitment and conviction is now squarely in ourselves. We must unconditionally love and honour ourselves and our contribution. New energetic boundaries are created that will infiltrate our emotional, mental and physical boundaries, too. Our self-love and self-care now teaches others what we will and won't stand for.

Living your truth with such integrity means you will no longer bend and break to the will of others. Discernment arrives. Reclaiming power in your own life, the focus shifts from reactive living to proactively influencing where the Magic Car goes.

Transformation has required you deepen your self-love and incorporate more self-care practices into your life, and these have strengthened your relationship with self. Now it's put to the test.

Test your conviction

Our divine life path will continue to unfold; lessons continuously arrive. Maintaining a relationship with our messengers helps navigate these new lessons, where we're no longer just reacting to what life throws at us but consciously, proactively co-creating the path ahead.

Tests will arrive asking us to hold our ground. Every interaction, thought and emotion influences our frequency and vibration; our energy field, our body as a conduit, is in constant flux. We could easily lose our new set point if we're not consciously and continuously choosing it. Sustaining this new set point may be a little difficult in the beginning. While up-levelling my perception of myself as an author as I worked on the book, I had to convince myself of this new truth by feeling it in my body. Daily. Feeling off-centre is our litmus test to show us where we're veering out of alignment, so we can quickly course-correct. Once the set point is locked in, it's harder to veer away.

As we send our new energetic set point out into the world, it will now respond to us. What is not a match falls away — just as my advanced teachings and mentoring had to subside. We must see this as another storm and not rush to attach to what is falling away.

Even when it does all fall away, hold faith in an unwavering conviction in the outcome. Don't drop or lessen the frequency. Don't crumble in the wake of outer-world change; you haven't got it wrong and your life does not need immediate tending to. See the process through by holding your set point through the storm. Life is reorganising itself to meet the new you.

Trust the process. Allow the outer world to reorganise itself to support the truth you're holding within. Stay the course, choose your truth, commit to seeing the process through and hold faith that all of life is reorganising itself to deliver to you what your energy now commands of it.

Once we've restored ourselves, which comes from energetically reworking our Four Bodies to match the feeling of our manual (and continuing to follow the threads of guidance we receive in the process), our chakras begin to spin and overflow with the true essence of who we are.

This energy now guides our thoughts, feelings, decisions, actions and behaviours. Day-to-day decisions can be filtered through the question: 'Will this bring me closer to, or further away, from my desired *feeling*?'

Now — follow your bliss! Reach for those high vibes, which are only now possible because of the groundwork you laid first to clear and heal the way. Without it, the true manifestation of your life path cannot take hold.

Guidance from your SST now shifts focus from the inner transformation, to the outer world doing and *being*. The direction of the In and Out Flow shifts, and what we now energetically send out into the world will change. What we attract to us, and how we respond to it, will be different, too.

The stretch of becoming

Every new divine whisper, every soul call, requires a new version of you to step up. It's time to arrive as this new you. This stretch of becoming the new you is akin to standing on one ledge, trying to get across to the next ledge — maybe like two ladders side by side. You can't just jump over; it's quite a stretch, higher and to the side. This is how it feels when we realise we must move from where we are to where we want to be. While the energetic transformation occurs, our human self just feels discombobulated between two states.

On the first ledge, everything is known and familiar. We can see where we're going, onto the next rung, but we're not quite sure *how* to get there. Sure, our mind will have some ideas — but so does our SST.

We're being asked to step into a new potential, a future beyond our current frame of reference, beyond anything your mind has known before — which also means your mind is about to freak out. But, if we let the energy weave its magic, we'll know how soon enough.

By the time we arrive on the new ledge, we must be holding the frequency of the new more than we're holding the frequency of the old. Until we're holding the conviction of the new us, we cannot arrive as the new version of us.

CASE STUDY — MARIA

Remember Maria? Unemployment prompted an inner transformation as Maria came back into alignment with her truth: to creatively express through music. Maria's guidance asked her to approach a local school, suggesting she run a creative music program for its students.

This was so outside Maria's comfort zone, but she knew in every fibre of her being it was what she had to do. Maria connected to this truth within her body, *feeling* it within her body. She filled her entire body with that feeling as she approached the school — and subsequently as she taught the classes they agreed to let her run. Maria started to feel more comfortable with the freedom she now had to express, and it showed up in other ways.

Maria felt more expressive in her new home, decorating it with far more colour than she'd dared to before. Connecting to the earth and her plants filled Maria with so much joy and energy — she began singing in local shows and competitions. Her life suddenly filled with new opportunities, people, events and activities. This new life was responding to the new Maria. When she felt herself losing the connection to herself, she came back to her practices. When new decisions arose, she checked if it helped her feel the way she wanted to feel, or not.

Maria's outer world matched her new inner state — and it hadn't come because she'd plotted and planned a well-worn path. Maria stayed focused on her inner world, rather than getting caught up in what was happening *outside* of her and reacting to it. She could now see that her outer world had shifted and changed *because* of her inner world. She was the cause, not the effect.

CHOOSE YOUR ADVENTURE — CONNECT WITH YOUR TRUE SELF

In this exercise, you'll connect with your true self, casting that vision forward to your future self, or the potential of your future true self. Use the Sacred Space technique from page 85.

Arriving in your Sacred Space, hold the intention to meet with your true self, or a future version of you who can guide this process. Visualise the new version of you, the part of you that is already bringing forth and living the life you're here to live. Meet with this version of you, enquiring with some of the prompts on the next page, or questions of your own.

Here are some journaling prompts to consider:
- Notice how your future self appears to you. Are there obvious changes to your appearance?
- How would you describe their demeanour?
- What can they tell you about this future place? What are they doing there? Who is with them? How do they live?
- Ask them how they got there, from where you are now.

Another similar tool is to write yourself a letter from the perspective of your future self. Simply imagine yourself in twelve months' time, and have that version of you write you a letter from the future, describing where they are, what they're doing and how they got there. This can be a particularly fun exercise each birthday or new year. Gary and I used to do this on our anniversaries — it was always fun reading back the previous year's, to see how much had actually materialised.

Be sure to date and record your experiences — and set a reminder to come back and read them later.

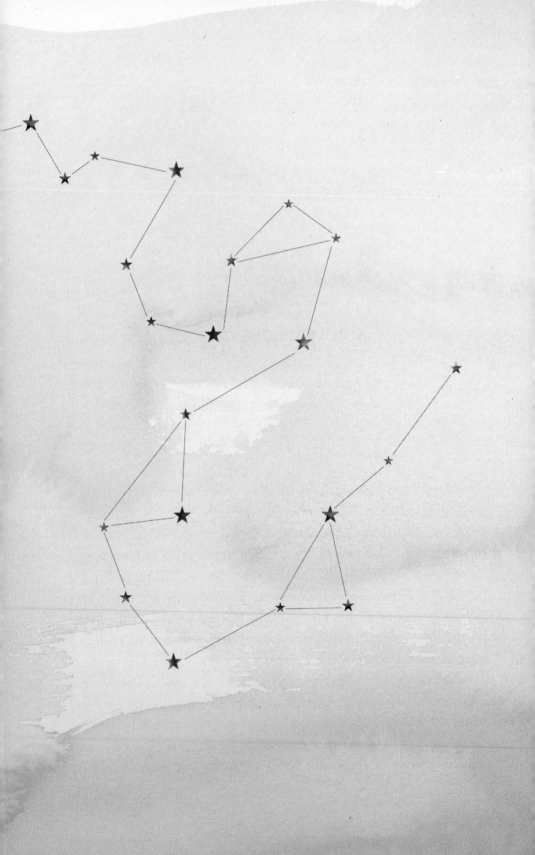

CHAPTER 21

MANIFESTING

Our last rental home (the house prior to our forever home) was a beautifully renovated property and I was convinced we were going to buy it off the owner. I knew it was far outside our budget, so a few months prior to the end of our lease, I started working with my energy to manifest the funds to make an offer on the house. I set the price point as my new internal set point, running the frequency of the purchase price through my In and Out, Up and Down Flows. Drawing closer to the lease renewal, it became apparent the owner wouldn't sell and instead wanted to return to her property. We were set to move yet again.

Putting my disappointment aside, Gary and I now had to find our new house, purchase the property, vacate the rental, settle here and move within just a few short weeks. Considering we'd tried and failed at this several times over the previous few years, it felt the odds were stacked against us. But I held faith we'd secure our house in time.

Another hurdle appeared. We actually didn't physically have the money required to purchase the kind of home we desired for our family. Undeterred, I kept working with the energy — which was tasked for the higher price bracket of the property we were renting. I knew the money would somehow show up.

Sitting at Mum's one afternoon, we were joking about pooling resources and having my parents live with us. We pulled out a real estate app on my phone and started dreaming as we scrolled through the listings. Before long, I found a newly posted property just a few streets from our current rental. I noticed it had a self-contained studio. I showed it to Mum, laughing, but she quickly saw potential in the home for my family (sans grandparents). Gary and I went to inspect it.

As soon as we walked in the front door, I turned to the right, noticing a stained glass window with two red roses on it. Granny's nod of approval — not only because of the obvious rose connection, but my parents had also had those exact roses on their front door in our family's home (the one Mum sold after Granny's death). Every time Granny walked through my parents' front door, she'd tap on their rose window and nod.

Suffice to say, this is the home I'm writing from today. It's the same home Chris had given me snippets of many years before, with the shed, French doors and studio space. I even recently found a note on my mobile phone dated 28 April 2013 (four years before we purchased), that listed every single feature of this new home, plus more.

Financially, things worked out. The only reason this house appeared in my app search was because it had just decreased in price, bringing it into our price bracket. The banks played nicely and we had some extra money turn up that month to add to our deposit. We just scraped in — for a little less than the figure I'd been manifesting to purchase our rental property from the landlord.

Manifesting isn't just about having material objects you desire; it has to be soul-aligned. And, as I've already shared, I've long-known that our home and my purpose are intertwined. But manifesting didn't come just because we wanted it — it took years of energetically clearing the way and moving through lessons before what was meant for us was able to find us, and vice versa.

Living 'on-purpose' by proactively creating our path, rather than reactively clearing it, moves us into the Manifest phase of the Guidance Cycle. After an intense inner journey, you're now ready to outwardly create and attract into your experience a match for who you really are — and all you have to do, is continue being you.

What is manifesting?

Remember the pyramid of champagne glasses? Creating such an abundant flow of champagne attracted an abundance of thirsty people. Simply put, this is manifesting: having our inner state or flow dictate what we experience in the outer world. As I described in the last chapter, I created an abundant flow of clients as I worked on the book, even if they weren't logically aware of why they were drawn to work with me.

Clearing, healing and restoring through the Guidance Cycle alters our inner world, causing an effect on our outer world, which was originally born out of our previous inner state. Look at your outer world today — this is the result of your inner state, just recently. To change it in the future, change your inner state, today.

But change it to match your soul's divine life path — no one else's, and certainly not your mind's ideas for you. Manifesting from a false self just creates more falsity; true self breeds more truth.

Manifesting is often grossly misunderstood and poorly applied. All too often, it's approached as a mental exercise, not an energetic one, serving the whims of our mind, not the desires of our soul. When your inner world is an energetic match for what's in your soul's blueprint, you'll start to attract all the things you need to support you in this mission — the people, resources, supports and opportunities, as well as the lessons and environments to continue to refine your vibe.

I don't subscribe to the notion that you can have *anything* you want just because you want it. It must be soul-aligned or contribute to the agreements of our blueprint. Our minds may demand a manifestation only to serve itself; this can either leave us falling short in our manifestation, or actually managing to manifest our mind's desire to only subsequently learn a massive lesson. An example here might be thinking we need to manifest more money to solve our problems, only to have it arrive and realise it didn't solve anything.

However, if what we desire to manifest is in alignment with our soul, we can harness the full power of our intention — because the energy of our intention will be backed by our thoughts and behaviours as stored in our chakras, setting an energetic resonance. When aligned, we manifest more powerfully than when there is misalignment among our desires, intentions, energy and behaviours. It's not enough to hold 'good vibes only'; instead, those vibes must arise from cleared, healed and restored energy and Four Bodies.

I do not subscribe to instant gratification or instant manifestation. Divine timing is at play. Life is geared to steer us into lessons, not egotistic satisfaction. The bigger the dream, purpose or vision, the longer it may take because of the depth of lessons, experiences and inner rewiring required to create the resonance for its match.

Your team of advisors will still direct you through the lessons and the inner transformation to bring your desires and purpose closer — but not through wishful thinking alone; they'll send you back through the Guidance Cycle, refining your vibration.

What is the Law of Attraction?

In spiritual speak, this process is known as the Law of Attraction. For brevity, we can describe this as like attracts like. We draw to ourselves the opportunities, experiences and material possessions we desire by holding ourselves as a *vibrational* match for those desires. Like vibration attracts like vibration; like thoughts do not attract like objects.

Often, this law is mistaken as 'do good things = receive good things'. It's the intention, belief and energy *behind* our actions that counts here, not the actions, thoughts or beliefs themselves.

> **Self-reflection:** Ever given a gift out of obligation? Maybe you tend to say yes when you really mean no. Where else in your life are your actions not in alignment with your desires and truth? Powerful manifestation requires this alignment, integrity and discernment.

Inner states attract outer states. Stagnant, blocked chakras from old emotions, beliefs, stories and behaviours influence your manifesting more than your positive thinking. Clearer, open, free-flowing chakras, as the result of clearing, healing and restoring our Four Bodies, attract clearer, open and free-flowing outer states.

In order to truly manifest our divine life path and truth, we must *first* clear the way of everything that is not aligned with that. The Process of Remembering is paramount; we need to clear the way of who we're not, remember who we are, then set our energy to that truth.

Being in the flow

Up and Down, In and Out Flows of energy have improved as you've moved through the Guidance Cycle. Not only has the quality of your own life force increased, but now you're running more and more of the same resonance of your own manual. What you're putting out into the world is now your soul-aligned self.

According to the Law of Attraction, you must now receive the same frequency in your outer world. You now, quite literally, draw to you the people, places, opportunities and circumstances matching your manual — to help you live out this purpose and divine life path.

Welcome to the slipstream. Our body (all Four of them) serves as an energetic conduit for these frequencies to radiate out of us, and to be received back in.

> It's not enough to simply *attract* what we desire into
> our lives; we must make manifest (i.e. bring into
> physical form) what wants to move through us,
> from soul, and has been called here to Earth.

Take this book, for example. I couldn't just attract this book into form; it would have to have existed in the outer world first for me to draw it to me. This would also be true of my courses, teachings, oracle cards and meditations. I also did not sit here feeling the book, alone. I wrote, edited and rewrote this book every damn day. I played an active role in its manifestation into physical form.

> Thus, manifesting is not just attracting to us what
> we want in life, but creating the circumstances to
> birth our unique contributions into the world.

By listening to our divine whispers, we will be asked, sooner or later, to express this energy through us and put it into form. For Maggie, yoga and meditation were restorative tools she could then teach others. Emma's frequency birthed forth her daughters. Maria created a body of work around musical therapy.

What wants to come into form through you? With these forces coursing through your body — from soul and Earth, spirit and human — what do you wish to channel this energy into? The Law of Attraction will bring you the people, places and opportunities to support you in your creation.

Set the magnet

Because your feelings influence the outer world experience, how you felt can explain what life dealt you. Changing your circumstances comes by changing how you feel — and once you feel in alignment with your truth, you need to vibrate and operate from that truth more often.

Cultivating this feeling within as often as possible now becomes the goal. Because asking is done *energetically*, not mentally, your truth and its frequency must be cultivated in your body in order to sustain it for longer periods of time.

Your truth becomes your transmission. This is the vibration or frequency you send out into the world. It must be expressed into the world through your thoughts, beliefs, actions and, eventually, the physical manifestation you create.

This transmission commands an equal force be returned to you, bringing more of the same. You attract to you the people, opportunities, finances and all other conditions matching what you transmit and express. The Law of Attraction will already be responding to the call.

You'll continue encountering lessons. When life's storms swirl around you, don't focus on what's swirling — it'll only attract more confusion. Instead, stay focused on the feeling you want to create. Now you must hold your transmission in the face of new storms and stand in the conviction of your truth.

Majority rules

Just as one small drop of coloured dye in the ocean won't make much difference to the overall colour, one occasional limited, blocked or negative thought, emotion or action won't undo all the positive, open, flowing thoughts. Life carries on and we continue to respond. Your dominant set point is more important.

Similarly, the occasional positive affirmation, or occasionally holding the vibration of your desire won't overcome years of negativity and self-loathing. You can't blindly follow your bliss. You'll need more coloured dye to make an impact — or to have excavated your inner world via the Guidance Cycle.

Continue to observe your Four Bodies, but now you're tasked with monitoring your set point. Now you know your truth, this becomes the guiding factor. When your feelings are off-kilter, you know how to come back to alignment — but you had to find the alignment first. Now, with some tweaking you can more easily course correct.

Don't give up on your dreams too early. Divine timing is at play, not your mind's time frame. Hand on heart, I've had these moments too — but my most deeply held belief is that I am living out my purpose and I do already know what that is. My momentary doubt is a small drop of dye in an ocean of faith.

Where lessons, purpose and manifesting meet

Alignment with our divine life path means we must be willing to manifest our lessons, too. Deep in our truth, we already know we must continue to learn and grow. Attempting to use the Law of Attraction to avoid difficulty won't work for long. Lessons cannot be avoided permanently; they eventually resurface. Besides, this intention would affect the internal resonance anyway, defeating the purpose and actually bringing you the lesson you wanted to avoid.

Lessons and purpose trump manifesting from the mind. Manifesting what you *think* you need to make you happy won't make soul happy. Even if you manage to manifest it, you'll have a harder time, as you still need to learn the lesson associated with it.

And, then, sometimes life just serves us up a big old surprise. I cannot fathom how I would have attracted Cathy's visitation, for example. Chris tells me it was destined. My soul's agreement with Cathy's was far bigger than our earthly Law of Attraction. Major pivot points and plot twists still turn up — and they may just need to be chalked up to something far bigger than us.

CASE STUDY – Jenny

Jenny, another client of mine, desired a new job that would also allow her to focus on her passion project in health and wellness. With a background in administration, Jenny thought an administrative full-time position in the wellness industry she was passionate about would fit the bill. She knew she wanted to feel vital and revived in her work, and felt the industry would help offer that.

Instead, life served Jenny up a part-time job opportunity, albeit in wellness, that would require her to move. Before talking with me, Jenny was ready to turn the offer down. But, as we looked a little more closely, we could see the opportunity here for her.

The job offer, while part-time, was aligned with her passions and would give her a chance to work on the front line more. It was also in a location rich with like-minded people, living a more holistic lifestyle Jenny craved. Rationally, it wasn't the right job; intuitively, it would serve up much more than Jenny had anticipated.

Testing the job against the feelings she desired — vitality and revival — Jenny knew it was the right job to take. She then set about tasking the Universe to bring her other opportunities to support her financially. In this community, Jenny's own passion project took off. Soon, she didn't need the part-time job at all.

At the surface level, Jenny created the perfect job and environment for this moment. She also wound up in the perfect classroom to begin turning her own passion project — her vocation — into a financially viable business. By following her threads, Jenny landed in the right place, at the divine right time to continue living out her life path. She used the Law of Attraction to help her bring forth what was inside of her.

CHOOSE YOUR ADVENTURE –
SET YOUR MAGNET

 To help you set your magnet, I've included some journal
prompts and practices below.

Review all the intuitive data you have regarding your path and purpose.

- How does this truth feel to you? How would you describe it?
- Can you encapsulate this feeling in one word?
- Can you pull that energy into your body?
- Where do you feel it in your body?
- How long can you hold this feeling before another takes over?
- What other feelings disrupt or interrupt you connecting with your set point?

Cultivating this feeling more often sets and strengthens your
manifesting magnet. Try these techniques to help you enlarge
your magnet.

- Spend time each day holding this feeling — in meditation, on public transport, in your meetings or with your children.
- How often do you feel it? How long can you hold it for?
- What happens when you hold it? How do others respond as you hold this feeling?

Over time, life will begin to respond to this feeling the more you hold it.

- What starts to fall away or become chaotic in response to you holding this feeling?
- Can you still hold this feeling in the eye of the storm?
- How might this be working for you, not against you?

Now work with this feeling to guide you forward. Ask it, as you would any other messenger, for its wisdom.

- Why is this feeling here?
- How does this feeling wish to be expressed?
- What day-to-day decisions would you make if this were your default position?

Can you make those decisions now, or take aligned action? Start small and play with this in your life.

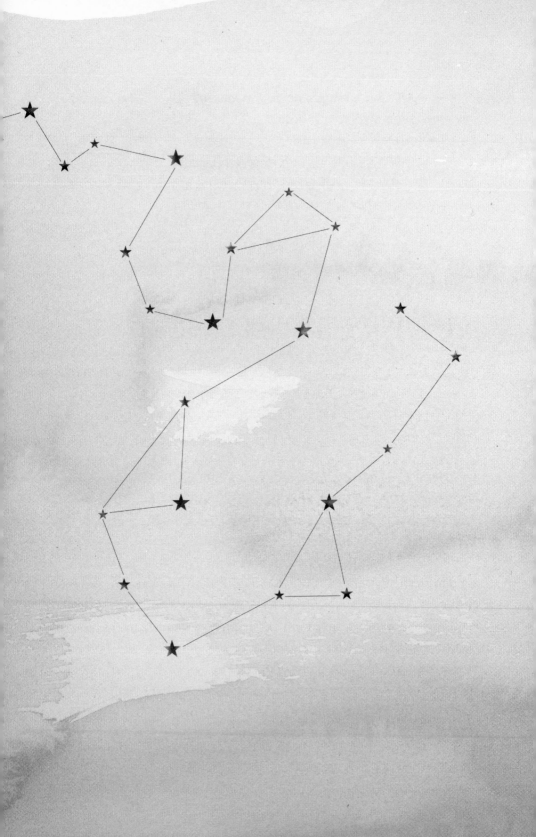

CHAPTER 22

★

EXPRESS YOURSELF

I joke that I've always worked in communications — I've just shifted from marketing communications to spirit communications. Expressing is a huge part of my purpose; my soul (and human self) majors in it. Yet, we all have a vital need to express.

Outside of my work, I express in other ways. I love to sing. I wouldn't say I'm particularly good at it, but I love it. As an interior design enthusiast, I'm often rearranging furniture or dreaming up new ways to accommodate our family. While not necessarily interested in fashion, I also like to express myself through my personal style. I dress how I feel. My physical body soon tells me when I haven't moved enough, or I'll have several signs to get back to walking and yoga.

Expressing isn't always easy, and this has been reinforced while writing this book. Plenty of times in my life I haven't expressed my truth — I didn't express who I really was while pursuing PR; far too often I've said yes when I really meant no; I've silenced my views for the good of the group. Perhaps you have your own examples, too?

Other times I've had to heal as my truth came out, like when I announced to the world I was psychic; during a client reading, while delivering messages I'd rather not relay; or when letting go of friendships that in my heart I knew weren't a fit for either of us.

Expressing our truth isn't always easy. It can terrify us. New fears arise at this point, so we need to clear, heal and restore in new ways as we hold our magnetic set point. Anything that's not a match for our truth, whatever it may be, must make its way out, too. And it creates a chain reaction in our outer world.

Will I be loved? Will I belong? Will I be accepted? Am I enough? It all comes up for review again here.

The good news is, though, we've set our new magnet — those who love us for us, will turn up. The places we belong appear. Our truth is accepted and respected. What we have to offer is enough, and is gratefully received. But most of all, this comes in the outer world because we've fostered it within.

Transmission and expression

By harnessing our energy, we've created a new transmission. Our bodies, our energetic conduit and transmitter, now send our transmission out into the world, via the In and Out Flow.

Others will respond to our transmission, to the frequency that now pulses out of us, and to the truth that is clearly evident. Some will resonate at the same transmission and will be an energetic match for us. For others, though, our transmission may be uncomfortable. This has its place too, for we now present a mirror to those people, prompting them to increase their own vibration, should they choose to. Creating such energetic resonance within us is not enough; it's what we now do with it that counts.

Yes, we are energetic beings — but we've come into
physical form. Thus, our own transmission, vibration
and frequency need to also come into physical form.
We must channel this heightened energy into the
projects, businesses, relationships, habits and
activities that best suit our transmission.

Self-reflection: Has your guidance already suggested how your
transmission is to be channelled? Perhaps into a project? An
activity? A practice? A business? How does your transmission
want to come into physical form?

How we express may also be guided — so much of my life has focused
on writing and communicating in one way or another. I've received the
call of the times, suggesting where to focus my transmission in any
given moment. Maggie loves restoring harmony. Emma channelled
her energy into her health. Maria spent time gardening. What do you
love to do? How can you express your truth?

When you don't express

An In and Out Flow suggests that for the circuit to complete, we
must be sending energy out. Without expressing, we also cannot
receive the inflow; the circuit won't complete. We cannot complete
our manifestation and attraction, then, if we're not expressing, too.

Start small. Expressing your truth may not be easy, but we have to
start somewhere. My journal provided an avenue for me to express and
move my truth somewhere before it ever was verbalised and shared en
masse. Where can you start small in your life?

No matter where we start, we must simply start. When we don't
express, we block up the in and out flows we've just worked so hard
to unclog. Stifling and suppressing our expression simply blocks up

our Four Bodies once more, stores the stagnation in our chakras and begins to knock us off-kilter again. Don't go backwards now! Although, sometimes this is the lesson, as I've also learned the hard way.

Not voicing my truth in both the small and big moments, compounded. Like our dye dropping in the ocean, one small denial of truth might not make an impact, but over time all those drops will add up and clog your energetic circuits, before it appears in your outer world once more.

For years, I denied my psychic abilities. At times, I've tried to minimise the visibility I know Chris is asking me to have. Luckily, our body responds to this, again sending us not-so-good-feeling feelings as a result. And within we go again.

Imagine what this accumulated denial of truth does to your body and energy flows. Over time, the outer world shuts down and closes off — a reflection of your inner state. For me, it contributed to depression, disconnection and disillusionment.

Beyond our personal implications, when we don't express, we aren't fulfilling our purpose collectively, which is to help serve the other souls who are waiting to hear from us. Right now, somewhere, other souls are contracted to learn from you. It'd be shame, for you and them, not to fulfil the agreement.

Creativity in motion

Creativity is how we're asked to express. Our life is a creative expression, sent forth in motion from Source. That same Source moves through us, asking us to continue creating on its behalf.

Every single thought, breath and action is a creation. Powerful creations are born through us every time we intend to move energy into another form. We needn't limit our understanding of creativity then as purely being artistic.

Creativity supports life. Quite literally. Even when we're not creating literal physical life within us, we are giving life to our ideas, thoughts, beliefs and intentions — and when they are aligned with our soul's path, we are creating from our soul.

Now, I'm not suggesting we must all become artists. Art and creativity are not the same thing. Nor am I suggesting we must create for anyone other than ourselves, although, in time, we will likely be guided to. For now, I'm asking you to create for creativity's sake.

In her book *The Artist's Way* Julia Cameron recommends a weekly Artist Date as a way of re-energising the creative juices. These solo dates may lead you to an art gallery, a new class, a live music event, a zoo, a bookstore — anywhere! The idea is to stimulate new ideas, interests and joy outside your usual frame of reference. Try it. Remember when I suggested having fun as a foundational tool to this approach — it's likely to gain importance here.

After the gruelling excavation of our inner transformation, this is the fun part! Of course, this can be happening simultaneously with the inner transformation; you needn't wait to have fun. But I've observed there is usually a very deliberate point in the process where we will feel we want to start afresh.

New people. New ideas. New social circles. New classes. New activities. New clothes. New diets. New routines. New house. Whatever area, or combination of areas you look at changing, you'll know when it's time to start the exploration and creativity phase.

This phase is not necessarily about having all the answers or the entire plan mapped out in a logical or linear fashion. Instead, this phase is about trying new things and exploring where they take you with a childlike curiosity and wonder for the world. This becomes easier and easier the more you've been clearing on the inside — and indeed, the outlet can assist the inner transformation when the work becomes hard.

This is not about fixed ideas or conditions on the exploration. This isn't about guaranteed outcomes, but rather surrendering to the moment and where you're being called. Be curious about why you're being called there. So many times, I've seen my clients drawn to a particular class or workshop, not because of what they learn there, but of who they meet. When I think back to why I ended up working at the online travel company, it was not so much about the work experience, it was so I would meet my husband and a number of dear friends.

If we can remain open to there being any possible outcomes for us following our intuition at this point — it may not be why we think it is. And in time, probably sooner than you think, you'll see just why you're being led from class to class and idea to idea.

Stay light. Don't overcommit or over-invest in this phase. You'll know when you're ready to go all-in.

CASE STUDY – Maria

Let's revisit Maria's story. Maria's guidance prompted her to express through her music, gardening and decorating her home. Guidance didn't tell her to go straight into developing her musical therapy program. Instead, she knew that would come the more she focused on her own joy of music, gardening and home decorating.

By expressing in these ways, new ideas arrived for Maria. Music, gardening and home decorating all provided Maria more opportunities to feel good, breeding more good feelings. However, something else happened, too. Feeling good, expressing and creating cultivated more stillness, space and silence. In those introspective moments Maria began to receive greater directions herself, not via sessions with me, regarding the very program she was to develop.

In the work Maria did with the children at her new school, she began noticing patterns. She observed what happened when the children applied certain practices at certain times. Maria's musical program developed because of her expression in a

> multitude of ways, not because she mentally mapped out the program.
>
> Maria lived out her guidance, and thus her life path. Without doing this, she couldn't have fulfilled her purpose.

The lessons in this phase

Expressing gives rise to a whole new bunch of lessons. As our truth makes its way out of us, it kind of bumps into all the lessons we learned during the first phase of the cycle, from the outside, in. Universal lessons may arise here, too, prompting us to deal with comparison, visibility, vulnerability and indeed the core question: can we be loved for being who we really are? Are we enough?

Entire books have been written on each question. I don't wish to reinvent the wheel here. Instead, here's a quick snapshot of the lessons. Of course, when and if you meet them (or others) you'll use exactly the same process from earlier in the book. You have the tools now.

On acceptance

Don't waste time on how someone else sees you; their perception is not the truth of who you are, but instead who *they* are right now. How someone else responds to your truth, your creation and expression really says more about them, than you. Based on the principles of the Mirror Technique, what another sees in you, or thinks, believes or feels about you, is a reflection of their own internal state. It's not about you, but what you represent *to them*. Your expression and creation simply provides a mirror, pointing others inward. You become a teacher to their soul.

On comparison

We each have our own unique programming and experience of life. It seems rather futile to compare our experience to another's path and experience. Yet, we still wonder if we are worthy enough to bring forward what's buried within us. If we don't, we have forgotten why we were born to begin with.

On visibility

Many of us dim our light for fear of outshining another. Perhaps we don't want to shine bright for fear of attracting too much attention. Either way, reducing our visibility is never a loving act; it stems from fear. Vibrating at our unique resonance, being happy and feeling comfortable in our truth provides a mirror to others, prompting them to find the same within themselves. And we want more of us to be shining our unique lights — it's why we came here, after all.

On vulnerability

During a recent live event, a participant asked me about vulnerability. As the event wasn't recorded, I paid attention to the answer I channelled. When we interact with others from our vulnerability, we are interacting without the masks of our false selves. If we want to encourage true and meaningful connections, we must be willing to be vulnerable — because we will be met by vulnerability in others in return. Therein real human connection lies. We can't find it on a glossed-up social media highlight reel.

On self-love and compassion

When it comes to self-love, Louise Hay wrote the book. Quite literally. If you want to strengthen your love and acceptance, start with her work in *You Can Heal Your Life*. As she tells us, on the topic of self-love and acceptance, being self-critical hasn't worked to improve our love of self. We cannot berate ourselves to a better relationship with self; we must love our way there. What might happen if we try it this new way?

Common to all these lessons, and with most others that arise here as you express, is *fear*. And we know that fear is head-based, not heart- or soul-based. Thus, come back to the basic foundations, work with your SST and process the fear within.

Honour your contract

I know I'm not for everyone. And, I hate to break it to you, but you might not be for everyone, either. Energetics and our soul contracts influence this, though, not necessarily our likeability as people.

Take this book as an example. The transmission it holds won't be for everyone. Many of the topics I've touched on have been explored elsewhere, and will be again, no doubt. But I trust that my unique take, my expression, of this content will reach the people it needs to reach.

This is true of anything we create, and even of who we are. But when we are creating and expressing our purpose, and bringing our soul's purpose into form (whether as a book, a business, a project etc.), there are other souls who have also been sent forth, remembering they're looking for this lesson.

Purpose and lessons meet. My purpose may help others learn their lessons. My lessons have been learned by others offering up their purpose. This combination was agreed to at the soul level, not just based on our human likeability.

Continuing to work with our own manuals and divine life paths ensures life will bring us the other souls we've incarnated to work with, and vice versa. For someone with a marketing and PR background, this takes the pressure off completely — there are others guaranteed to receive what I put out. No amount of marketing alone can change that — only my energy and the readiness of those ready to receive it.

Polishing and perfecting our expression in order to be accepted, whether by one or by the masses, is futile. Can we trust soul didn't lead us here to only lead us here? Instead, we've been sent forth with more than enough to fulfil what we came here to do.

CHOOSE YOUR ADVENTURE –
UNLEASH YOUR EXPRESSION

 Remember your set point from the last chapter? Connect with this feeling again. Use the following journal prompts to work with this feeling.

- How does this feeling want to be expressed?
- Is there an overarching purpose — a project, business or activity that wants to be explored? Work with your SST to unravel this thread.
- How else does this feeling want to be expressed, day-to-day?
  - How does this feeling want to dress?
  - How would it style your home, room or office?
  - What fragrance would it wear?
  - How does it suggest you eat?
- What comes up to challenge this feeling? Fears? Beliefs?
- Using the Mirror Technique, what are these lessons teaching you?

You might also like to go into your Sacred Space (use the technique on page 85) and ask your SST for information about how to express, and what you're learning as you fulfil your purpose.

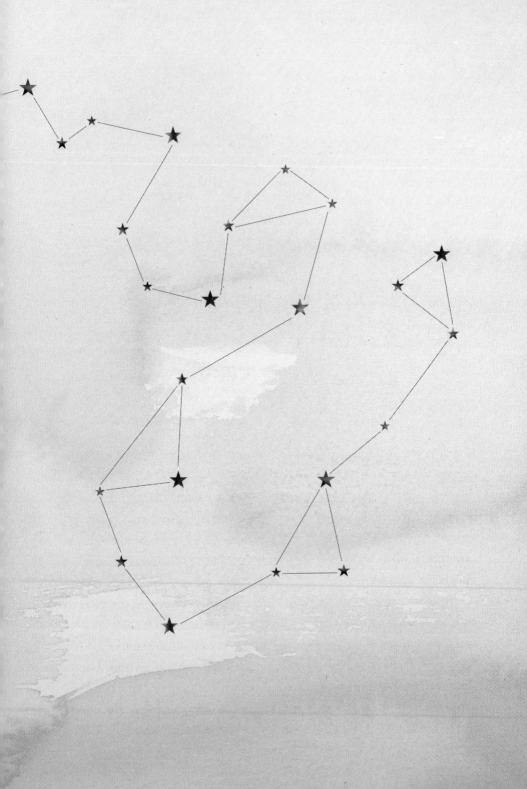

★

CHAPTER 23

PITFALLS &
TROUBLESHOOTING

I can't pretend living this way is a breeze. Multiple times I've cried, questioned my sanity and wondered why on earth I continue to live this way. Chris has driven me nuts. I've felt let down, misguided and betrayed. Predictions haven't eventuated (*yet*). Surprise twists and turns arise, even when Chris has clearly foretold, 'This won't come about the way you think it will.' Perhaps you'll experience this, too, as many of my clients also have.

My soul chose to go in deep with this work. I've held my ground with such faith and conviction, while many thought I was foolish. Not everyone can see what I see — nor does everyone *want* me to see what I see. Friends have pulled away, although others always arrived. I don't always fit neatly into other people's ideas; I challenge and confront people without ever saying anything. Conversely, some see me as entertainment (although, Chris doesn't take to this too kindly). You may not have these specific pitfalls, of course, but as you journey with your own lessons and purpose, you're bound to have your version of them.

Suffice to say, living this way presents challenges. Even the pitfalls teach us when we apply the Mirror Technique. With a decade of experience under my belt, and this being my life's mission, I've experienced many pitfalls — and troubleshooted them — which I share in this chapter. I've also included frequently asked questions I receive.

Have you flicked to this chapter before working through the previous ones? Please go back! This chapter can't be used to bypass the growth (although, you may need to troubleshoot your avoidance!). Your intuition and SST should be your first line of enquiry — and then, if all else fails, and you need to appease your mind (we are human after all), then come here for troubleshooting.

Here are the most common pitfalls and frequently asked questions.

My guidance didn't come true

Yet. Some of my guidance has taken years to come to fruition. There are a number of reasons this might occur.

- Timelines aren't set in stone; our free will and choices (and those of others) can alter outcomes.
- Check your interpretation. Was the guidance incorrect, or was your understanding of it wrong? What can you learn from this?
- Ask for more information on the timing — does something else need to clear, heal or restore before this manifests? Is divine timing at play?

Here's some additional channelled guidance on this topic:

'To the idea of the certain insights and information not coming to fruition, we typically see it is on the part of the person not playing their part in the co-creation of their own life. It is not enough to simply know a particular outcome or future, and wait for it to land in your lap. We usually offer the

guidance in order to help you navigate there — to help you realise what trajectory you are on and what you can do to continue or alter that pathway.

'We cannot make something happen; much of that is your job. And what you make happen is not just as simple as the effort or work you put into something, but far more to do with the energy and intention you put behind it.

'To have the energy and intention behind something be aligned with the outcome we've suggested — or the outcome possible according to your blueprint — we encourage you to do the inner work. The inner transformation across the Four Bodies is paramount in bringing you towards the very thing you desire (or away from what you do not desire). Without the involvement of the upgrading and up-levelling of the human involved, not everything in the blueprint is possible — and sometimes this is the very lesson and area of exploration a soul has chosen. Not actualising yourself is a pain no soul wants to bear, and yet many will still choose to come here and not actualise.

'If you remain disconnected from yourself, your lessons and purpose, you won't see all the abundance encoded here for you and waiting just simply to make its way to you. Similarly, just because you desire something enough, it won't come to you if it is not aligned with your soul and a match for the frequency you are radiating.

'In this way, there is no match for the knowledge unless the knowledge has been integrated and transformed through the human conduit first.'

I followed my guidance, but it's no better where I am now

Guidance doesn't guarantee a destination or outcome, other than leading us wherever we need to go to learn our lessons. Winding up somewhere we didn't want to be means guidance is asking us to look for the lesson. You might like to revisit Mandy's story in Chapter 8.

Perhaps it's a stepping stone (see 'My guidance didn't come true'), leapfrogging you into the destination via an alternate classroom. It's not over yet.

Check in with your SST — why have they led you here? What growth is possible here? Who are you meeting here? What are you letting go of here? And how is this leading you forward?

Sometimes, this happens to highlight that we still have head-based expectations about a heart-based process.

I've already learned this lesson

Perhaps. Perhaps not. Lessons will repeat until we truly learn them, and explore them from every angle. It's not enough to just *know* our lessons, we must integrate them as a new, lived experience, too.

Use the Mirror Technique to explore the lesson. Why are you here again? What's different this time? What can you learn here? What else may need to be cleared, healed or restored? Are you clearing, healing or restoring on one of the other Four Bodies this time?

Ask your SST why the lesson is back. Can they show you a higher perspective?

Remember, a life lesson is for life; it will come up again and again. Is this repeating lesson just a life lesson in disguise?

I followed the steps, but didn't get my outcome

Spirituality isn't just a new, trendy to-do list. Just because you've meditated, pulled oracle cards, gone to yoga, saged your home and set new moon intentions, doesn't mean you're guaranteed the outcome you desire. Sadly, this is just ego in disguise finding a new means to the same egotistic ends.

Ask yourself, have you done the inner work?

These tools are not the change; it's within. So, if you haven't gone inwards, or moved through the Guidance Cycle and the inner transformation, then these tools won't be nearly as effective as they could be.

Whenever I've thrown my hands up in the air and told Chris I've done everything he's asked me to do, inevitably I realise I've fallen into some trap — either by being the good girl and doing the 'right' thing; waiting for permission; giving away my power (to guidance or the external tools); attaching to some outcome from ego. Often in my realisation, I learn the lesson, and move through the frustration.

Don't hand over your power (the new permission)

Many of us, women particularly, struggle with permission. We're 'good girls' waiting to be directed, or allowed to act.

Struggled with this? Then please be mindful of it cropping up in your relationship with your intuition and SST. Unwittingly, I've seen people defer permission to their guides, never making a single decision in their own life before running it through their SST. Sadly, I've wasted a great deal of time doing just this.

While I encourage you to run everything through the filter to begin with, I also caution you that if it becomes a bottleneck or slows you down, it has become a problem. Our intuition should build to a cursory check-in on everyday occurrences, so that the bigger choices require more time for reflection.

We have free will. We don't need our SST's permission to act. We must find the balance between guidance and directives.

My partner/friend/colleague/significant other isn't on the same path as me

Thank goodness! They're on their own path. We cannot pretend to know how someone is, or isn't, learning their lessons. We also don't know where someone is on their soul journey, if we are only looking at them at the human level. We don't know how evolved someone else is, or isn't. In fact, it's none of our business.

Wherever there is judgement, there is an opportunity for us to use the Mirror Technique and go within. What part of us wants our significant other to be 'on the same path'? Why? What's in it for that part of us? Can you be who you are without validation and acceptance from an external source? Can they be who they are, unconditionally?

Depending on the circumstances, of course, there may be times where such discrepancies mean it's time to make choices that align with your truth — but before acting from ego, be sure to check your guidance. Typically, I've seen such relationships naturally fade out. The people that stay are likely to be encoded in our blueprint, and our greatest teachers. Love them hard and thank them for bringing you the challenge.

I didn't think spiritual people did (insert your thing here)

I've heard some weird and wacky ideas on this. Spiritual people shouldn't make money, eat meat, curse, get angry, make mistakes, be human.

'Spiritual people' are just people. Human. Like the rest of us — they're making decisions for themselves based on their own path, lessons and purpose.

Just because we can access guidance, commune with our soul or reach for higher beings on tap, it doesn't make us any more 'godlike' than anyone else. We've just remembered there's more to our humanity than meets our physical eyes. And we're learning lessons and experiencing this wild Earth classroom just like the next person — 'spiritual', or not.

We are all spiritual beings, despite our expression or application of this spirituality. We are spiritual because we exist, not because of the choices and behaviours we choose. Be careful not to measure yourself or others based on expectations of what spirituality should look like.

Like the previous pitfall, we cannot pretend to know someone else's path. We cannot assume their soul journey for them. And we must be very cautious not to trip up on spiritual superiority.

Whenever we hold ideas about this work, pathway or journey, we can come back into our beliefs and mindsets and work to open the current restrictions beyond anything we've ever logically known before.

It's not time to act

Sometimes, I've heard this used as a delay tactic. 'Oh, I just intuitively feel it's not the right time/sign/opportunity for me,' I might hear from someone, while the exact thing they've been waiting for is staring them in the face. (Ahem! Chris reminds me I've done this, too.)

Vigilance catches fear. See the next pitfall for more.

Conversely, we can intuitively know when we need to take action, and don't. Or we delay our action. This can delay the outcome; I have certainly seen that if we delay long enough, we can miss the window of opportunity and the guidance no longer stands. What is meant for us, though, won't pass us by — see, 'Will I miss my chance?' for more.

Be sure to check in with the season or cycle you're in (Chapter 24) to see if there are additional influences at play.

How do I know it's guidance and not ego

You might not at first. Trial and error can be useful — and this is why I suggest you start small first, on less impactful decisions.

Guidance will feel open, loving, unconditional and expansive. But it can also push us beyond our comfort zones, in fact, it probably should. Usually, the guidance doesn't go away; we will still feel drawn to it over time.

Fear will want to keep you safe, cautious, comfortable, limited and known. Fear can shift and change, depending on the situation.

Sometimes, our ego is also very clever at adapting to our newfound guidance, and can use it to trick us. If we are unsure, we can ask for more guidance, or a sign to confirm our feelings.

Will I miss my chance?

Our soul blueprint is encoded with the lessons, purpose, soul mate relationships and karma that need to be explored in this lifetime. We cannot miss out — although our choices, decisions and free will can influence the timing, outcome and particular classroom we wind up in.

We cannot guarantee *how* we learn something. We may have a particular opportunity in front of us — say a job offer — that we can choose or not. Either way, the lesson that job would present to us will still turn up.

In my case, it wasn't the job at the online travel agency that was as important as *who* I'd meet there. I'd been approached several times to apply; life really wanted me to get over there. And, after I married Gary, I realised why.

Since then, he went on to work at another company where I'd missed out on a job years before. If I'd got that job, our paths may have crossed. More recently, he's started a job at a company whose office is a few doors down from the PR agency I once worked in.

Timings and classrooms can change, but life is always working for you. What is meant for you — at the soul level — can never truly pass you by.

I'm experiencing a huge change, but my old supports no longer work

Over the course of the past year, Isla has moved from her basic first reader books to chapter books. She's learned what she needed and has moved on. So it is with the tools and healing modalities we use to support the journey.

Here's a little secret: I don't rely on the tools from Chapter 6 half as much as I used to. They were indeed where I started — and where I still encourage you to start — but they are only a starting point. Not a crutch.

As you'll see in the next chapter, we move through cycles with this journey. As we move beyond the spiritual awakening and into a soul awakening, we also move from human-level healing to soul-level healing. They require different supports and tools (and we already know it's not the tool itself that does the work, but us).

Don't feel bad if you outgrow a modality or practice — just please check in to make sure that you have, indeed, outgrown it and that you aren't just experiencing some sort of avoidance. I hear far too many people say, 'Oh, meditation didn't work for me,' as an excuse to quit.

There are a few things that will become everyday (or almost everyday) practices. Meditation is likely to be one of them, along with energy work and the inner work. Whatever you need in between will be guided intuitively — but your SST will let you know when you've reached this point.

Jesus didn't have an Instagram account

I started blogging before it was popular in Australia — before people made money from it, before there was Instagram, before businesses began using Facebook. Fast-forward to now, and so many people are using technologies to support their purpose and vocations — clearly, myself included.

My point here is not about the use of social media or the technologies themselves, but rather, would we still be pursuing these vocations if we couldn't tell everyone about it? Would it still be cool to pursue the thing that is driving you forward if you couldn't make money from it, or tell a few hundred thousand people across the globe about it?

So I joke: Jesus didn't have an Instagram account — and yet his life's work, his healing, his compassion and his teachings on forgiveness have stood the test of time. In fact, he did this work *despite* it being unpopular and uncool at the time. He paid the ultimate price for his choice, commitment and conviction.

Our soul's work is not necessarily for the consumption of other people. It is not to be validated or liked by others, although it's amazing when that is the case, but it's not the reason *for* it. It may be a by-product of it, but we must bring through what is in our hearts, what we are being called to do — even when it is uncool, unpopular, scary and terrifying. *Especially* then.

I find this all so contradictory

Yup, I hear you. In the beginning, I couldn't work out which adage to listen to at which point, either. I just kept coming back to the present moment and what I was guided to do then. There's no point working on manifesting if you haven't done the clearing, healing and restoring first. We can't fix a soul-level wound with a physical modality. My hope is that this book helps you realise that there is a very specific process we move through; when we know where we are along the pathway, we are better placed to know which supports we need. Of course, there's always higher guidance, too.

Soul came to Earth, in human form, to experience duality; it doesn't exist in the non-physical dimensions. Sometimes the contradiction is the lesson.

I just feel stuck

Feeling stuck can be heavy, confusing and stifling, like you're 'off your path', going backwards, or going nowhere at all. Don't let this fool you into thinking it's a sign to stop, avoid, circumvent, rework, overcome, or some other such idea.

Our discomfort, avoidance, resistance and fear can also disconnect us from ourselves and guidance — right when we feel we need it the most.

Thinking our way out of our feelings isn't going to work. Chances are it's the thinking that got us into this state to begin with! Instead, we need to *feel* our way through our feelings. Sit with the 'stuckness' and really feel it, before it subsides. This is true of any of emotion — we must feel them so they pass.

Using the Mirror Technique, try to identify what the stuckness reflects to you. Where can you clear, heal, restore or manifest? What needs to be expressed here? Check whether the stuckness is actually calling you within or if it's actually just something making its way out. Ask the stuckness itself what it needs; you might just be surprised by the answer.

There's a reason I don't want to feel all of this

There's usually a reason we don't want to feel everything. Doing the inner work will, at some point, ask us to face old traumas, either from this lifetime or past lifetimes. Depending on your specific circumstances, some of this may require additional support from qualified professionals. Ask your SST to guide you to the perfect support for this.

No matter the level of pain or trauma, we use tactics to numb, withdraw and disconnect from emotions we don't want to feel. And here I am, asking you to feel them all over again!

We not only disassociate from the pain physically, mentally and emotionally, but also spiritually. Energetic disassociation means we inadvertently send our energy off elsewhere. Trauma at the soul level can fragment our soul and leave it outside — disconnected from our body. When this happens, we may also need qualified healers and practitioners to help us weave the energies back together. It's not just enough to heal physically, mentally and emotionally; we also need to do the deeper energetic healing to restore complete wholeness.

We don't always feel ready to leave this perceived safety, although spirit will nudge us along when it's time. Ask for guidance and assistance to find the supports you need as you do this inner work.

 **CHOOSE YOUR OWN ADVENTURE –
TROUBLESHOOTING YOUR OWN PITFALL**
Didn't find your pitfall here? Take it to your SST. Journal, meditate or pull an oracle card. Perhaps you actually need to seek additional outside help from someone who can see your path (not just provide head-based advice).

CHAPTER 24

★

SEASONS & CYCLES

While my relationship with Chris is constant, it certainly ebbs and flows. Occasionally, Chris' guidance feels stop-start, sometimes due to one of the pitfalls I shared in the last chapter, which I can troubleshoot through. Other times, the ebb or subsequent flow signals a change in the season or cycle of our relationship. Chris' silence during my most recent book/business storm flagged a changing of the season; the years I spent channelling and mentoring groups through the advanced teachings was another cycle, requiring a different pace and inward focus.

Not understanding this, at first I just got mad at Chris. Sometimes the information flowed, sometimes not. Sometimes there was so much for me to action, then nada. My mind blamed him as the keeper of all wisdom. Not surprisingly, a lesson reflected to me here: this new approach to living is not a constant uphill trajectory.

Personal growth cannot be pursued at a constant steep incline; there's a seasonality to it all — my life, work and relationship with Chris, too. The flow of guidance itself is a pretty good indicator of the personal season or cycle we're in. Once again, we're asked to come back into sync with our natural rhythms from Chapter 6.

Chris reminds us: *'You can't harvest in the summer what wasn't planted in the spring, and there's no point planting in winter's inhospitable soil.'*

Other cycles we operate within became clearer to me. Not just the Guidance Cycle, but bigger collective cycles influencing our path. Obvious influences include our own life cycle and Mother Earth's seasons, but cycles of menstruation, lunation and broader astrological cycles piqued my interest, too. During this phase of channelling the High Council of Sages, they shared details with me of the collective energies that work in waves of expansion and contraction to move us all into new seasons and cycles of collective growth and expansion. This guided journey isn't individual, but shared.

Harmonising with our own personal rhythms and collective influences is key. This requires a far more feminine approach; masculine tendencies for constant growth, output and outcomes won't work within a cyclical system asking for balance of give and take, work and play. Such harmonisation also asks us to harmonise these aspects of our human and soul selves; they must unite and work as one, not just as two opposing forces. Understanding and working with our seasons and cycles starts to bring broader context to our guidance and divine life path. Nothing's as linear as it seems, or as the mind demands it to be.

Our path is not linear, but cyclical

To our minds, our divine life path appears rather linear and sequential, a one-step-after-the-other kind of pathway. Time rolls on; let's move forward. Life unfolds lesson-to-lesson, situation-to-situation, in a sequential, chronological fashion.

To soul, the pathway is more like a spiral staircase. We cycle in an upward trajectory, revisiting the same view (or life lesson, or classroom) over and over, albeit from a different perspective. As we move up and around the staircase, we also spin in minor rotations, somewhat akin to the Moon's cycle within a year's spin of the Earth's axis. Within this cyclical pathway are many other micro cycles within macro cycles. For example, within our life cycle from birth to death (a macro cycle) we can see we progress through the Guidance Cycle (a more micro cycle). However, within the Guidance Cycle itself, we might cycle on either a macro or micro rotation.

For example, working through the book, we've experienced a macro Guidance Cycle — an overarching arc of transformation. Since leaving PR more than a decade ago, I cleared, healed, restored and manifested to get to this point today, of producing this book. However, within that major cycle, I've completed many smaller rounds of the Guidance Cycle, all contributing to the overall arc. At any given moment, you may find yourself within a key phase of the macro Guidance Cycle — say, restoring — but still have clearing and healing happening in the background (like with your daily chakra maintenance), while much materialises outwardly from your inner process.

Zooming out further, there is a macro cycle across all of soul's human lifetimes, which I call the soul journey; the micro cycles are each individual lifetime soul incarnates into. From a human perspective, our macro cycle is the life cycle from birth to death; for soul it's from birth to death and back to birth again. To soul, this human lifetime is really a micro cycle.

Suffice to say, much is moving and shifting beyond our human frame of reference. It is far greater than the linear trajectory we think our life plan ought to take.

Life seasons

We must attune to nature's seasons of spring, summer, autumn and winter, but also, beyond this, attune to our life's personal seasons. Macro and micro cycles spin here, too. Life spans us through four phases (akin to the seasons) as we move from birth, growth, maturity and into death. However, despite our chronological age, we can experience those seasons within seasons. With every clearing of the Guidance Cycle, we experience a death and destruction; with every manifestation, we experience a birth. This can come at any life phase, just as with each year of chronological age we will experience each of Mother Nature's seasons. Additionally, women experience one of the seasons on an almost weekly basis via the menstruation cycle.

As Chris reminded us at the top of this chapter, 'You can't harvest in the summer what wasn't planted in the spring; there's no point planting in winter's inhospitable soil.' The macro and micro seasons of life naturally influence our experience of our lessons and purpose, so please don't beat yourself up if you feel your personal growth isn't progressing as you think it should. There really is a time for every purpose (and lesson).

Soul seasons

Beyond our life's seasons are many soul seasons across the soul journey from lifetime to lifetime. Overlooking such a journey with a bird's-eye view, we would see from the first incarnation of an infant soul how it begins a process of accumulating lifetimes. We'd see it moving through its lessons and growth as a soul, lifetime after lifetime, and reaching maturity as an old soul (where we get the phrase 'old soul' from) after which it no longer incarnates, and operates instead on the higher spiritual planes (like spirit guides). As such, we can have infant souls, young souls, mature souls and old souls incarnating on the planet at any given time.

Depending on the soul's age, a human may live out its lessons and purpose in quite different ways — yet another reason we cannot compare our outer human experience with someone else's. We're all at varying stages of the process. An infant soul, for example, is focused on surviving and acclimatising to life on Earth. It may not have the same burning desire to change the world as a mature soul does.

Remember Jane, who approached me after a live event, confused about her soul's purpose? She felt she couldn't bring anything to fruition because she was constantly healing. Clairvoyantly looking across her entire soul's timeline, I could see her soul was in a very mature phase, tying off loose ends and completing karma in this lifetime. She didn't have the impetus for grand, outward outputs; it wasn't her soul's season.

We don't all move into our purpose in the same way in each lifetime. What I've outlined here is possible for us all, but the breadth and depth we each take it to will vary. Some clients tell me they don't have such big, grand visions, and I suspect this could be why; they're simply not yet in the soul season to warrant one.

Balancing cycles and seasons

Knowing your seasons and cycles helps contextualise not only your lessons and purpose, but also how your human self is being asked to show up in each and every moment, or across the lifetime itself. Depending on the phase of season or cycle, you may be asked to come into the masculine (output and giving) or the feminine (input and receiving). This applies not only across micro seasons and cycles — there's a time for sleep and a time for work and play — but also across your lifetime, or indeed your entire soul's timeline.

Like Jane, you may not be in a lifetime where you need to produce or offer something so grand; this may be a lifetime to purely receive, learn and experience. Conversely, as I suspect is the case for me, your lifetime may be asking you to produce a great deal, so yours may be a more masculine or purpose-driven lifetime.

While entire lifetimes can take on a predominant focus, each phase of the seasons and cycles also has a masculine or feminine emphasis. My reference to feminine and masculine energy has nothing to do with gender or sexuality, but instead the make up of give and take. Feminine energy is usually far more inward, introspective, reflective, intuitive, creative and cyclical, while masculine energy is more linear, extroverted and outcome-oriented. Our minds tend to use a more masculine approach, while soul is more feminine. It's counter-productive to use masculine energies on a feminine phase, and vice versa.

Collectively, we are moving out of a vast period of history with an emphasis on the masculine and patriarchy. This is shifting and changing. All genders are now being asked to individually recalibrate the balance of masculine and feminine within, so as to shift the energies universally.

We must recognise when we're called to be in our feminine: receiving, creating, learning and intuiting, and when we are to be in our masculine: giving, servicing, producing and acting.

Earth Campus provides this duality to soul that cannot be experienced in the non-physical dimensions. Soul not only wanted this duality, but all of our souls have incarnated at this time in history to experience such a shift in duality on a mass scale. We each have an important role to play.

Swings and roundabouts

As a collective, we're being asked to reinstate our femininity once more. We're all being asked to slow down, move inward, and connect to ourselves and Earth a little more. We're moving away from constant work outputs that have us feeling depleted and burnt out. Even our addictions to social media ask us to constantly look outward to others, and the nature of our busy modern life requires that we constantly give of ourselves in unhealthy ways. This also feeds into the collective spiritual awakening occurring now.

Over time, I observed we move more like a pendulum at first, before we swing into our own cycles. Back in my PR days, masculine energy fuelled me; I was head-based, output-oriented and burnt out. Then, giving readings and running my online hub was purely based on feeling and intuition for the first few years. The constant output during my PR days wasn't balanced with a rejuvenating input, nor was the constant creative expression in my business' early days supported by the systems and structures it needed. I'd gone from one extreme to the other instead of finding balance between them.

As with our heads and hearts, human and soul selves, we must balance the interplay of our dualities, masculine and feminine included. Working to the seasons and cycles, and the natural way one gives way to the other, takes all the pressure off. Harmony is reinstated.

The swinging pendulum will move from extreme to opposite extreme, before finding its middle ground.

The human experience

Consider a spectrum: at one end is our human experience, at the other, soul. Working with the materials in this book, our SST helps scale the human end of the spectrum up closer to the soul end of the spectrum. The same is true for soul — as the human self increases its vibration, we're able to access more of soul directly, without the assistance of our SST.

In this way, the human self moves through a process, as does the soul self. When the two processes — the array of many seasons and cycles come together and meet in the middle — we find the balance and integration of soul and spirit with human and Earth.

Naturally, our perception is typically through the human lens (although this may change the further along the spectrum we slide). But as we veer more towards the middle, we become far more aware of our soul journey and the vast array of soul-level data at our disposal. Suddenly, our vaults open wider and more of our manual can be received.

Other impacting cycles

Do you feel like there's just so much more going on than you'd imagined? There is! Many other collective cycles may influence our divine life path and soul journey. I'm particularly interested in some astrological and numerological cycles, but you may find you're drawn to other cycles, too. To help reinstate the feminine, I've also long worked with both the lunar and menstrual cycles.

Before we get into this discussion, though, let me be clear that these external influences do not control our path; we are not energetic victims. However, they are *influences*. Awareness can contextualise why things may be unfolding the way they are for you. These are also not the only influences, of course, so if you find yourself intuitively drawn to understanding other cycles, too, follow that thread.

Astrological

Soul chooses the precise timing of our births. When meeting with our blueprint guides and higher masters, astrological placement is taken into consideration in preparing our blueprint. Soul will wait for the exact conditions to enter Earth, so that all is set up to support that blueprint.

Consider this in the context of fertility issues, and suddenly there's another factor at play: the perfect timing of entry for the soul awaiting incarnation. Certainly, my three miscarriages were divinely timed, as was the arrival of each of my girls. One loss in particular set about a particularly deep healing journey for me, all divinely timed in the greater scheme of my life's lessons and work. My children, and their souls, had a frame of reference for their own soul's journey, far beyond the timing desired by Gary and me.

Astrological placement can influence the collective themes and experiences of humans on Earth. Working with a complete birth chart, which reveals the planetary alignments at the time of birth, is far more important than any individual planet placement, or even star sign. (For your own birth chart, try a free online generator.) Such a chart, and a skilled reader, can give the full picture. For that reason, looking at which zodiac sign the Moon is in, or which planet is retrograding where is only a partial story — what does it mean against your personal chart?

My sun sign (another term for birth or star sign, which is the zodiac sign the sun was passing through when I was born) is Scorpio. This gives a cursory glance, or the headlines, of my life, but it's not the full astrological picture. It's not by chance I have Pisces rising (psychic abilities and the underworld) and a Leo moon (expressing emotions), nor any other placement in my chart. By working with my own chart, and following planetary placements and movements, I can see timings and themes at play, and how it's going to influence me.

For example, I use Mercury retrograde (periods when the planet appears to move backwards in relation to Earth) to revisit ideas and plans, but I avoid signing contracts or making technological upgrades then. As Mercury is the planet for communication, plans and transport, when it appears to move backwards, so, too, can our life in these same areas. Coincidentally, Jupiter has moved into Sagittarius — an auspicious time for both spirituality and publishing. Another reason my own timings never stood a chance.

Numerological

Numerology provides additional context to our astrological charts. I've observed over the years that the patterns of the year's numerology match up to what's shown in my personal birth chart and, more importantly, the guidance from Chris. More recently, my collective energy forecasts seem to weave all these cycles together, too.

Numerologically speaking, we move in cycles of nine years, both collectively and individually. Essentially, each year has a numerological meaning attributed to it. To discover the number of a year, you simply add up the numbers of the year. For example, 2019 would be 2+0+1+9=12. You reduce this again, so 1+2=3, giving you a three year. We each have a Master Personal Number (mine is 11, or 2) based on our birth date and year. We can also calculate our Personal Year by taking our birthdate with the *current* year. For 2019, my Personal Year is a four. There are many free resources online to help you then interpret what each year will symbolically focus on.

I use this cycle as more of a broader understanding as to why some projects and passions have a longer life cycle than others. I've often wondered if this numerological cycle is akin to one of the rotations around the staircase, although I don't think it's as fixed as that.

Lunar cycles

The lunar cycle is another astrological cycle I observe, but I'm not stringent with it. Over the course of the Moon's cycle, there are both masculine and feminine phases ideal for certain activities. There are many micro phases within one full moon rotation, and many people observe each phase. I've outlined these phases below, however, I tend to observe the new and full moons, and a general feeling of the waxing and waning moon. See how you're called to observe this cycle.

Waxing moon — new moon to full moon
New ideas, concepts and beginnings ripen here as the Moon gets brighter and bigger in the night sky, representing illumination. This two-week waxing phase links with fertility, both creatively and reproductively, but of course, physical conception is governed by your own personal menstrual cycle (see page 302). Culminating with the full moon, this phase is masculine, or outward, in nature.

Waxing moon phases:
- **New moon (masculine):** hailed as a time for new beginnings, but also clarity and revelation. Perfect for starting new projects, however, not all information will have yet come to light.

- **Crescent (feminine):** receive more information, insight and intuition here as a plan or course of action relevant to the ideas from the new-moon phase.
- **First quarter (masculine):** time to trust, especially yourself and timing. Focus on creative self-expression.
- **Gibbous (feminine):** insight or confirmation on how to proceed, but without an entire picture of the full moon just yet. Trust.

Waning moon — full moon to new moon

Having reached full moon, it now wanes, or appears to decrease in size and light in the night sky. This two-week window takes us into our shadow aspects and inner world — a great time for introspection. More feminine in nature, this is the time to turn inward; explore your inner world and Four Bodies through journaling, oracle cards and meditation. By the time the waning moon once more becomes a new moon, there is a sense of release and completion.

Waning moon phases:

- **Full (masculine):** illumination! All is revealed — a full picture, and the potential shadows. Tweak your new-moon plans and ideas now with this clarity.
- **Disseminating (feminine):** collaboration is now key. Birth ideas or share the concepts.
- **Last quarter (masculine):** completion and transitioning now, preparing for phase end. Intuition is again strong. The final 'push' towards finalising the original idea or goal.
- **Balsamic (feminine):** release and give thanks, before looking ahead once more with the new moon. What must be left behind and what will you carry forward? You are likely to feel withdrawn and once again turn inward at this point.

Look up the Moon phases for the coming month and mark them in your diary. Plan your creative work and social engagements according to the Moon and journal your results — you'll be amazed at the difference it makes. And remember to start small; a little will still go a long way.

Menstrual cycle

Menstruation cycles mirror the lunar cycles just outlined, and I do encourage you to do further reading in this space. Although this cycle mirrors the lunar cycle, please do not worry if they don't sync up. And please do not worry if you're no longer menstruating, either. Like all we've discussed here, your own rhythms are far more important than falling in line with an ideal. I pay attention to both my menstrual and lunar cycles as I navigate my days, weeks and months. With my own menstrual cycle, for example, I know there are days where my ability to channel and give readings will be lessened, and others where it's heightened. I try and work to these, granted, this is perhaps a little easier for the self-employed. Revisit Chapter 6 and see where you can add small elements of this into your routine, too.

Each week of the menstrual cycle mirrors the seasons, while ovulation mirrors the new moon and bleeding the full moon. While we can work with the menstrual cycle for obvious fertility and reproductive means, I share it here as a means to explore when you are also more naturally intuitive and creative, versus when you're more outward and productive.

On the next page is a basic outline of the cycle and how to work with its rhythms.

Phase 1 — Menstruation phase: winter

This is a very gentle, inward phase of releasing and letting go. Shedding the past, whether physically, mentally, emotionally or spiritually (thus, closely linked to the clearing phase of the Guidance Cycle). Rest and recuperation is required here. Projects, plans and production aren't the focus, but tending to yourself and your inner world.

Phase 2 — Follicular phase: spring

After winter, this is a good time to reconsider projects and new ideas. Your energy levels pick up across your Four Bodies, with insights and awareness creeping in a little easier. Typically, this may be a more physical and mental time, a little more outward than last season. Akin to the healing and restoring phase, this phase is not quite full manifestation, but preparing for it.

Phase 3 — Ovulatory phase: summer

Building from the last phase, this is another brilliant time for outward focus. Productivity and action feature strongly here. Perhaps not as focused on feminine creativity and intuition, this is a very outward-focused phase of doing and action.

Phase 4 — Luteal phase: autumn

Things begin to wind down again, especially the closer to menstruation you get. Focus turns inward once more, contemplating, reflecting and connecting dots. Questions for guidance will arise here. Self-care is needed more as you're preparing for the winter.

Track your own cycle for a few months to notice what is true for you. You can also glean a great deal of information about your Four Bodies through this process, too.

**CHOOSE YOUR ADVENTURE —
WHAT SEASON ARE YOU IN?**

Have some fun syncing with your seasons and cycles. Below are some suggestions to get you started. Your SST may have already pointed you towards some of these suggestions, too. If so, pay close attention.

1. Enquire with your SST about your soul seasons and life seasons. Meditate, journal or pull oracle cards for insights.
2. Use a free online birth chart generator to create your own astrological birth chart. Research the current and upcoming planetary placements and what it might mean for you. You might even like to have an astrology reading with someone you trust.
3. Track your own menstrual cycle (or lunar cycle if you're not menstruating) and observe the peaks and troughs in your cycle. How do you receive guidance in those phases?
4. Work out your Master Personal Number and Personal Year in numerology and look up their meanings.

As you see these bigger cycles, compare these notes to any impressions and directions you've had from your SST, or reflections in your journal. Watch for patterns emerging.

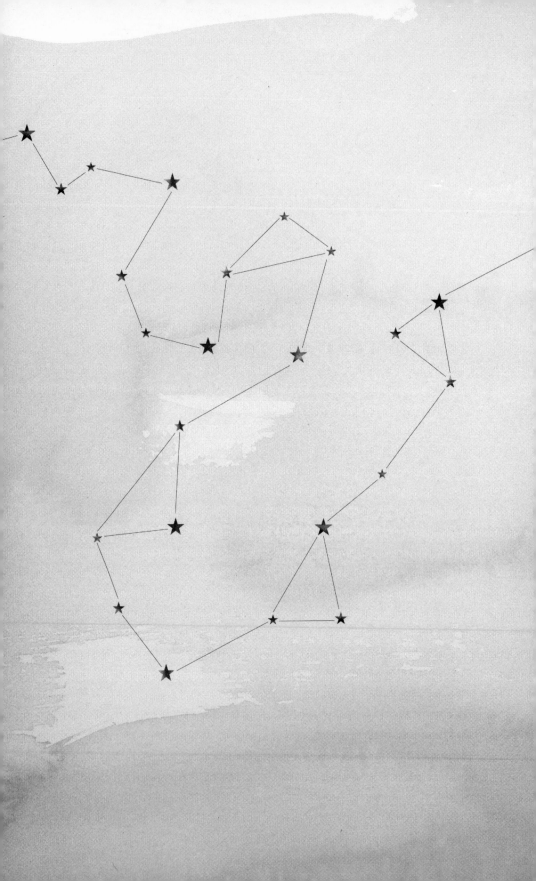

CHAPTER 25

GUIDED PATHWAY

Life is remarkably different as a result of this new approach. Daily, I work with my energy and its four flows; I see the outer world as a reflection of my inner state; I attune to my guidance frequently while still taking day-to-day action, trusting the overarching vision is manifesting. Again and again, I choose, with conviction, this path and way of living. My life has become the embodiment of what my soul has always known, but my logical mind often struggles to understand.

Around the time I was pregnant with Rose, and the first drip-feed of information came from the High Council of Sages, I was shown another important cycle at play as we progress with this guided living. The material I channelled didn't focus on the importance of intuition and spirit guides; instead, it led me into the realm of soul. Chris explained I'd moved through this cycle, now opening a portal to the soul realm, to access and sustain it in my field for longer and longer periods of time. There was a meeting and merging of the human and soul selves, as I'd progressed along my own spectrum. It was the culmination of the inner work of all the years before.

I'd entered new territory altogether. Reams of information channelled through, explaining the advanced teachings I mentioned earlier. Spirit tasked me to share these teachings with my clients, many of whom had already been through a spiritual awakening and were now commencing a soul awakening, just as I had. Such a soul awakening takes our awareness beyond ourselves as spiritual beings connected to spirit guides (the work of a spiritual awakening), but into the realm of soul and all the wisdom residing here. As you complete the first cycle with this book, you'll likely move through your spiritual awakening (or revisit and complete it). Spirit will no doubt guide you to work through this book again as your soul awakening begins. We'll talk more about soul awakening in the next chapter; in this one, we will explore the cycle we've just been through.

Working with the processes of this book, you've begun radically transforming your life. You've already laid the foundations for a brand new lifestyle approach, one where your mind is not in total control, but rather a faithful servant to the inner and higher guidance available to you. More becomes available to you now, dependent on the foundations you've laid. And, if needed, we will now strengthen and reinforce these foundations to help you receive even more.

Your new normal

You picked up this book because you knew it was time for change, and a new way to create that change in your life. Throughout the book, we've gone deeper into the process I've clairvoyantly and physically witnessed, experienced and channelled over the past decade. You've instilled a new rhythm and pace in your life that matches your own natural flow and supports your communication with guidance. Your new stillness, space and silence allow your inner voice to be heard, for you to observe and interpret the subtleties of your inner landscape. Your SST has come to the fore; you've developed a relationship with your team of advisors.

Not only are you guided in each and every moment, but there is an overarching direction — a thread pulling you deeper into your own soul's blueprint, and the reason you're here. You've gone inward, working with your energy to clear, heal and restore it. You've seen the knock-on effect in your physical, mental, emotional and spiritual bodies. You now also know that any ailment or symptom in any of these bodies, or your outer world itself, is a nudge to look inward, to clear, heal and restore again.

Simultaneously, you've been drip-fed details of your unique soul blueprint — the energetic imprint of your soul's lessons and purpose in this lifetime. Your internal navigation and SST have worked to it all along; now you are, too. Remembering and recognising who you really are, you begin to make choices to act in such a way to transmit and express this truth. You've arrived. And you trust all of life supports you in your transformation, and the transmission of your truth.

Life can never be the same again. Your SST and your soul have not led you here to only lead you here. Now, you must continue forward with this new way of living. You must continue to walk this guided pathway, one intuitive step at a time.

The guided pathway

This process is akin to a 'Choose Your Own Adventure' book. Each choice and decision you've made has been your own, and you've worked with your SST to make these decisions. You could think of them as tour guides along your pathway. They've helped you prepare for the spiritual journey — this inner work, the revelation of your soul's blueprint is really just the beginning. Now, you must live it; a new adventure begins.

Your guides have led you through the first phase of the journey, an initiation of sorts, preparing you for what's ahead. The terrain changes here as there are new tour guides and new supports for this next phase of the journey. The energetic weather even changes; you'll begin to feel the effects of new energies at play. If you're not aware you've wandered into this new neighbourhood, you could be caught off guard. A new soul season dawns at this point, along with a new cycle for the human self. The two ends of the spectrum have met in the middle, initiating a new life, or rebirth.

Earlier, we pictured a spiral staircase, however, I usually think of this concept as a mountain. The pathway the human self walks around the mountain is not linear; it's a circular track around and up the mountain (thank goodness the trajectory isn't too steep!). Our progress together in this book thus far has taken us from base camp, where we prepared to climb our mountain. We gathered our SST as tour guides, who further prepared and equipped us for the individual journey ahead. Your intuition (your map) and your true self (your compass) have been tasked towards your North Star.

From there, you set off around the first cycle of the mountain. Here, you strengthened your relationship with guidance, worked with your energy, inner and outer worlds and your Four Bodies to receive details of your lessons and purpose. On and on you hiked, clearing the way to receive more of the blueprint the higher up the mountain you got. By continually clearing, healing and restoring, you've raised your vibration, or ascended the mountain.

Now the terrain changes. There's a new cycle. We're atop the mountain, waiting for soul to descend, beginning our soul awakening, or what Chris calls the second spin of the Guidance Wheel.

The Guidance Wheel

The Guidance Wheel explains our awakening and remembering of our higher, multi-dimensional natures. Not to be confused with the Guidance Cycle, the Guidance Wheel is more of a macro cycle to the micro Guidance Cycle. Both the Guidance Cycle and the Guidance

Wheel are cogs; the constant rotation of the Guidance Cycle spins the Guidance Wheel. Clearing, healing and restoring facilitates more guidance to be received, leading us ever deeper into our inner transformation. We move beyond our human-level healing to soul-level healing, integrating all our past lives. We strengthen our soul gifts, contracts and mission, deepening our understanding and transmission. All our work to date with the Guidance Cycle has naturally been edging us through the Guidance Wheel, preparing us for soul-level integration.

The Guidance Wheel is comprised of four spokes, or central pillars. If each isn't strengthened equally, the wheel can't turn, as it's too lopsided. One pillar naturally gives way to the others, so they are feeding into and spinning one another constantly, as the wheel spins around. Thus, the central themes of the Guidance Wheel must be equally catered for in order for us to advance along in the adventure.

The four spokes, or central pillars, of the Guidance Wheel are:

1. *Guidance* — your intuition, higher guidance from SST and soul.
2. *Layers* — your inner and outer worlds; your Four Bodies.
3. *Energy* — your chakras and aura; In and Out, Up and Down Flows.
4. *Blueprints* — your soul and Earth blueprints.

Completing the progress in this book thus far completes the first round of the Guidance Wheel. You strengthened your Guidance pillar, courting your intuition and SST. Guidance led you into the Layers of your being; your inner and outer world, your Four Bodies. Here, the Guidance Cycle cleared, healed, restored and manifested across these Four Bodies. You increased your vibration to receive the vibration of your blueprint.

Following the path, you ascended the mountain, equipping your energy circuits for the changing altitude. Now, atop the mountain, new frequencies (like altitudes) swirl around you, descending from the cosmos above.

Another cycle now begins, and the Guidance Wheel spins again. Available guidance now expands; new layers and portals open up within you; the energy you work with changes; and new elements of your blueprint are revealed. Here, you move beyond your spiritual awakening — the ascent of the mountain — to the soul awakening — and the descent of soul's frequency into your awareness and body. We'll explore this more in the following chapter.

The Guidance Wheel

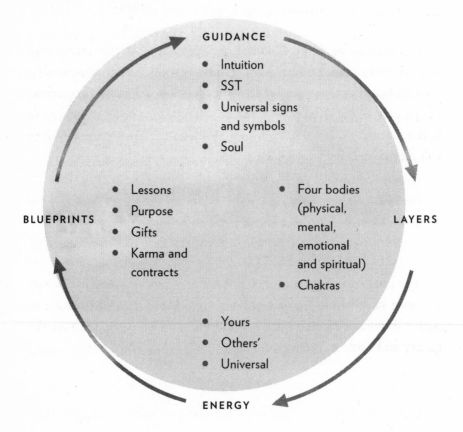

GUIDANCE

- Intuition
- SST
- Universal signs and symbols
- Soul

BLUEPRINTS

- Lessons
- Purpose
- Gifts
- Karma and contracts

LAYERS

- Four bodies (physical, mental, emotional and spiritual)
- Chakras

ENERGY

- Yours
- Others'
- Universal

Do I really need to jump these hoops to reach soul?

Oh, how I wanted to play in the realm of soul before I was ready! Of course, we can access the soul realm — we've received snippets from our manual, we've worked with our blueprint guides — but this doesn't mean we can fully sustain and maintain these soul-level frequencies within our human form. This requires full expanse of the Guidance Wheel.

> There are many ways to reach soul. This framework
> will help us do so en masse, collectively up-levelling
> and upgrading our awareness as a whole.

Chris, and the High Council of Sages, suggest this framework will support us collectively and individually as so many of us awaken spiritually and at the soul level — there are few earth guides explaining the process. What is, of course, meant as a very personal experience can indeed operate within a framework. Ultimately, following the guidance you receive will help you play your part.

> Of course, we're never truly separate from our soul —
> it is the energy and frequency of our soul that we want
> to weave into our denser, earthly, human frequencies.

The goal is to meet and merge these energies and frequencies like we never have before, en masse. For us to achieve this, Chris suggests such a framework is necessary — otherwise, it's like trying to take the galaxy and force it into a pinhead.

A GALAXY INTO A PINHEAD

Imagine yourself standing at the top of a mountain, like the one you've just been ascending. You look like a tiny pinhead atop such a vast, high mountain. Above your head is the entire galaxy (the information from your soul and beyond), which now wants to make its way down from the cosmos and into the tiny, little pinhead (your human form). How can such a pinhead open itself to receive the vastness of the cosmos?

We must expand our pinheads! It's not enough to just reach the cosmos; we need a framework to ensure our pinheads are expanded and robust enough to receive the cosmos. Chris will often explain it to me another way: our body is like a 40-watt bulb now trying to take in 1000 megawatts. The bulb is likely to blow, unless it is upgraded.

Not only will these frameworks allow for the pinhead, or bulb, to open to the megawatts, but there is also a specific process happening from the other side to manage the flow. Soul has its own process of descending into our realm.

Our human self has increased its vibration enough to begin to pull down threads from the cosmos — the very threads you began to follow back in Chapter 12. One of these is the thread leading you deeper into your blueprint; it gives you a sense of the bigger purpose, vision and legacy you're here to uphold. Our guidance in the next turn of the Guidance Wheel will again ensure we move further into our inner transformation, shifting our 40-watt bulb, or our tiny little pinheads, into vast open channels ready to receive the fullness of the cosmos, or the data from the soul realm.

CASE STUDY – **Maggie**

I continued working with Maggie on and off for most of my career. More recently, Maggie's vision for her work with women and corporates has expanded greatly. In the first spin of the Guidance Wheel, Maggie created a business providing programs and retreats for busy corporates, especially working mothers.

Maggie's inner transformation, however, didn't stop. Like you, she now had an ongoing new lifestyle approach, one that continuously guided her within. The Guidance Wheel continued to spin, adding to her understanding as she upgraded her energy and brought forth what she'd received of her blueprint. Maggie's lessons to date had already given way to a very purposeful body of work — but now, as she started to receive more details of her blueprint, a great legacy for this work arrived.

It was no longer enough to share the retreats and corporate wellness programs herself. Maggie's soul began directing a bigger vision into place. Maggie felt the call to train up others to facilitate the programs, developing her own trainings to train teachers in her method. Maggie also felt this was work not only to share with corporates, but with other workplaces, too, particularly schools. This had never originally been part of the vision on the first round of the Guidance Wheel, but as Maggie strengthened her energy by listening to her guidance, she received even more of the blueprint over time.

At the time of writing, Maggie is still receiving insights from soul for this next round of soul work. We're yet to see how it will unfold in the physicality of her divine life path. But I hold every faith our world will soon see wellness programs for education providers in a very different way.

My own Guidance Wheel

Like Maggie, my Guidance Wheel spun around. By being present in each and every moment, by following the call of the times and offering what I was guided to offer in each of those moments, I've been able to use my soul gifts to humbly help many people. My mind, at times, has wanted this to be fixed in a particular form. 'Choose a business model, Helen, and stick to it,' I've thought, most likely thanks to my business background.

Hindsight is a wonderful tool once it becomes available to you. For many years, I've had the pieces of the bigger vision, the legacy of my work. For many years, I've also known that when this book is finally brought to life, and sent out into your hands, dear reader, that my own soul work would land. Anchor. And commence a whole new cycle and transformation for my being. To think that each of you reading this is helping to uphold my own soul agreements is remarkable to me. Thank you for playing your part.

As I've journeyed with the inner transformation (from the inside out), which this book has required of me, more and more of the next iteration of my purpose has revealed itself. Much of it looks like the speaking and mentoring Chris has long since shown me, but now new pieces of the puzzle and legacy are emerging, too. A new beginning is born out of this wildly adventurous experiment I began all those years ago.

 CHOOSE YOUR ADVENTURE —
WHERE ARE YOU IN YOUR JOURNEY?
Take a moment to consider your own Guidance Wheel. I've created a free resource for you to download, so you can plot your progress with the Guidance Wheel. You'll see a version of it on page 317.

Within each quadrant of the wheel, within the Guidance, Energy, Layers and Blueprint pillars, mark on the relevant dotted line your progress in that area. The closer you mark to the centre of the circle, the lower your score. The closer you mark to the outer perimeter, the higher your score. For example, if you've fostered a wonderful relationship with your SST, you might plot yourself somewhere towards the outer concentric circles. If you're not yet receiving the details of your blueprint, though, you'd score that lower.

Once you've got the four points plotted, connect the dots. This will reveal how easily your wheel is likely to spin. If it's off-kilter, it's going to be harder and clunkier, right?

This exercise also helps you understand where you may need to focus your attention, or it may simply highlight how your SST has been moving you through your energy and layers and why you might not yet have the details from your blueprint. Don't lose faith! Ask your SST to help you move through each of the four pillars, to strengthen your wheel and move you forward. Always trust yourself and the process, knowing that your process and experience will always be true to you — it may not look like anyone else's.

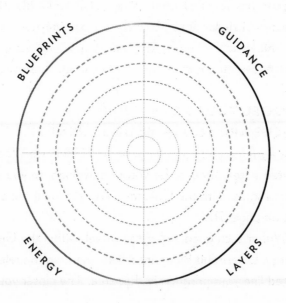

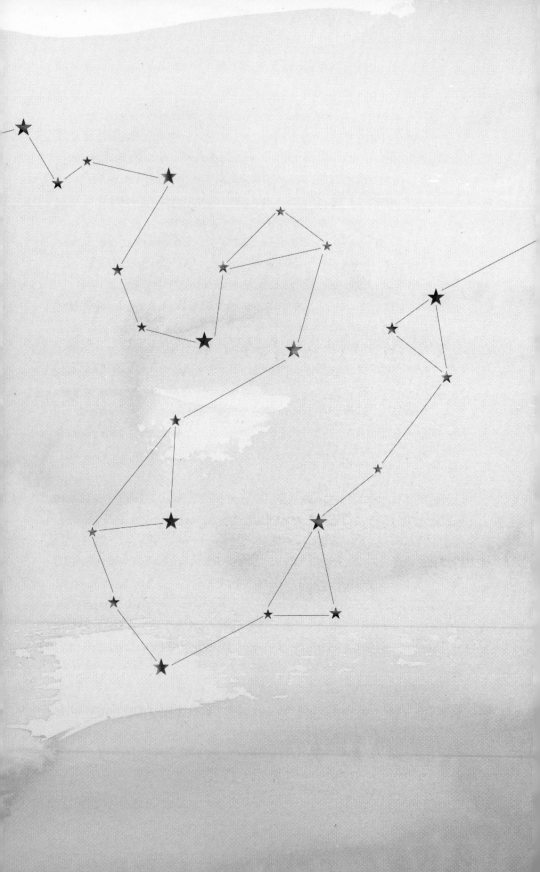

CHAPTER 26

SOUL JOURNEY

Streaming new insights from spirit, albeit now higher guides, I set about applying all I was learning via automatic writing. A new channel opened up, taking me beyond Chris and the High Council of Sages — I'd gone to the realm of soul. Here, I met new guides. My Soul Council (spirit's equivalent, in the soul realm) arrived, expressions of my soul appeared, rather like the feelings and future self we work with in Chapter 20. Revisiting similar concepts, this felt different; I realised I was in the soul realm, working with my human self, not the other way around.

SPIRIT SPEAK

A **Soul Council** is just like an SST, but in the soul realm. Rather than made up of spiritual beings, a Soul Council is comprised of many aspects or expressions of our soul, each sharing gifts, wisdom, knowledge and truths.

New healing occurred with a rather intensive inner transformation. I ventured into many of my soul's past lives, retrieving lost fragments of my soul. Wounds from this lifetime, like my fear to reveal myself as psychic, had roots in these previous incarnations. In many lifetimes, my soul explored themes of spiritual teaching, healing and even a lifetime as a witch. The pain and trauma from this contributed to my reaction as a young child upon recognising my grandfather (and my mother's anguish). Soul knew those circumstances would elicit that response; it was chosen by soul. This new round of healing took me into multi-dimensional healing chambers, where I convened with the souls of my soul mates, reviewing — sometimes completing — our soul contracts.

Clearing, healing and restoring across my soul's timeline allowed new information to pour in. Soul began channelling new materials, much of which I haven't yet publically shared, as they feed into a later portion of my work and purpose. This clearing, healing and restoring wasn't happening in my chakras; new energy centres opened up within me. I weaved new soul-level frequencies through my body — and my physical body couldn't keep up. My health blew out; I gained weight. My nervous system needed rewiring.

No wonder Chris told me to step back from it all! My human self needed time to catch up with the soul adventure I'd been on. In truth, I had disconnected from my body during my escapades into higher realms. It was time to come back down to Earth.

This was the personal detour I went on when I first committed to this book, around the time of Rose's arrival. Both personally and professionally, I needed this exploration before this book could come to life. It's quite different from where I once thought it would go, but all in divine timing and order.

Many forces are at play in our lives. Just as our human self has explored this process from a very human, tangible, earthly dimension, soul is journeying here from beyond to meet and merge with us.

May I caution you here, dear reader, don't rush to this point. Soul and spirit will guide you in your own divine timing. Perhaps this may not even come in this lifetime! But, gee, if I'd known back then what was happening, it might have been so much easier. So, I share this chapter not because Chris tells me the masses are ready, although certainly many individuals are, but because when we know where we're going it can help appease our logical mind. Spirit wants us to carry on, not give up.

From spiritual awakening to soul awakening

The Guidance Wheel spins, moving us from our spiritual awakening to our soul awakening. Of course during our spiritual awakening, we've no doubt connected with our soul — but not like this. In our soul awakening, the soul begins to descend, making its way down that spectrum, meeting the human self at the other end, whose energy can now receive this soul. Just as we've followed a process to prepare for soul, soul has journeyed to meet us here. Soul has a journey and process all of its own.

We're standing atop the mountain, the pinheads that we are. Now, soul starts to make its way down to us, descending threads from the galaxy and weaving them in and around our pinhead, while we are simultaneously expanding said pinhead. Don't worry, we're still guided through this process — but it's most unlike the first phase of the journey. Tools and modalities from my personal healing toolkit no longer cut it; you'll need to expand the toolkit from Chapter 14. Human-level healing won't work with soul-level frequencies.

Soul journey

Let's come back to our spectrum. At one end is our human experience making its way to soul at the other end. Meanwhile, soul moves along its own pathway, to us. Just as the human self ascends to reach soul, soul descends to reach us. As we learned earlier, what you seek is seeking you.

This descending is rather like us receiving snippets of information, first, through our intuitive instructions, our SST, and the energy and expression of our purpose itself. Beyond this are many other layers of our soul (just like the layers of our Four Bodies) making their way down the spectrum and into our awareness the closer we get to being a vibrational match to it. Our soul purpose expands in scope to a rich legacy our soul wishes to impart in this lifetime.

Preparing for such knowledge, we're prompted into more transformation. Our healing journey begins to expand from healing our Four Bodies, to healing across our many lifetimes. Past life and soul-retrieval work are common at this level, although you may be guided to it during the spiritual awakening.

Many of my lifetimes were explored, healing past hurts, pains and traumas that fed into this lifetime's experiences. Previous past life traumas with psychic ability contributed to the family of origin my soul chose this time; old wounds around expression (I was once a singer, captured on stage; in other lifetimes I failed to speak up as a leader) needed to be healed, freeing my expression in this lifetime.

Soul needed to clear, heal and restore as it became manifest in this human form, with full integration and realisation in this lifetime — no small feat.

CHANNELLED GUIDANCE – the travelators
This takes our Mirror Technique to a whole new, multi-dimensional level. Another excerpt of channelled guidance helps explain:

'Imagine that mirrored above the Earth, in what you may conceptualise as a heaven or higher space or place, another journey is unfolding. It isn't bound to your earthly clocks, but on an infinite time frame. At this higher level, things move smoothly,

easily, for there is no density as there is on Earth. On Earth, as humans, you're moving in a time-space reality different to the higher realms, including the realm of soul. (For this reason, it is often difficult for us to give Helen accurate time frames according to Earth time.)

'As humans open to spirit and are taking more guided action, the speed at which they begin to move increases. They begin to move beyond the time-space reality and fall into a slipstream of sorts. It's almost like you're on conveyors, or travelators, in airports. When you jump onto one, your human body needn't move, but you can begin to overtake those walking alongside the travelator. This is how someone who is moving through a spiritual awakening appears from our perspective alongside someone bound by 3D time and space.

'Now, imagine that same person moves forward into another period, where they can speed up their time again, this time to be in sync with the speed of soul in the higher dimensions. There is a rapid leap in their understanding, energy and perspective of their life. For a brief moment in time, they've opened to a higher frequency and slipstream. Yet, until now, that slipstream has not been able to be maintained. This is changing. The human and soul realms were too far apart — they are now coming closer. And so, for an individual, the speed with which they can come into the slipstream of their soul is unprecedented.

'It also means that soul is, in effect, using these waves of acceleration to bring through these higher and higher frequencies. This is happening to individuals, but also happening on a collective level, too. As more and more individuals are flooded with this higher energy, they more rapidly remember who they are and why they are here, thereby activating those around them in the process.

'Over the course of many, many lifetimes, soul has been waiting for generations to reach this point. This is a unique opportunity in the history of your people — and one that can significantly impact the direction of the population. If everyone were able to tap into these pockets and frequencies, remember who they are and live on-purpose, the world would change with rapid speed. When you all remember who you are, and live from there, there is an important part for everyone to play in the larger ecosystem.

'As you move through the opening and healing already outlined here, you are effectively putting yourself onto these travelators. You clear the density so you can accelerate into these slipstreams. To find them, work with your own SST. And then, once on an accelerator, you will receive the essence of the blueprint able to reach you at that point in time.'

Soul is on its own journey on these higher planes. On Earth, when we follow guidance to clear our heavy energies in order to tap into higher frequencies, we can match progress in the non-physical dimension. Then our divine life path rapidly launches again.

Second turn of the Guidance Wheel

Now we experience a second spin of the Guidance Wheel, taking our experience into the soul realm, beyond the human experience. In this round, however, the focus of each of the pillars alters to adjust to the soul level.

On the second rotation of the Guidance Wheel, as we journey with our soul awakening, we experience these four pillars in a new way:

* **Guidance** — now moves beyond intuition and spirit guides to soul guides such as your Soul Council and the expression of your soul.

- *Layers* — you begin to work with layers beyond your inner and outer worlds and your Four Bodies, which now span your soul's timeline.
- *Energy* — no longer your own life force, chakras and aura, but the soul frequencies, and the expanded impressions from the blueprint.
- *Blueprint* — expands here, too, and the other templates reveal more of themselves to you.

SPIRIT SPEAK

An **expression of your soul** refers to certain threads or themes, gifts or wisdom that your soul has developed over its many lifetimes. Your soul then draws on certain expressions as it weaves its way into this particular lifetime, akin to influencing a song by selecting certain chords.

New guidance — soul guides

Akin to spirit guides, you are now guided in the realm of soul. Your Soul Council, akin to your SST, is comprised of many expressions of your soul (an essence, aspect or frequency of your soul developed across the timeline of your soul now weaves its way into your human experience) and many soul guides, much like your spirit guides.

For example, I have expressions of my soul as woman, mother, teacher, business owner and leader (among others). Working with the energy of your expression in Chapter 22 was a precursor to this. You may have started to receive impressions of a future self, or you can ask to be connected. This is likely a first meeting with an expression of your soul. Soul sends you these impressions, like your future self, as a particular frequency to embody in your life. Over time, you'll meet numerous expressions of your soul. You can interact with the expression of your soul just as you have with your intuition and SST.

My future self appeared via clairvoyant images and visions of a future version of myself. I was outside the scene, looking in. I paid attention to how I looked, how I held myself, what I desired, who I shared it with, how I lived. I recognised myself, but not as I am now. This 'future me' was an expression of my soul — my true self leading me forward into the vision and version of myself I was destined to become; a dangling carrot of future potential.

Just as I got to know Chris, I got to know her — *remember* her — and take her advice on how to live *as* her. In this way, I moved from an abstract idea of the future to a real, lived experience of who I was born to be. I'd become my own guide, and my SST became my back up, not the main show (sorry, Chris!).

 Self-reflection: Ask to meet your future self in your Sacred Space. Notice who comes to you, respecting who and what is revealed in each meeting. Spend some time getting to know each other, then honour what is asked of you.

Try not to intellectualise this, or rush into this new relationship. Soul guides are more likely to come to you in the first instance. When they arrive, simply work with them as you have your SST — but notice their guidance; their energy and directions will feel so very different.

New energies — soul funnel

As soul descends and the galaxy makes its way down from the cosmos, it is corralled through a series of funnels. Layers of the galaxy make themselves known to us in human awareness, and new and higher frequencies are received around our purpose, legacy and lessons. I clairvoyantly see them as threads, drip-feeding their way to us by dropping from the cosmos and into our awareness. These soul threads gain a gravitational pull as they come down into our bodies and earthly energies — they are rather like the guidance threads from Chapter 12.

These seemingly separate threads weave together in our bodies, creating a beautiful soul tapestry, if you will. In truth there are more threads than this, which begin to descend and weave together, knitting a beautiful, full picture — a rich energetic imprint — of who we really are. Here, soul is fully aligned and activated in our lives.

Soul threads will also guide you deeper into the healing across the soul timeline (past life healing, soul retrieval). A new toolkit develops. You'll follow the threads of guidance in order to heal and bring your purpose into form.

New layers — Guidance Gateways

New energies must work their way through new layers in our being. Chakras were the focus of the spiritual awakening, but now new portals and energy centres linked to the soul dimension activate and open within you. I call these Guidance Gateways. These gateways are portals through which these soul threads and the details of the soul funnel can drip into our earthly energies.

Guidance Gateways, like chakras, need to be worked with as you pull through the In and Out, Up and Down Flows, except this time you're running soul frequencies into the circuit, and the gateways will be the litmus test to the soul-level healing required.

Perceiving the gateways may not be possible immediately. Even with my more advanced students, this work can take a little time. It certainly will only be sustained after moving through the first Guidance Wheel — and soul has a way of ensuring you enter into the frequencies you need, and not a moment too soon.

New blueprints — the chambers

Here, you're well and truly inside the vault — only to discover there are multiple chambers residing within. You remember far more details of your blueprint here, such as the nature of your gifts and the legacy you're assigned to imprint upon Earth.

Here, we connect with our expression anew — this time, it comes to us via what I call soul seeds. New ideas are conceived as these seeds integrate within your body, in the form of energetic knowledge that needs to gestate (as you undergo new soul-level inner transformations). This knowledge will eventually be birthed and made manifest through you.

SPIRIT SPEAK

Soul seeds refer to the beginnings of ideas, projects, businesses and even children aligned with your soul blueprint. We become custodians of these soul seeds to conceive, gestate, birth and then grow them.

We saw with Maggie, for example, how her work changed shape and form, depth and breadth with the arrival of her soul seed. As I write, she is still in a gestation phase and cannot rush to birth this new work. It will require her to clear, heal and restore; first tidying any residue at the human level, before deep-diving into the soul realm.

I believe this book — and the teachings I've been channelling for the past few years — are soul seeds at various stages of conception, gestation, birth and growth. I will be guided on their subsequent process through their own life cycles. Such soul seeds are their own energetic entity, complete with blueprints of their own.

Chris' guidance to close my business activities inadvertently led me into my own soul-level healing — your SST can still lead you here! But the process you'll go through will feel different; same process, new dimension.

Collective journey

Throughout this book, our goal has been to connect with our guidance and live our divine life path. Soul has led the charge, even when its messengers arrived via our body or SST. So, what I'm about to say may sound counterintuitive, as we're never really truly separate from our souls — but soul resides on a different dimension than we do here on Earth.

Such a guided journey is designed to bring us *more* of our soul, more often, for more people at once. The effects of this are already being felt on our planet at this time. We're living through a period of huge collective spiritual awakening, whether we are aware of it or not. Just as our individual journey had us excavate our beliefs, behaviours, expectations and judgements, we are now doing this on a collective scale, too. It sure ain't pretty or comfortable, but it's desperately needed if we desire a new way forward. Like the bear hunt, the only way through it, is through it.

Mass awakening, ascension of energy and increasing collective consciousness enables this new wave of soul frequencies to make their way to Earth. Our capacity to reach for more of the frequencies from the realm or dimension of soul has increased — but we haven't necessarily known what to do with this (if we've been aware of it at all). I know it's part of my own soul purpose to help us through this process because when we are all connected in this way, life here is remarkably different. We'll all have achieved our common purpose, to truly actualise soul on Earth.

 ## CHOOSE YOUR ADVENTURE –
YOUR SOUL AWAKENING

Spirit will guide you into your own soul awakening; trust you will access this realm when the time is right. For now, visit your Sacred Space and ask your SST to make any introductions that are now possible.

Using the technique on page 85, go into your Sacred Space. In today's visit, ask your SST to prepare you to meet your soul guides and expression of your soul. If you're not able to meet with them today, ask your SST about what steps are still needed to bridge the gap. You'll receive more guidance about where you are in the Guidance Wheel and Guidance Cycles.

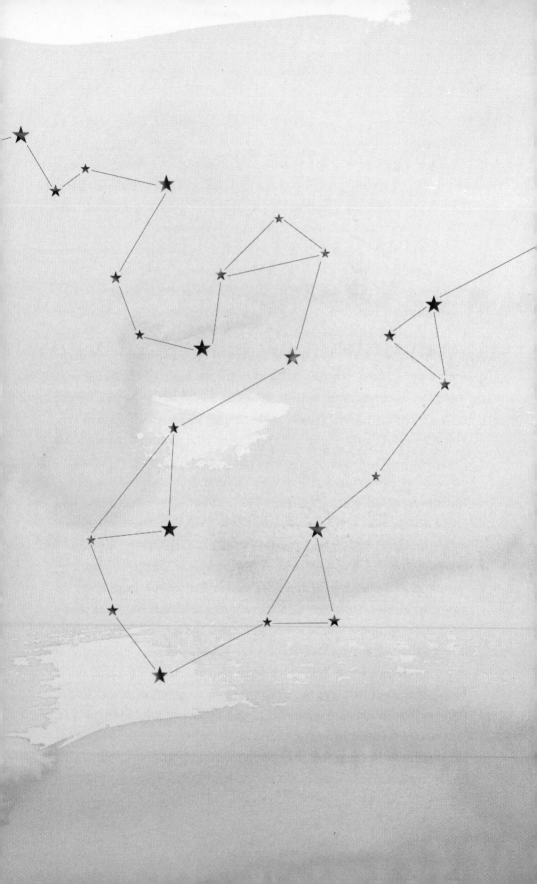

CHAPTER 27

ONWARD JOURNEY

Sitting down to write this chapter, emotions bubble up, tears well and I realise how sad I am to reach the end. This book was always so much more to me than putting words to print or sharing Chris' message; this has been the culmination of this wild spiritual and soul adventure, punctuating the period of my life that began the moment my aunt psychically visited me all those years ago. It's a full stop on a very long and, often at times, confusing process for me. And the emotion catches me off guard. Emotion, as we now know, is a messenger in and of itself. Feeling is the very premise underpinning this entire book. Honouring the changing of the seasons is important, is *needed*, in this process. Cycles keep on spinning; there's more just around the corner, but this moment must be honoured now, too.

Your own journey will also feature many endings. Every ending and completion naturally births a new beginning. There's excitement up ahead — for me and for you. Each macro and micro cycle serves up undulating emotions, each to varying degrees. Learning our lessons, integrating the energy and realising a new perspective and a new consciousness demands time, space and a sacred reverence for what is occurring. You cannot rush soul.

My ending in completing this book births a whole new journey for you, dear reader. As you've journeyed with these concepts and exercises, you've already begun unravelling your own divine life path. You've got to go all-in. This doesn't stop now just because the book does. Life will continue rising up to meet you, asking you again and again to choose your path, your soul and yourself. Choose wisely.

In passing you the baton, I trust there are many new, exciting possibilities ahead for you. As I suggested in the beginning, I hope these frameworks and suggestions now become a reference guide for you as your cycles keep on spinning and you ascend your own spiritual mountains and unfurl your divine life path. Refer back here as life comes rushing in. Every messenger, every intuitive hunch, every spirit communication may send you back here. Your inner transformation and recalibration of mind, body and spirit may send you back here. You have the tools now to support yourself through each phase of the spiritual awakening journey — and any time you feel you don't, ask your guides to send you what you need.

In sharing my personal highs and lows, I've tried to best equip you for the onward journey with everything I've personally and psychically gathered along my pathway. Before we part ways, there are a few last key recommendations or onward guiding principles I wish to share.

Always evolving

Life will never really be the same again. Once you've started, you can't go back. You can certainly choose your own adventure, but you cannot un-know what you now know; you cannot un-see what you have seen.

Many times, half-laughing, half-crying, I've questioned: 'Why do I continue to do it this way?' No matter how many childlike tantrums my ego has, I ultimately know soul will win; I don't want to let soul down, or let myself down. Somehow or other, once my tantrum is over, I wake up again, only to ask my team of advisors — in spirit and soul — 'What do I need to know today?' And on the cycle rolls.

Looking back over the various stories I've shared of Maggie, Mandy, Maria, Emma, Alice and Jenny, I hope you've seen that there are many divine life pathways we may walk. Yours is just as valid, important and needed. We haven't arrived here by chance; we are not just the by-product of our parents' relationship, but the meeting and merging of soul and Earth, our Father Sky and Mother Earth, who called us here to contribute to our collective uprising. Our parents (and their blueprints) were the vehicles, not the cause.

While there is much healing, processing and energetic upgrading in this journey, it can be fun, too. Indeed, this is often the lesson! May your onward journey be one of continual self-discovery, from a place of childlike wonder and curiosity. You are magical and wondrous, after all.

While having fun along your onward journey, please bear the following in mind.

When you think you know, you don't

Yes, you're nearing the end of a book titled *You Already Know* and here I am now cautioning you that when you think you know it all, you really don't. The operative word here is *think*. In my experience, I've seen that we cannot get too comfortable with what we *think* we know along this guided pathway. Soul's been at this a while! And will continue to be at this for lifetimes to come. As soon as you think you know all there is to know about your path, purpose, lessons and life — beware! A new cycle will sneak up, prompting you to consider all options again, this time by *feel*. Our minds adjust with the process, too, and can become quite sneaky in trying to regain control.

Can you now see how multi-dimensional, wondrous, infinite and magical you are? By definition, such an infinite, expansive being cannot ever truly be done meeting every aspect of themselves. Our work is never done.

Forget everything you know, once more

Of course I'm not suggesting truly forgetting all you just learned, but rather, to now put it into perspective. Let it have its place. If we attach too much to the journey, we experience it through the mental plane alone. While there is a framework and arc to our trajectory, we cannot map this out. Our spiritual unfolding will not run to ego's schedule.

Instead, we must observe and respond, knowing our journey is not random and ad hoc, but that it fits within the framework, even if our rational minds cannot fathom that while in the eye of any of our personal storms. And, if at any point we cannot feel where we are, the framework itself can provide a signpost, pointing you to the tools and practices required at that time.

It's not a quick fix

What I've shared in these pages has emerged over a decade of personal, dedicated daily work. While our spiritual and soul awakenings are speeding up (this doesn't need to take you a decade!), we certainly can't expect to complete this kind of deep spiritual work in the time it has taken you to complete this book. Just as with any of the other tools I've shared here, the book is the tool, not the rule. The real work is over to you.

Please don't be someone who only reads this book but doesn't apply what you learn here; the healing is not in the reading of the book, but in applying what you've learned. Just as with our guidance, it's not enough to know this theory or the frameworks you're moving through. The integration and transformation comes from actually integrating and transforming. From establishing a new rhythm in your life, working with your SST and intuition daily, following the threads of guidance into your own personal healing toolkit and processes, as well as building out a vision and understanding of the next physical steps to take as you move in the direction of your soul's vision and purpose.

Devotion and dedication wins out, especially in those moments when you want to give up and give in. The healing is actually in the pain and discomfort of change. The healing comes when we can move beyond the limiting mental reference that 'this must be hard' — your arrival and soul birth can actually be ecstatic. All of life cheers you on and supports you in this quest. You are not alone. There is a vast, multi-dimensional realm of possibility and support available to you in each and every moment. This can fuel your growth.

But it takes time. The more we work with our multi-dimensional selves, the more we realise Earth-based time is just a construct here — we exist beyond it. In a realm not bound by time, space and physical matter, where the 'all that is' just *is*; you already exist in the full, integrated richness of your potential. It is already real, somewhere. Your job is to bring it into physical form. Translating an energetic imprint into physical form takes time on the earthly plane.

My childhood vision foretelling I would be an author to this moment with this book in your hands took nearly thirty years to come into form. While the book has taken time to materialise, I continued to live out my purpose in whatever way was before me. I continued to give readings, write, teach, channel and share my soul's message wherever and however I was called to (or not) in each moment. Fine-tuning layers and layers of energy manifested this part of the vision as a lived experience; the culmination of my process through the Guidance Cycle's clearing, healing and restoring.

Plenty of experiences have happened in my life that haven't make it into this book. And you certainly don't need to wait thirty years for a vision to come to reality! Indeed, I've fallen in love, married and birthed two beautiful children (and moved through the loss of three miscarriages). We've bought and sold properties, travelled, laughed, cried, grieved, loved. *Lived*. I've grown and closed and shifted and re-emerged in my business. Suffice to say, I've lived a full and rich life while trusting that this vision — and every other vision in between — would come to pass. And when I look to see what's ahead for me, I know I'll do it all again in a heartbeat.

The more I've worked with my guidance, moved through my daily intuitive instructions, supported myself through the inner transformation, and showed up in each and every moment as present and as fully as I could, things rapidly gained momentum. A tipping point is reached, a buoyancy felt where our In and Out Flow and our Up and Down Flow find their harmony and level. Then, we see things rapidly alter.

 ### CHOOSE YOUR ADVENTURE — ONWARD JOURNEY

Turning the pages of this book, you've moved through this process in a rather linear fashion, but life (and our divine life path and soul journey) is more cyclical. You may be processing, clearing and healing in one life area, only to be restoring in another or manifesting elsewhere. Perhaps, in situ, you'll find there are periods of intensive healing, before guidance comes your way again. Or, maybe, like me, once you've turned on this inner navigation, you won't be able to switch it off again.

Please know that however life serves this up for you is perfect. It needn't fit the model I've outlined here. Your life and path will have their own unique timing and rhythm. Like Maggie, Emma, Mandy, Maria, Alice and Jenny, your life's lessons and purpose will be unique to you, but the *how* is shared. Your 'how' is guided, uniquely for you.

Along the onward journey, and to summarise the book, here's the process in one place:

- Work with your rhythms, cultivating stillness, space and silence. This is your new normal.
- Create rituals for review — new and full moons, calendar markers like the new year, birthdays, or winter and summer solstice.
- Build your relationship with your intuition and SST daily, in your morning or evening routine. How can you integrate it throughout the rest of your day, too?
- Look for mirrors as you interact with life. Let them point you within; journey with the healing, identifying if it's required physically, mentally, emotionally or spiritually.
- Run diagnostics on your Four Bodies, monitor your chakras and do the inner work you're guided to undertake, ensuring you restore balance and harmony to your inner world. This will always bring harmony, balance and flow to your outer world.
- Stay open, light-hearted and curious about who and what shows up. Know that life supports you; it's sending you the teachers and answers you need, but not always in the form your mind is looking for.
- Compile your intuitive data, working with your SST to build up a dossier of your lessons and purpose. Connect to the feeling of the purpose so it becomes your guide.
- Look for the changing call of the times, and the changing cycle and season, and adjust accordingly. This will prompt you back into your healing toolkit, likely asking you to draw on another tool or technique, or pointing you to another of the Four Bodies. Eventually, it will lead you into your soul awakening, where an entirely new framework and support is required.
- Come back to this book as life continues, using it as a reference for your life in situ. Life is likely to unfold differently, and in its own timing. Allow your SST to show you how best to use this book on your onward journey, as it may not be chronologically.

Finally, know that you are never alone. Your SST will guide you through the process — even when you can't tell exactly where you are and what's needed. It'll happen. If you're looking to build your own physical support team, I'd be delighted to support you. You'll find a number of the resources mentioned here on my website, along with deeper dive programs and events. Other teachers and guides will arrive for you, too. Everything and everyone contributes to your onward journey. No matter the guides, messengers or breadcrumbs arriving, you are your own most powerful guiding being. Everything I shared here was what you already knew, but now remember — and live — for yourself. What you already knew was within you all along.

RESOURCES

You'll find a treasure trove of additional articles, audio guides and supports on my website, helenjacobs.co. Below are the specific resources mentioned throughout the book, but new resources are regularly added to helenjacobs.co/resources.

Chapter 6 • The Little Sage Oracle Cards, page 68: helenjacobs.co/the-little-sage-oracle (also mentioned on page 160 in Chapter 13)

Chapter 8 • Dream interpretation resource, page 95: dreammoods.com

Chapter 9 • Chakra Balancing meditation, page 109: helenjacobs.co/guided-meditations/ (also mentioned on page 179 in Chapter 14)

Chapter 10 • My suite of guided meditations, page 119: helenjacobs.co/guided-meditations/
Meet Your Spirit Guide meditation, page 123: helenjacobs.co/guided-meditations/

Chapter 11 • Ground, Clear and Protect Your Energy meditation, page 129: helenjacobs.co/guided-meditations/

Chapter 15 • Energy Activation Visualisation, page 191: helenjacobs.co/resources

Chapter 24 • Astrological resource, page 298: astro.com

Chapter 25 • Guidance Wheel resource, page 316: helenjacobs.co/resources

ACKNOWLEDGEMENTS

Over many, many years, I've pondered writing such an acknowledgement in some future book I dreamed of writing. And yet, now I'm here writing it, I'm finding it quite the challenge. I'm amazed at all the serendipitous turns of events and people whom have all contributed in their own way to bring this book to life. It was always far bigger than me — and perhaps even bigger than what I can acknowledge here.

To be extremely esoteric about it, I could thank my soul for choosing this life, this purpose and this human experience. Zooming out to some cosmic level, I see my Aunt Cathy's life and death left a far bigger legacy for me, and for that I'm incredibly grateful. None of this would ever have been possible without Cathy's visit, and the agreements our souls must have had to make this happen. As she awoke in me a remembrance of my abilities, I got to understand my first meetings with my maternal grandfather and maintain an eternal connection with my grandmother. What a gift! As inadequate as my thank you feels, I'm truly indebted to this magical process of life and soul paths, and those of Cathy, Barney and Granny. I miss you all, but have you right here. This book is for you and all you see in me.

To my most wonderful co-creator, Chris — and the entire team of beings in spirit — thank you for walking every step of the way with me, nurturing, teaching, guiding and patiently steering me. I feel immense gratitude and I am beyond privileged to be able to do this with (and for) you every day.

Here, back in the material world, is a rather large contingent of physical supports that have also allowed this book to come into being.

I express a special and endless thank you to Gary, Isla and Rose as you all supported me along every step, encouraging and believing in me, especially when I couldn't. I feel lucky to do life with you. To my mum, Jackie, and my dad, Phil — orchestrating the in-house family publishing of my first book attempt at age seven paid off. You always knew I had it in me. And to Liz and Claire, my biggest supporters and defenders, you've always got my back. Here's to living out the next installment of our predictions!

To the entire team at Murdoch Books, thank you for taking a chance on this first-time author and bringing my childhood dream to life with such care and finesse. Particular thanks goes to my publisher, Kelly. Your advice at the outset to enjoy each stage of this process has only been possible because of the ease and delight felt while working with you, and the entire Murdoch team of editors, designers and marketers. It's been one of my life's best experiences!

Cassie Mendoza-Jones, you changed my life. You know what you did! Thank you for the countless chats and laughs during the writing process, for allaying my fears and questions and for kindly reading this manuscript while you nurtured your own divine creation. For all of it, and your friendship, I'm so grateful.

To the special circle of authentically soul-led women who came into my life at just the right time, your unique brand of magical soul midwifery helped me birth this work into form. Melissa Sandon, Sarah K Jones, Jenna Ward, Carly Stephan and Susana Frioni, I adore you all beyond words and I am so lucky to be seen and held by you.

Other than my immediate family, early copies of this manuscript were sent to Cassie Mendoza-Jones, Katie McKnoulty, Rebecca Van Leeuwan, Rachel Crethar, Melissa Sandon, Lorraine Murphy and Jack Delosa. Receiving your feedback meant the world to me and

I appreciate your time in reading through a very unrefined version of the book. Your feedback made it better!

Behind the scenes, an incredible team keeps things running while I hang out in the ether. Special thank you to Lauren Wright for *all* that you do and to Katie McKnoulty for helping to shape and communicate this work. Lorraine, your mentoring helped keep me organised and indeed to get some remarkable shit done!

My soul purpose is only delivered because other souls agreed to receive it. So, to each and every person who has engaged with my work over the past decade — from the very first practise psychic readings over cups of tea in my kitchen to the people the world over who've read my emails, attended events, bought my oracle cards, listened to my podcasts and meditations or attended a workshop, retreat or course, none of this is possible without you. Our soul work is always produced in tandem with those who are meant to help us learn, and each and every one of you encouraged this work to come forward. What an honour and privilege it has been to serve you.